Islam and the Bahá'í Faith

Islam and the Bahá'í Faith

by

Moojan Momen

GR

George Ronald
Oxford

George Ronald, *Publisher*
46 High Street, Kidlington, Oxford OX5 2DN

A catalogue record for this book is available from the British Library

ISBN 0–85398–446–8

Printed and bound in Great Britain by Biddles Ltd
www.biddles.co.uk

Contents

To my son,

who first put the thought of this book

into my mind

Introduction

This book is an attempt to present the Bahá'í Faith to Muslims. It is hoped that all Muslims will benefit from it in that most of the arguments presented are backed up by evidence taken from the text of the Qur'án and from the Traditions (*ḥadí<u>th</u>s*) of the Prophet Muḥammad (blessings and peace be upon him). I have in most cases used Traditions found in the six collections that are regarded by Sunni Muslims as the most reliable: al-Bu<u>kh</u>árí, *aṣ-Ṣaḥíḥ*; Muslim, *aṣ-Ṣaḥíḥ*; at-Tirmi<u>dh</u>í, *aṣ-Ṣaḥíḥ*; Ibn Májah, *Sunan*; Abú Dáwud, *Sunan*; an-Nasá'í, *Sunan*; as well those collections by other scholars who are regarded as having been reliable, such as Ibn Ḥanbal (*Musnad*), at-Tibrízí (*Mi<u>sh</u>kát al-Maṣábíḥ*) and as-Suyúṭí (*ad-Durr al-Man<u>th</u>úr*). Similarly, I have quoted only from the great classical commentators on the Qur'án such as aṭ-Ṭabarí, az-Zama<u>kh</u><u>sh</u>arí, al-Bayḍáwí and Ibn Ka<u>th</u>ír. In many cases, similar Traditions are to be found in the Shi'i collections and I have tried to point these out in the endnotes.

Since the inception of the Bábí and Bahá'í Faiths in Iran in 1844, the followers of these religions have been persecuted in many Muslim countries. Consequently, there has been little opportunity for the teachings of the Bahá'í Faith to be presented to Muslims in these places in a fair and unbiased manner. Most Muslims either know nothing about the Bahá'í Faith at all or else know only what they have learned from prejudiced and biased accounts. Most of what Muslims think they know about the Bahá'í Faith is in fact the misinformation and exaggerations that have been propagated in newspapers, magazines and books in Muslim countries. The Bahá'ís themselves have been prevented from publishing their own works on the Bahá'í Faith and they have not even been able to publish refutations of errors.

Where this book contains Bahá'í interpretations of verses of the Qur'án, the reader should note the difference between those interpretations that are from the writings of Bahá'u-'lláh, 'Abdu'l-Bahá and Shoghi Effendi, and are therefore considered authoritative by Bahá'ís (see p. 171), and other interpretations. Interpretations by Bahá'í scholars, such as Mírzá Abu'l-Faḍl Gulpáygání, Aḥmad Ál-Muḥammad and Dr Ṣábir Áfáqí, have been used in this book but the reader should note that such interpretations, no matter how distinguished the scholar, are not considered authoritative by Bahá'ís. The reader can distinguish these in this book by the fact that passages from the authoritative texts of the Bahá'í Faith are always introduced by a statement to that effect or by the name of the author in parentheses at the end, while statements by Bahá'í scholars are often introduced by words such as 'Bahá'ís consider that . . . ' It is important to note that Bahá'ís regard all of the writings of Bahá'u'lláh and the Báb to be the revelation of Allah's word. Therefore where reference is made to one of the books of Bahá'u'lláh and it is stated that 'Bahá'u'lláh writes . . . ' or 'Bahá'u'lláh says . . . ', for Bahá'ís, this is the equivalent to a Muslim saying 'In the Qur'án, Allah says . . .'

Except where indicated otherwise, I have used Yusuf Ali's translation of the Holy Qur'án, as this appears to be the most widely accepted among Muslims (although in a few places, where I have felt that it was clearer, I have used the translation of another Muslim, Marmaduke Pickthall, and very occasionally the translation of N. J. Dawood). The reader should be aware that, because of variations in the numbering of the verses of the Qur'án, any particular reference from this book that they seek may vary by as much as three or four verses depending on which text they consult.

Throughout the book, I have used certain words consistently so that the reader will always know what this term refers to. These terms are always given with an initial capital letter. The words which I have treated in this way are: Messenger (for *rasúl*, rather than Apostle), Tradition (for *ḥadíth*, rather than sayings or other terms) and the Qur'án (rather than other spellings such as Koran and Quran). I have, therefore, made these changes also in the translations of the Qur'án and Traditions that I have used. Muslims of a previous generation were happy to use the word God. Yusuf 'Ali, for example, used God in the original edition of his translation of the Qur'án. In the last few decades, however, it has become customary for Muslims to retain the word Allah rather than to use the translation God. Bahá'ís, however, prefer to use the translation God in order to emphasize the common ground between religions. In deference to Muslim preferences, I have used Allah throughout this book, except in passages translated from the Bahá'í scriptures.

It is customary among Muslims to give the Prophet's name with an honorific 'Muḥammad, peace be upon him' or 'may the peace and blessings of Allah be upon him'. This is also used with the name of other prophets. It has also been customary to follow the names of the first four caliphs with the honorific 'may Allah be pleased with him'. It is, however, also considered permissible just to use this honorific on the first occasion of the mention of the Prophet. Since the frequent recurrence of this honorific makes the text difficult to read, I have adopted the convention of using this honorific only on the first mention of the Prophet in each chapter. Since it is not a Bahá'í, Christian or Jewish custom to use an honorific in the English language, I have not used one for Bahá'u'lláh, Jesus or other Messengers of Allah. The Bahá'í scriptures in their original languages, Persian and Arabic, do, in fact, contain honorifics after the names of prophets and Messengers of Allah. When these were being translated into English, the honorifics were usually omitted as they were not considered part of the English usage. Instead, the proper respect for the Messengers of Allah was shown by capitalizing the pronouns relating to them. This is the convention used in many Christian texts in English and its use is intended merely to honour the Messengers of Allah, although it may appear to some Muslims that this usage gives too much elevation to the rank of the Messenger.

1

What is the Bahá'í View of the Prophet Muḥammad and of Islam?

Bahá'u'lláh, the founder of the Bahá'í Faith, displayed throughout his life the utmost respect for Muḥammad (blessings and peace be upon him) and the religion of Islam. The Bahá'í scriptures show the highest regard for the Prophet Muḥammad, for the Holy Qur'án and for the religion of Islam and Bahá'ís are instructed to honour these. Regarding the station of the Prophet Muḥammad and the effects of his coming to the world, the Bahá'í scriptures state:

> Blessing and peace be upon Him [Muḥammad] through Whose advent Baṭḥá [Mecca] is wreathed in smiles, and the sweet savours of Whose raiment have shed fragrance upon all mankind – He Who came to protect men from that which would harm them in the world below. Exalted, immensely exalted is His station above the glorification of all beings and sanctified from the praise of the entire creation. Through His advent the tabernacle of stability and order was raised throughout the world and the ensign of knowledge hoisted among the nations. May blessings rest also upon His kindred and His companions through whom the standard of the unity of God and of His singleness was uplifted and the banners of celestial triumph were unfurled. Through them the religion of God was firmly established among His creatures and His Name magnified amidst His servants.[1]

In the Kitáb-i-Íqán, one of the most important of the Bahá'í scriptures, Muḥammad is described as 'the Messenger of God',[2] 'that Essence of truthfulness',[3] 'that immortal Beauty',[4] 'that divine Luminary'[5] and as 'the Sun of Prophethood'.[6] The following is a passage of the Kitáb-i-Íqán describing the results of Muḥammad's mission:

> The following is an evidence of the sovereignty exercised by Muḥammad, the Day-star of Truth. Hast thou not heard how with one single verse He hath sundered light from darkness, the righteous from the ungodly, and the believing from the infidel? . . . These revealed words were a blessing to the righteous who on hearing them exclaimed: 'O God our Lord, we have heard, and obeyed.' They were a curse to the people of iniquity who, on hearing them affirmed: 'We have heard and rebelled.' . . . On the other hand, consider the welding power of His Word. Observe, how those in whose midst the Satan of self had for years sown the seeds of malice and hate became so fused and blended through their allegiance to this wondrous and transcendent Revelation that it seemed as if they had sprung from the same loins. Such is the binding force of the Word of God, which uniteth the hearts of them that have renounced all else but Him . . . Furthermore, how numerous are those peoples of divers beliefs, of conflicting creeds, and opposing temperaments, who, through the reviving fragrance of the Divine springtime . . . have been arrayed with the new robe of divine Unity, and have drunk from the cup of His singleness![7]

In the same book there is a passage dwelling at length upon the sufferings endured by Muḥammad at the hands of the people of his time and on his self-sacrifice and forbearance:

> For this reason did Muḥammad cry out: 'No Prophet of God hath suffered such harm as I have suffered.' And in the Qur'án are recorded all the calumnies and reproaches uttered against Him, as well as all the afflictions which He suffered. Refer ye thereunto, that haply ye may be informed of that

> which hath befallen His Revelation. So grievous was His plight, that for a time all ceased to hold intercourse with Him and His companions. Whoever associated with Him fell a victim to the relentless cruelty of His enemies.
>
> We shall cite in this connection only one verse of that Book. Shouldst thou observe it with a discerning eye, thou wilt, all the remaining days of thy life, lament and bewail the injury of Muḥammad, that wronged and oppressed Messenger of God. That verse was revealed at a time when Muḥammad languished weary and sorrowful beneath the weight of the opposition of the people, and of their unceasing torture. In the midst of His agony, the Voice of Gabriel . . . was heard saying: 'But if their opposition be grievous to Thee – if Thou canst, seek out an opening into the earth or a ladder into heaven.'[Qur'án 6:35] The implication of this utterance is that His case had no remedy, that they would not withhold their hands from Him unless He should hide Himself beneath the depths of the earth, or take His flight unto heaven.[8]

A passage in another of the Bahá'í scriptures laments the sufferings of Muḥammad thus:

> Ponder that which befell Muḥammad, the Seal of the Prophets, may the life of all else be a sacrifice unto Him. How severe the afflictions which the leaders of the Jewish people and of the idol-worshippers caused to rain upon Him, Who is the sovereign Lord of all, in consequence of His proclamation of the unity of God and of the truth of His Message! By the righteousness of My Cause! My Pen groaneth, and all created things weep with a great weeping, as a result of the woes He suffered at the hands of them that have broken the Covenant of God, violated His Testament, rejected His proofs, and disputed His signs.[9]

'Abdu'l-Bahá, the son and successor of Bahá'u'lláh as leader of the Bahá'í Faith (see pp. 208–11), spoke out on many occasions in front of audiences in the West in praise of the achievements of Muḥammad. To an audience of Christians in the United States in 1912, for example, he said:

> The Arabians were in the utmost state of degradation. They were blood-thirsty and barbarous, so savage and degraded that the Arabian father often buried his own daughter alive. Consider, could any barbarism be lower than this? The nation consisted of warring, hostile tribal peoples inhabiting the vast Arabian peninsula, and their business consisted in fighting and pillaging each other, making captive women and children, killing each other. Muḥammad appeared among such a people. He educated and unified these barbarous tribes, put an end to their shedding of blood. Through His education they reached such a degree of civilization that they subdued and governed continents and nations. What a great civilization was established in Spain by the Muslims! What a marvellous civilization was founded in Morocco by the Moors! What a powerful caliphate or successorship was set up in Baghdád! How much Islám served and furthered the cause of science![10]

In London, 'Abdu'l-Bahá reverted to this theme in an article written for a Christian journal, the *Christian Commonwealth*:

> So it was with the Arabian nations who, being uncivilized, were oppressed by the Persian and Greek governments. When the Light of Muḥammad shone forth all Arabia was brightened. These oppressed and degraded peoples became enlightened and cultured; so much so, indeed, that other nations imbibed Arabian civilization from Arabia. This was the proof of Muḥammad's divine mission.[11]

The Qur'án itself is frequently quoted in the Bahá'í scriptures and is regarded as the authoritative repository of the Word of Allah. The words of the Qur'án are stated in the Bahá'í scriptures to be 'that which the Merciful Lord hath revealed'[12] and 'the unfailing testimony of God to both the East and the West'.[13] Regarding the guidance given to the peoples of the world in the Qur'án, the Bahá'í scriptures state:

> All the things that people required in connection with the Revelation of Muḥammad and His laws were to be found revealed and manifest in that Riḍván [paradise] of resplendent glory. That Book constitutes an abiding testimony to its people after Muḥammad, inasmuch as its decrees are indisputable, and its promise unfailing . . . That Book is the Book which unfailingly leadeth the seeker unto the Riḍván [paradise] of the divine Presence, and causeth him that hath forsaken his country and is treading the seeker's path to enter the Tabernacle of everlasting reunion. Its guidance can never err, its testimony no other testimony can excel. All other traditions, all other books and records, are bereft of such distinction, inasmuch as both the traditions and they that have spoken them are confirmed and proven solely by the text of that Book.[14]

'Abdu'l-Bahá refers to the fact that the Qur'án preceded science in its knowledge of certain facts, such as those of astronomy.

> Thus, you know that before the observations of modern times – that is to say, during the first centuries and down to the fifteenth century of the Christian era – all the mathematicians of the world agreed that the earth was the centre of the universe, and that the sun moved . . . But there are some verses revealed in the Qur'án contrary to the theory of the Ptolemaic system. One of them is 'The sun moves in a fixed place', which shows the fixity of the sun, and its movement around an axis. [Qur'án 36:37] Again, in another verse, 'And each star moves in its own heaven.' [Qur'án 36:38] Thus is explained the movement of the sun, of the moon, of the earth, and of other bodies. When the Qur'án appeared, all the mathematicians ridiculed these statements and attributed the theory to ignorance. Even the doctors of Islám, when they saw that these verses were contrary to the accepted Ptolemaic system, were obliged to explain them away.

> It was not until after the fifteenth century of the Christian era, nearly nine hundred years after Muḥammad, that a famous astronomer made new observations and important discoveries by the aid of the telescope, which he had invented. The rotation of the earth, the fixity of the sun, and also its movement around an axis, were discovered. It became evident that the verses of the Qur'án agreed with existing facts, and that the Ptolemaic system was imaginary.[15]

In writings addressed to those from a Western Christian background, 'Abdu'l-Bahá defended Islam and the Prophet Muḥammad. He specifically refuted accusations that have traditionally been made by Christian leaders against Islam, such as the idea that Islam was war-like and had been spread by the sword and that Islam degraded women.[16] In defending Islam, he pointed out to Christians that, in the Qur'án, Jesus is mentioned respectfully and is praised greatly:

> I wish now to call your attention to a most important point. All Islám considers the Qur'án the Word of God. In this sacred Book there are explicit texts . . . stating that Christ was the Word of God, that He was the Spirit of God, that Jesus Christ came into this world through the quickening breaths of the Holy Spirit and that Mary, His mother, was holy and sanctified. In the Qur'án a whole chapter is devoted to the story of Jesus . . . In brief, in the Qur'án there is eulogy and commendation of Christ such as you do not find in the Gospel . . . Furthermore, it is significant and convincing that when Muḥammad proclaimed His work and mission, His first objection to His own followers was, 'Why have you not believed on Jesus Christ? Why have you not accepted the Gospel? Why have you not believed in Moses? Why have you not followed the precepts of the Old Testament? . . .'[17]

Furthermore, 'Abdu'l-Bahá pointed out that Muḥammad himself had treated Christians with great kindness and consideration and that this had also been the policy in early

Islam. It was only later that hatred between some adherents of Islam and Christianity arose.

> Muḥammad never fought against the Christians; on the contrary, He treated them kindly and gave them perfect freedom. A community of Christian people lived at Najrán and were under His care and protection. Muḥammad said, 'If anyone infringes their rights, I Myself will be his enemy, and in the presence of God I will bring a charge against him.' In the edicts which He promulgated it is clearly stated that the lives, properties and honour of the Christians and Jews are under the protection of God; and that if a Muḥammadan married a Christian woman, the husband must not prevent her from going to church, nor oblige her to veil herself; and that if she died, he must place her remains in the care of the Christian clergy. Should the Christians desire to build a church, Islám ought to help them.[18]

'Abdu'l-Bahá states moreover that the civilization upon which Europeans pride themselves and which they vaunt over the other peoples of the world was itself derived from Islam. He asserts that the impulse and the ideas that brought about the Renaissance in 14th- and 15th-century Europe had their origins in the Islamic world. They came to Europe as a result of the interactions between Christians and Muslims in Andalusia (Spain and Portugal) and were also taken back to Europe by the Crusaders following their exposure to the Islamic world for 200 years in the 12th and 13th centuries.

> In the early ages of Islám the peoples of Europe acquired the sciences and arts of civilization from Islám as practised by the inhabitants of Andalusia. A careful and thorough investigation of the historical record will establish the fact that the major part of the civilization of Europe is derived from Islám; for all the writings of Muslim scholars and divines and philosophers were gradually collected in Europe and were with the most painstaking care weighed and

debated at academic gatherings and in the centres of learning, after which their valued contents would be put to use . . . Furthermore, the laws and principles current in all European countries are derived to a considerable degree and indeed virtually in their entirety from the works on jurisprudence and the legal decision of Muslim theologians . . .

. . . To sum up, from 490 A.H. [1097] until 693 [1294], kings, commanders and other European leaders continually came and went between Egypt, Syria and the West, and when in the end they all returned home, they introduced into Europe whatever they had observed over two hundred and odd years in Muslim countries as to government, social development and learning, colleges, schools and the refinements of living. The civilization of Europe dates from that time.[19]

Shoghi Effendi, the second successor of Bahá'u'lláh as leader of the Bahá'í Faith (see pp. 211–12), also asserted the truth of Islam and stressed in particular the fact that, through the Bahá'í teachings, Queen Marie of Romania, a European Christian monarch, a descendant of Britain's Queen Victoria, had publicly proclaimed the truth of Islam. He presented this as evidence of the fact that the Bahá'í Faith must be regarded as a true friend and upholder of Islam.

As to Muḥammad, the Apostle of God, let none among His followers who read these pages, think for a moment that either Islám, or its Prophet, or His Book, or His appointed Successors, or any of His authentic teachings, have been, or are to be in any way, or to however slight a degree, disparaged. The lineage of the Báb . . . the glowing tributes paid by Bahá'u'lláh in the Kitáb-i-Íqán to Muḥammad and His lawful Successors . . . the arguments adduced, forcibly, fearlessly, and publicly by 'Abdu'l-Bahá, in churches and synagogues, to demonstrate the validity of the Message of the Arabian Prophet; and last but not least the written testimonial of the Queen of Rumania, who, born in the Anglican faith and notwithstanding the close alliance of her government with the Greek Orthodox Church, the state religion of her adopted country, has, largely as a result of the perusal of these public discourses of 'Abdu'l-Bahá, been prompted to proclaim her recognition of the prophetic function of Muḥammad – all proclaim, in no uncertain terms, the true attitude of the Bahá'í Faith towards its parent religion.[20]

Shoghi Effendi, in writing to Bahá'ís of European Christian origin, stated that it was a fundamental principle of the Bahá'í Faith that the religion of Islam, being later than that of Christianity, was a fuller, more complete revelation from God:

> From the standpoint of institutionalism Islám far surpasses true Christianity as we know it in the Gospels. There are infinitely more laws and institutions in the Qur'án than in the Gospel. While the latter's emphasis is mainly, not to say wholly, on individual and personal conduct, the Qur'án stresses the importance of society . . . When carefully and impartially compared, the Qur'án marks a definite advancement on the Gospel, from the standpoint of spiritual and humanitarian progress.[21]

Shoghi Effendi confirms 'Abdu'l-Bahá's assertion that the civilization of modern Western Europe was only possible because of the influence and spread of ideas from the Islamic world.

> The so-called Christian civilization of which the Renaissance is one of the most striking manifestations is essentially Muslim in its origins and foundations. When medieval Europe was plunged in darkest barbarism, the Arabs regenerated and transformed by the spirit released by the religion of Muḥammad were busily engaged in establishing a civilization the like of which their contemporary Christians in Europe had never witnessed before. It was eventually through Arabs that civilization was introduced to the West. It was through them that the philosophy, science and culture

> which the old Greeks had developed found their way to Europe. The Arabs were the ablest translators, and linguists of their age, and it is thanks to them that the writings of such well-known thinkers as Socrates, Plato and Aristotle were made available to the Westerners. It is wholly unfair to attribute the efflorescence of European culture during the Renaissance period to the influence of Christianity. It was mainly the product of the forces released by the Muḥammadan Dispensation.[22]

Finally, Shoghi Effendi urged the Bahá'ís of the West to strive to gain a better knowledge and understanding of Islam. He considered that such knowledge was an essential background for a proper understanding of the Bahá'í Faith itself.[23] Lamenting that there was 'so much misunderstanding about Islám in the West',[24] he also considered that the Bahá'ís should 'uphold Islám as a revealed Religion' and said that 'the mission of the American Bahá'ís is, no doubt to eventually establish the truth of Islám in the West'.[25]

In summary, the teachings of the Bahá'í Faith unreservedly accept the claim by the Prophet Muḥammad that he was a Messenger of Allah. All Bahá'ís can fully assent to the classical wording of the Shahádah and can state that they believe that 'There is no god but Allah and Muḥammad is the Messenger of Allah'. Bahá'ís also accept the Qur'án, in the form in which it is current among Muslims, as the pure and unadulterated word of Allah. The Bahá'í teachings thus affirm that Islam is a true religion revealed by Allah.

2

Spiritual and Ethical Teachings

With regard to teachings relating to the spiritual world, the beliefs of Islam and the Bahá'í Faith are very similar. This is not surprising as Bahá'ís believe that they came from the same source. Like Islam, the Bahá'í Faith teaches of a God who is the Ultimate Reality.

God (Allah)

Both Islam and the Bahá'í Faith are agreed on their descriptions of Allah. The characteristics of Allah that are common to both religions include the fact that there is only one God – Allah.

Islam	Bahá'í
There is no god but He: that is the witness of Allah, His angels, and those endued with knowledge . . . There is no god but He, the Exalted in Power, the Wise. (3:18) Allah has said: Take not (for worship) two gods: For He is just One Allah. Then fear Me (and Me alone). (16:51)	Beware, beware, lest thou be led to join partners with the Lord, thy God. He is, and hath from everlasting been, one and alone, without peer or equal . . . He hath assigned no associate unto Himself in His Kingdom, no counsellor to counsel Him, none to compare unto Him, none to rival His glory. To this every atom of the universe beareth witness, and beyond it the inmates of the realms on high . . . (Bahá'u'lláh)[26]

Allah is regarded in the both the Qur'án and the Bahá'í scriptures as the Creator and Sustainer of this World of Being in which we exist.

Islam	Bahá'í
Your Guardian-Lord is Allah, Who created the heavens and the earth in six Days, and is firmly established on the Throne (of authority). He draweth the night as a veil o'er the day . . . He created the sun, the moon and the stars (all) governed by laws under His Command. Is it not His to create and to govern? (7:54) Praise be to Allah, who created (out of nothing) the heavens and the earth . . . He adds to Creation as He pleases: for Allah has power over all things. (35:1)	All praise to the unity of God, and all honour to Him, the sovereign Lord . . . Who, out of utter nothingness, hath created the reality of all things, Who, from naught, hath brought into being the most refined and subtle elements of His creation . . . Nothing short of His all-encompassing grace, His all-pervading mercy, could have possibly achieved it. How could it, otherwise, have been possible for sheer nothingness to have acquired by itself the worthiness and capacity to emerge from its state of non-existence into the realm of being? (Bahá'u'lláh)[27]

Both Islam and the Bahá'í Faith consider Allah to be All-Powerful, the Almighty Lord and Sovereign of Creation. Allah does whatever He wills and none can ever question or oppose Him.

Islam	Bahá'í
Lo! power belongeth wholly to Allah. He is the Hearer, the Knower. (10:65)[28] To Allah belongeth all that is in the heavens and on earth . . . He forgiveth whom He pleaseth and punisheth whom He pleaseth. For Allah hath power over all things. (2:284)	He, verily, is the Lord of strength and of might. The changes and chances of the world, and the powers of the nations, cannot frustrate Him. He doeth what He pleaseth, and ordaineth what He willeth through the power of His sovereignty . . . No God is there but Him, the Almighty, the Great . . . Praised be God, the Lord of the worlds! (Bahá'u'lláh)[29]

Islam	Bahá'í
Seest thou not that Allah hath created the heavens and the earth in Truth? If He so will, He can remove you and put (in your place) a new Creation. Nor is that for Allah any great matter . . . Allah doeth what He willeth. (14:19–20, 27)	He ordaineth as He pleaseth, by virtue of His sovereignty, and doeth whatsoever He willeth at His own behest. He shall not be asked of the things it pleaseth Him to ordain. He, in truth, is the Unrestrained, the All-Powerful, the All-Wise. (Bahá'u'lláh)[30]

Allah also possesses perfect and complete knowledge and wisdom.

Islam	Bahá'í
That ye may know that Allah hath knowledge of what is in the heavens and on earth and that Allah is well acquainted with all things. (5:100)	He is in truth the Dayspring of divine precepts and commandments and the Fountainhead of knowledge and wisdom, while all else besides Him are but His subjects and under His rule, and He is the supreme Ruler, the Ordainer, the All-Knowing, the All-Informed. (Bahá'u'lláh)[31]

The Messengers of Allah

One important concept that both the Islamic and Bahá'í scriptures agree upon is the fact that Allah cannot be said to be incarnated in any human form. The Bahá'í scriptures, for example, state:

> Know thou of a certainty that the Unseen can in no wise incarnate His Essence and reveal it unto men. He is, and hath ever been, immensely exalted beyond all that can either be recounted or perceived. From His retreat of glory His voice

is ever proclaiming: 'Verily, I am God; there is none other God besides Me, the All-Knowing, the All-Wise.'[32]

The Qur'án states that direct contact between Allah and human beings is impossible. It records, for example, that Moses asked to see Allah. Allah then demonstrated the impossibility of this by revealing Himself to a mountain, whereupon the mountain was turned into dust (7:143). Because Allah is unknowable and human beings cannot have direct contact with him, Allah has from time to time revealed His Will to human beings and guided them through a succession of Messengers (*rasúlín, rusul*) that He has sent to the world. The Qur'án depicts these figures as coming to the world from time to time in a series.

> We gave Moses the Book and followed him up with a succession of Messengers; We gave Jesus the son of Mary clear (Signs) and strengthened him with the holy spirit. (2:87)

Similarly, the Bahá'í scriptures state:

> The door of the knowledge of the Ancient of Days being thus closed in the face of all beings, the Source of infinite grace, according to His saying: 'His grace hath transcended all things; My grace hath encompassed them all' hath caused those luminous Gems of Holiness to appear out of the realm of the spirit, in the noble form of the human temple, and be made manifest unto all men, that they may impart unto the world the mysteries of the unchangeable Being, and tell of the subtleties of His imperishable Essence.[33]

Thus both the Qur'án and the Bahá'í scriptures show that, in order to help us in our development both spiritually as individuals and socially as an ever-advancing human civilization, Allah has sent from time to time a Messenger (*rasúl*) with a teaching from Him. Each of these Messengers of Allah teaches of the one who went before. He affirms and expands on the message of the previous prophets:

> And in their footsteps We sent Jesus the son of Mary, confirming the Law that had come before him. We sent him the Gospel: therein was guidance and light and confirmation of the Law that had come before him: a guidance and an admonition to those who fear Allah. (5:49)

Each of these Messengers of Allah also foretells of another figure who is to come in the future. Thus, for example, Jesus says:

> And remember Jesus, the son of Mary, said: 'O Children of Israel! I am the Messenger of Allah (sent) to you confirming the Law (which came) before me, and giving Glad Tidings of a Messenger to come after me, whose name shall be Aḥmad.' (Qur'án 61:6)[34]

Unfortunately, humanity's record has not been good. Each of these Messengers that come from Allah has faced persecution at the hands of the people to whom he was sent:

> Then sent We Our Messengers one after another: every time there came to a people their Messenger, they accused him of falsehood: so We made them follow each other (in punishment). (23:44)

In the Bahá'í scriptures there is also reference to the persecutions of the prophets of Allah:

> Consider the past. How many, both high and low, have, at all times, yearningly awaited the advent of the Manifestations of God in the sanctified persons of His chosen Ones. How often have they expected His coming, how frequently have they prayed that the breeze of divine mercy might blow, and the promised Beauty step forth from behind the veil of concealment, and be made manifest to all the world. And

> whensoever the portals of grace did open, and the clouds of divine bounty did rain upon mankind, and the light of the Unseen did shine above the horizon of celestial might, they all denied Him, and turned away from His face – the face of God Himself. Refer ye, to verify this truth, to that which hath been recorded in every sacred Book.[35]

These Messengers have even faced death at the hands of the people of their time because those people did not want to hear the message that had been sent from Allah:

> We made a covenant of old with the Children of Israel and We sent unto them Messengers. As often as a Messenger came unto them with that which their souls desired not (they became rebellious). Some (of them) they denied and some they slew. (Qur'án 5:73)[36]

And yet, after a time, because these Messengers brought the teaching of Allah and they represented His Will, their message did eventually triumph and was accepted by the people.

The Purpose of the Messengers of Allah and the Nature of Religion

The Qur'án states, regarding the nature of true religion:

> And they have been commanded no more than this: to worship Allah, offering Him sincere devotion, being True (in faith); to establish regular Prayer; and to practise regular Charity; and that is the Religion Right and Straight. (98:5)

> Whatever ye are given (here) is (but) a convenience of this Life: but that which is with Allah is better and more lasting: (it is) for those who believe and put their trust in their Lord; Those who avoid the greater crimes and shameful deeds, and, when they are angry, even then forgive; Those who hearken to their Lord, and establish regular prayer; who

> (conduct) their affairs by mutual Consultation; who spend out of what We bestow on them for Sustenance; And those who when an oppressive wrong is inflicted on them (are not cowed but) help and defend themselves. (42:36–9)

Thus religion is essential for righteousness and beneficence to prevail among human beings and for society to be well-ordered. 'Abdu'l-Bahá, the son of Bahá'u'lláh, explains that for this to occur, humanity is in need of a divine educator, a Messenger of Allah who brings the divine teachings that educate the individual and order society.

> If the earth is not cultivated, it becomes a jungle where useless weeds grow; but if a cultivator comes and tills the ground, it produces crops which nourish living creatures . . . The same is true with respect to animals: notice that when the animal is trained it becomes domestic, and also that man, if he is left without education, becomes bestial, and, moreover, if left under the rule of nature, becomes lower than an animal, whereas if he is educated he becomes an angel . . .
>
> Then it is plain and evident that man needs an educator, and . . . he must be at the same time their material and human as well as their spiritual educator – that is to say, he must teach men to organize and carry out physical matters, and to form a social order in order to establish cooperation and mutual aid in living . . . In the same way he must establish human education – that is to say, he must educate intelligence and thought in such a way that they may attain complete development, so that knowledge and science may increase . . .
>
> He must also impart spiritual education, so that intelligence and comprehension may penetrate the metaphysical world, and may receive benefit from the sanctifying breeze of the Holy Spirit, and may enter into relationship with the Supreme Concourse . . .
>
> It is clear that human power is not able to fill such a great office, and that reason alone could not undertake the responsibility of so great a mission. How can one solitary person without help and without support lay the foundations

> of such a noble construction? He must depend on the help of the spiritual and divine power to be able to undertake this mission. One Holy Soul gives life to the world of humanity, changes the aspect of the terrestrial globe, causes intelligence to progress, vivifies souls, lays the basis of a new life, establishes new foundations, organizes the world, brings nations and religions under the shadow of one standard, delivers man from the world of imperfections and vices, and inspires him with the desire and need of natural and acquired perfections. Certainly nothing short of a divine power could accomplish so great a work.[37]

Thus the purpose of the Messengers of Allah is to educate humanity and in particular to educate humanity in the religion of Allah. And the purpose of the religion of Allah is to assist the advancement of both the individual human soul and human society in general.

Progressive Revelation

Concerning the Messengers of Allah, the Qur'án teaches that they are all one and that no one should make any distinction between them.

> Say (O Muslims): We believe in Allah and that which is revealed unto us and that which was revealed unto Abraham, and Ishmael, and Isaac, and Jacob, and the tribes, and that which Moses and Jesus received, and that which the Prophets received from their Lord. We make no distinction between any of them, and unto Him we have surrendered. (2:136)[38]

The Islamic Traditions (*ḥadíths*) confirm this point that the Messengers of Allah are one and the essential truths of their religions are one.

> The prophets are paternal brothers; their mothers are different, but their religion is one (Al-Bukhárí).[39]

The Bahá'í scriptures reiterate and emphasize this point:

> Beware, O believers in the Unity of God, lest ye be tempted to make any distinction between any of the Manifestations of His Cause, or to discriminate against the signs that have accompanied and proclaimed their Revelation. This indeed is the true meaning of Divine Unity, if ye be of them that apprehend and believe this truth. Be ye assured, moreover, that the works and acts of each and every one of these Manifestations of God, nay whatever pertaineth unto them, and whatsoever they may manifest in the future, are all ordained by God, and are a reflection of His Will and Purpose.[40]

The Qur'án treats disbelief in any one of these Messengers as if it were disbelief in all of them. For example, the Qur'án refers to the people of Noah as though they had disbelieved 'the Messengers', when they had only disbelieved in one Messenger, Noah:

> And the people of Noah – when they rejected the Messengers, We drowned them, and We made them as a Sign for mankind . . . (25:37)

The Bahá'í scriptures make the same point:

> Be thou assured in thyself that verily, he who turns away from this Beauty hath also turned away from the Messengers of the past and showeth pride towards God from all eternity to all eternity.[41]

Each of the Messengers of Allah, as described above, confirms and expands upon the teachings of those Messengers that came before him but he also changes some of the laws and teachings that had previously been given. Thus, for example, some laws were given to the Jews and were abrogated by later Messengers of Allah (see Qur'án 6:146). Similarly Jesus says, in the Qur'án:

> And (I come) confirming that which was before me of the Torah, and to make lawful some of that which was forbidden unto you. I come unto you with a sign from your Lord, so keep your duty to Allah and obey me. (3:50)[42]

Any change that these Messengers of Allah make in the divine teachings results in an improvement, making the teachings better and more appropriate to the time:

> None of Our revelations do We abrogate or cause to be forgotten, but We substitute something better or similar; knowest thou not that Allah hath power over all things? (2:106)

It is the changes that each Messenger makes that are the source of differences between them. These changes, however, result not from any deviation from the principle of the unity of the Messengers but rather from the differences in the human condition at the times that they appear on earth. They come to the world at different times, when humanity is in different stages of its social development and facing varying spiritual and social problems. And so each of them has a specific mission to address the problems that confront humanity at that time. The Qur'án also refers to the fact that only Allah Himself is unchanging while all earthly affairs are transient, and so Allah is every day occupied in some new undertaking.

> All that is on earth will perish: But will abide (for ever) the Face of thy Lord – full of Majesty, Bounty and Honour . . . Every day some new task employs Him. (55:26–7, 29)[43]

The Bahá'í scriptures also state that the teachings of the Messengers of Allah have been appropriate to the needs of the time in which each has appeared. The Bahá'í scriptures liken the Messengers of Allah to divine physicians:

> The Prophets of God should be regarded as physicians whose task is to foster the well-being of the world and its peoples, that, through the spirit of oneness, they may heal the sickness of a divided humanity . . . Little wonder, then, if the treatment prescribed by the physician in this day should not be found to be identical with that which he prescribed before. How could it be otherwise when the ills affecting the sufferer necessitate at every stage of his sickness a special remedy? In like manner, every time the Prophets of God have illumined the world with the resplendent radiance of the Day Star of Divine knowledge, they have invariably summoned its peoples to embrace the light of God through such means as best befitted the exigencies of the age in which they appeared. They were thus able to scatter the darkness of ignorance, and to shed upon the world the glory of their own knowledge.[44]

It is through the teachings of the successive Messengers of Allah that humanity is enabled to 'carry forward an ever-advancing civilization'.[45] This, then, is the nature and purpose of true religion. In the Bahá'í scriptures, it is likened to a set of clothes that humanity wears. Although these clothes are very necessary for humanity, they eventually become worn out and so a new set of clothes is needed.

> And now concerning thy question regarding the nature of religion. Know thou that they who are truly wise have likened the world unto the human temple. As the body of man needeth a garment to clothe it, so the body of mankind must needs be adorned with the mantle of justice and wisdom. Its robe is the Revelation vouchsafed unto it by God. Whenever this robe hath fulfilled its purpose, the Almighty will assuredly renew it. For every age requireth a fresh measure of the light of God. Every Divine Revelation hath been sent down in a manner that befitted the circumstances of the age in which it hath appeared.[46]

The knowledge that is with Allah is infinite. The Messengers of Allah cannot give humanity all of this knowledge on one occasion; humanity would not be able to bear it. Therefore on each occasion that a Messenger of Allah comes he gives that part of the knowledge of Allah which is suitable for that particular time. The Qur'án refers to the fact that the Messengers only communicate a little of what they could reveal:

> They ask thee concerning the Spirit (of inspiration). Say: 'The Spirit (cometh) by command of my Lord: of knowledge it is only a little that is communicated to you (O men!).' (17:85)

> And there is not a thing but its (sources and) treasures (inexhaustible) are with Us; but We only send down thereof in due and ascertainable measures. (15:21)

The Bahá'í scriptures similarly state that what is revealed by each of the Messengers is only that part of the knowledge of Allah which humanity can cope with at any particular time.

> O Son of Beauty! By My spirit and by My favour! By My mercy and by My beauty! All that I have revealed unto thee with the tongue of power, and have written for thee with the pen of might, hath been in accordance with thy capacity and understanding, not with My state and the melody of My voice.[47]

We can summarize the above passages from the Qur'án by saying that there are two aspects to the station of these Messengers of Allah. On the one hand, they are all equally the representatives of Allah; they all reveal Allah's Will and guide human beings in their spiritual development. Therefore, Allah states in the Qur'án: 'We make no distinction between any of [the Messengers]' (2:136).[48] On the other hand, each of these Messengers has altered some of the laws and teachings of the previous Messengers in accordance with the needs of the time and this is the source of differences among the

Messengers ('some of [the Messengers] We have caused to excel others,' Qur'án 2:253[49]). In the Bahá'í scriptures, this matter is explained thus:

> These Manifestations of God have each a twofold station. One is the station of pure abstraction and essential unity. In this respect, if thou callest them all by one name, and dost ascribe to them the same attribute, thou hast not erred from the truth . . . For they one and all summon the people of the earth to acknowledge the unity of God . . . They are all invested with the robe of Prophethood, and honoured with the mantle of glory . . .
>
> . . . If thou wilt observe with discriminating eyes, thou wilt behold them all abiding in the same tabernacle, soaring in the same heaven, seated upon the same throne, uttering the same speech, and proclaiming the same Faith . . .[50]
>
> The other is the station of distinction, and pertaineth to the world of creation, and to the limitations thereof. In this respect, each Manifestation of God hath a distinct individuality, a definitely prescribed mission, a predestined Revelation, and specially designated limitations. Each one of them is known by a different name, is characterized by a special attribute, fulfils a definite Mission, and is entrusted with a particular Revelation . . .[51]

This passage of the Bahá'í scriptures goes on to say that, although the Messengers of Allah are in their essence one and the same, it is because of this difference in their missions that people have imagined differences among the Messengers themselves and thus religious misunderstandings and conflicts have arisen.

> It is because of this difference in their station and mission that the words and utterances flowing from these Well-springs of divine knowledge appear to diverge and differ. Otherwise, in the eyes of them that are initiated into the mysteries of divine wisdom, all their utterances are, in reality, but the

> expressions of one Truth. As most of the people have failed to appreciate those stations to which We have referred, they therefore feel perplexed and dismayed at the varying utterances pronounced by Manifestations that are essentially one and the same.[52]

Allah has also, from time to time in the past, sent a prophet (*nabí*), whose purpose was to call people back to Allah and to the teachings of the Messenger of Allah when they have strayed. Bahá'ís and Muslims both believe that, in the process of humanity's development, the age of prophets is now over. Humanity has advanced to the stage where there is no longer a need for prophets to appear after each Messenger of Allah in order to call people back to the teachings of Allah.

The Human Soul and Its Development

The Qur'án states that Allah created human beings and placed them upon the earth as Allah's vicegerents and trustees upon the earth (2:30). Our goal while on earth is to obey Allah's Will and to become righteous individuals.

> O ye people! Adore your Guardian-Lord who created you and those who came before you, that ye may have the chance to learn righteousness. (2:21)

The Bahá'í scriptures also teach that Allah's purpose in creating humanity and placing us upon the earth is that we may develop in the way that Allah wishes:

> Out of the wastes of nothingness, with the clay of My command I made thee to appear, and have ordained for thy training every atom in existence and the essence of all created things . . . And My purpose in all this was that thou mightest attain My everlasting dominion and become worthy of My invisible bestowals.[53]

The path for the spiritual development of the individual is described in much the same way in the scriptures of both religions. In order to progress human beings must follow the teachings of the Messengers of Allah. These include observing the laws that they have given (such as daily prayer, fasting, reciting the scriptures and other matters; for the Bahá'í laws, see chapter 7) and striving to develop spiritual qualities and virtues (some of these are described on pp. 27–31).

The Bahá'í teachings state that each individual has two aspects to his nature: the animal aspect that clings to the things of this world and a spiritual nature that strives for spiritual perfection. The Qur'án also indicates the same idea:

> Relate to them the story of the man to whom We sent Our Signs, but he passed them by: so Satan followed him up and he went astray. If it had been Our Will, We should have elevated him with Our Signs; but he inclined to the earth and followed his own vain desires . . . so relate the story; perchance they may reflect. (7:175–6)

This concept is amplified in the Bahá'í writings. 'Abdu'l-Bahá explains the two natures of human beings thus:

> In man there are two natures; his spiritual or higher nature and his material or lower nature. In one he approaches God, in the other he lives for the world alone. Signs of both these natures are to be found in men. In his material aspect he expresses untruth, cruelty and injustice; all these are the outcome of his lower nature. The attributes of his Divine nature are shown forth in love, mercy, kindness, truth and justice, one and all being expressions of his higher nature. Every good habit, every noble quality belongs to man's spiritual nature, whereas all his imperfections and sinful actions are born of his material nature. If a man's Divine nature dominates his human nature, we have a saint.[54]

It is up to us to develop our spiritual, our divine nature while we are in this world so that we may be more ready for the life after death (for the Bahá'í teachings on how to acquire these virtues, see chapter 5).

Life after Death

Both the Islamic and Bahá'í scriptures agree that our lives do not end with our death. Rather death is just the first step in a long journey taken by our soul in worlds beyond this world. Both religions agree that what our fate is in the next world depends both on our actions while we are in this world and upon the grace of Allah.

Islam	Bahá'í
As for those who disbelieve I shall chastise them with a heavy chastisement in the world and the Hereafter; and they will have no helpers. And as for those who believe and do good works, He will pay them their wages in full. Allah loveth not wrongdoers. (3:56–7)[55]	Thou hast decided between all created things, causing them who are devoted to Thee to ascend unto the summit of glory, and the infidels to fall into the lowest abyss. (Bahá'u'lláh)[56]

However, in the Bahá'í scriptures it is explained that heaven and hell are words that signify spiritual states and are not physical places. When humanity was in its childhood, it needed simple explanations of spiritual realities that could be easily understood and so the prophets talked of heaven and hell and drew graphic descriptions of these places. They described heaven as somewhere that was as wonderful as any human being could imagine and hell as somewhere more terrible than any human being has ever experienced. In this age, however, when the whole world has been explored and human beings have even been into space and have seen into the farthermost recesses of the universe, modern humanity has realized that there is no physical place that is heaven or hell. The Bahá'í scriptures explain that this was a parable to indicate that if one follows the teachings of the Messengers of Allah, one draws nearer to Him and this is the true source of human happiness, a wonderful experience that can be called heaven or paradise. If one ignores and goes against the divine teachings, one becomes a prisoner of the satan within each of us, the animal self, and this is hell.

> They say: 'Where is Paradise, and where is Hell?' Say: 'The one is reunion with Me; the other thine own self, O thou who dost associate a partner with God and doubtest.'[57]

The Ethical Teachings of Religion

Since Bahá'ís believe that Islam and the Bahá'í Faith both come from the same God, it is not surprising that many of the ethical teachings given in the two religions are the same. Allah's Will that human beings should acquire certain virtues and perfections has not altered over the centuries.

Islam	Bahá'í
CLEANLINESS	
For Allah loves those who turn to Him constantly and He loves those who keep themselves pure and clean. (2:222)	God hath enjoined upon you to observe the utmost cleanliness, to the extent of washing what is soiled with dust, let alone with hardened dirt and similar defilement. Fear Him, and be of those who are pure. (Bahá'u'lláh)[58]
JUSTICE	
O ye who believe! Stand out firmly for justice as witnesses to Allah, even as against yourselves, or your	The best beloved of all things in My sight is Justice; turn not away therefrom if thou desirest Me, and

Islam	Bahá'í
parents, or your kin, and whether it be (against) rich or poor: for Allah can best protect both. Follow not the lusts (of your hearts), lest ye swerve and if ye distort (justice) or decline to do justice, verily Allah is well-acquainted with all that ye do. (4:135)	neglect it not that I may confide in thee. By its aid thou shalt see with thine own eyes and not through the eyes of others, and shalt know of thine own knowledge and not through the knowledge of thy neighbour. Ponder this in thy heart; how it behoveth thee to be. Verily justice is My gift to thee and the sign of My loving-kindness. Set it then before thine eyes. (Bahá'u'lláh)[59]

Kindness to parents

Thy Lord hath decreed that ye worship none but Him, and that ye be kind to parents. Whether one or both of them attain old age in thy life, say not to them a word of contempt, nor repel them, but address them in terms of honour. And, out of kindness, lower to them the wing of humility and say: 'My Lord! bestow on them Thy Mercy even as they cherished me in childhood.' (17:23–4)	Say, O My people! Show honour to your parents and pay homage to them. This will cause blessings to descend upon you from the clouds of the bounty of your Lord, the Exalted, the Great. (Bahá'u'lláh)[60]

Truthfulness

Allah will say: 'This is a day on which the truthful will profit from their truth: theirs are Gardens, with rivers flowing beneath, – their eternal Home: Allah well-pleased with them, and they with Allah.' (5:122)[61]	Adorn your heads with the garlands of trustworthiness and fidelity, your hearts with the attire of the fear of God, your tongues with absolute truthfulness, your bodies with the vesture of courtesy. These are in truth seemly adornings unto the temple of man, if ye be of them that reflect. (Bahá'u'lláh)[62]

COMPASSION AND KINDNESS

Islam

Muḥammad is the Messenger of Allah; and those who are with him are strong against Unbelievers, (but) compassionate amongst each other. Thou wilt see them bow and prostrate themselves (in prayer), seeking Grace from Allah and (His) Good Pleasure. (48:29)

Serve Allah, and join not any partners with Him; and do good – to parents, kinsfolk, orphans, those in need, neighbours who are near, neighbours who are strangers, the Companion by your side, the wayfarer (ye meet), and what your right hands possess [slaves]: for Allah loveth not the arrogant, the vainglorious . . (4:36)

Bahá'í

The Almighty beareth Me witness: To act like the beasts of the field is unworthy of man. Those virtues that befit his dignity are forbearance, mercy, compassion and loving-kindness towards all the peoples and kindreds of the earth. (Bahá'u'lláh)[63]

Under all conditions, whether in adversity or at ease, whether honoured or afflicted, this Wronged One hath directed all men to show forth love, affection, compassion and harmony. (Bahá'u'lláh)[64]

DETACHMENT FROM THE THINGS OF THIS WORLD

Islam

Fair in the eyes of men is the love of things they covet: women and sons; heaped-up hoards of gold and silver; horses branded (for blood and excellence); and (wealth of) cattle and well-tilled land. Such are the possessions of this world's life; but in nearness to Allah is the best of goals (to return to).

Say: Shall I give you glad tidings of things far better than those? For the righteous are Gardens in nearness to their Lord, with rivers flowing beneath; therein is their eternal home; with Companions pure (and holy); and the good pleasure of Allah. (3:14–15)

Bahá'í

O Son of Being! Busy not thyself with this world, for with fire We test the gold, and with gold We test Our servants.

O Son of Man! Thou dost wish for gold and I desire thy freedom from it. Thou thinkest thyself rich in its possession, and I recognize thy wealth in thy sanctity therefrom. By My life! This is My knowledge, and that is thy fancy; how can My way accord with thine? (Bahá'u'lláh)[65]

Islam	Bahá'í

GENEROSITY

Islam	Bahá'í
By no means shall ye attain righteousness unless ye give (freely) of that which ye love; and whatever ye give, of a truth Allah knoweth it well. (3:92)	O Children of Dust! Tell the rich of the midnight sighing of the poor, lest heedlessness lead them into the path of destruction, and deprive them of the Tree of Wealth. To give and to be generous are attributes of Mine; well is it with him that adorneth himself with My virtues. (Bahá'u'lláh)[66]

LOVE AND UNITY

Islam	Bahá'í
And hold fast, all together, by the Rope which Allah (stretches out for you), and be not divided among yourselves; and remember with gratitude Allah's favour on you; for ye were enemies and He joined your hearts in love, so that by His Grace ye became brethren. (3:103)	The Great Being saith: O ye children of men! The fundamental purpose animating the Faith of God and His Religion is to safeguard the interests and promote the unity of the human race, and to foster the spirit of love and fellowship amongst men. (Bahá'u'lláh)[67]

OTHER VIRTUES

Islam	Bahá'í
It is not righteousness that ye turn your faces towards East or West; but it is righteousness – to believe in Allah and the Last Day, and the Angels, and the Book, and the Messengers; to spend of your substance, out of love for Him, for your kin, for orphans, for the needy, for the wayfarer, for those who ask, and for the ransom of slaves; to be steadfast in prayer, and practise regular charity; to fulfil the contracts which ye have made; and to be firm and patient in pain (or suffering) and adversity, and throughout all periods of panic. Such are the people of truth, the Allah-fearing. (2:177)	Be generous in prosperity, and thankful in adversity. Be worthy of the trust of thy neighbour, and look upon him with a bright and friendly face. Be a treasure to the poor, an admonisher to the rich, an answerer of the cry of the needy, a preserver of the sanctity of thy pledge. Be fair in thy judgement, and guarded in thy speech. Be unjust to no man, and show all meekness to all men. Be as a lamp unto them that walk in darkness, a joy to the sorrowful, a sea for the thirsty, a haven for the distressed, an upholder and defender of the victim of oppression. Let integrity and uprightness

Islam

Thy Lord hath decreed that ye worship none but Him . . . And render to the kindred their due rights, as (also) to those in want, and to the wayfarer: but squander not (your wealth) in the manner of a spendthrift . . . Kill not your children, for fear of want: We shall provide sustenance for them as well as for you. Verily the killing of them is a great sin. Nor come nigh to adultery: for it is a shameful (deed) and an evil, opening the road (to other evils). Nor take life – which Allah has made sacred – except for just cause . . . Come not nigh to the orphan's property except to improve it, until he attains the age of full strength; and fulfil (every) engagement, for every engagement will be enquired into (on the Day of Reckoning). Give full measure when ye measure, and weigh with a balance that is straight: that is the most fitting and the most advantageous in the final determination. And pursue not that of which thou hast no knowledge; for every act of hearing or of seeing or of (feeling in) the heart will be enquired into (on the Day of Reckoning). Nor walk on the earth with insolence: for thou canst not rend the earth asunder, nor reach the mountains in height. Of all such things the evil is hateful in the sight of thy Lord. These are among the (precepts of) wisdom, which thy Lord hath revealed to thee. (17:23, 26, 31–9)

Bahá'í

distinguish all thine acts. Be a home for the stranger, a balm to the suffering, a tower of strength for the fugitive. Be eyes to the blind, and a guiding light unto the feet of the erring. Be an ornament to the countenance of truth, a crown to the brow of fidelity, a pillar of the temple of righteousness, a breath of life to the body of mankind, an ensign of the hosts of justice, a luminary above the horizon of virtue, a dew to the soil of the human heart, an ark on the ocean of knowledge, a sun in the heaven of bounty, a gem on the diadem of wisdom, a shining light in the firmament of thy generation, a fruit upon the tree of humility. (Bahá'u'lláh)[68]

3

The Claim of Bahá'u'lláh

If the teachings revealed in the Bahá'í scriptures are very similar to those in the Qur'án as demonstrated in the previous chapter, what then is the purpose of Bahá'u'lláh's coming? How can Muslims understand who Bahá'u'lláh is? What does he claim to be? What station does he claim? As we have previously seen (see pp. 14–15), the Qur'án depicts a series of Messengers from Allah coming one after the other. Muḥammad (blessings and peace be upon him) is himself stated in the Qur'án to be a Messenger come after a break in the series of Messengers:

> O People of the Book! Now hath come unto you, making (things) clear unto you, our Messenger, after the break in (the series of) Our Messengers, lest ye should say: 'There came unto us no bringer of glad tidings and no warner (from evil)': but now hath come unto you a bringer of glad tidings and a warner (from evil). And Allah hath power over all things. (5:21)

Muslims can thus understand Bahá'u'lláh as a further Messenger from Allah in this same series of Messengers who have come to guide humanity whenever this has been necessary. He claims that his coming was prophesied in all of the scriptures of the past. He claims that the books that he has revealed are the Word of Allah for this age. This claim can be summarized in Bahá'u'lláh's own words:

He Whose advent hath been foretold in the heavenly Scriptures is come, could ye but understand it. The world's horizon is illumined by the splendours of this Most Great Revelation. Haste ye with radiant hearts and be not of them that are bereft of understanding.[69]

God is My witness that this Wronged One hath had no purpose except to convey the Word of God.[70]

The Bahá'í scriptures teach that the pattern described in the Bible and the Holy Qur'án, whereby Allah has sent from time to time a message, has been continued in our time by Bahá'u-'lláh's coming. Each time that humanity has needed guidance from Allah because of changing circumstances, Allah has sent that guidance in the form of a Messenger. In this day also, when humanity's circumstances have changed more than at any comparable period in the past, Allah has sent Bahá'u'lláh with a new message. The Messengers of Allah are likened in the Bahá'í scriptures to heavenly doctors who come to diagnose and prescribe the correct medicine for the spiritual ills of the world (see pp. 137–8). The Bahá'í scriptures claim that Bahá'u'lláh has brought the divine remedy which will cure the ills of the world today; he is thus the divine doctor sent by Allah with the medicine for the spiritual ills that afflict humanity today.

The Prophets of God should be regarded as physicians whose task is to foster the well-being of the world and its peoples, that, through the spirit of oneness, they may heal the sickness of a divided humanity. To none is given the right to question their words or disparage their conduct, for they are the only ones who can claim to have understood the patient and to have correctly diagnosed its ailments. No man, however acute his perception, can ever hope to reach the heights which the wisdom and understanding of the Divine Physician have attained. Little wonder, then, if the treatment prescribed by the physician in this day should not be found to be identical

> with that which he prescribed before. How could it be otherwise when the ills affecting the sufferer necessitate at every stage of his sickness a special remedy?[71]

Muslims have raised objections to the claim of Bahá'u'lláh based upon their understanding of the Qur'án. They maintain that Muḥammad is stated in the Qur'án to be the 'Seal of the Prophets' (33:40) and thus to be the last prophet of Allah. On the basis of this they consider that Allah has precluded the possibility of further prophets coming after Muḥammad. They point out, moreover, that in the Qur'án, Islam is stated to be the 'complete' religion which Allah has chosen for humanity (5:3, cf. 3:17, 3:79). If it is complete, they argue, there is no need for any further religion from Allah. Based on such passages, these Muslim scholars have rejected the claims of Bahá'u'lláh and some have even called for a persecution of the followers of Bahá'u'lláh on this basis. We will now consider these objections and the Bahá'í response to them.[72]

The Seal of the Prophets

Bahá'ís believe that the objections raised by Muslim scholars are based upon a misunderstanding of the Qur'án. This is particularly so with regard to the matter of the verse of the Qur'án that states that Muḥammad is the 'Seal of the Prophets':

> Muḥammad is not the father of any of your men, but (he is) the Messenger of Allah, and the Seal of the Prophets (*kh͟átam an-nabiyyin*): and Allah has full knowledge of all things. (33:40)

> *Má kána Muḥammadun abá aḥadin min rijálikum walákin rasúl alláh wa kh͟átam an-nabiyyin. Wa kána 'lláhu bi-kulli sh͟ay'in 'alíman.* (33:40)

The Claim of Bahá'u'lláh

The time fore-ordained unto the peoples and kindreds of the earth is now come. The promises of God, as recorded in the holy Scriptures, have all been fulfilled . . . Happy is the man that pondereth in his heart that which hath been revealed in the Books of God, the Help in Peril, the Self-Subsisting. Meditate upon this, O ye beloved of God, and let your ears be attentive unto His Word, so that ye may, by His grace and mercy, drink your fill from the crystal waters of constancy, and become as steadfast and immovable as the mountain in His Cause. (Bahá'u'lláh)[73]

Verily I say, this is the Day in which mankind can behold the Face, and hear the Voice, of the Promised One. The Call of God hath been raised, and the light of His countenance hath been lifted up upon men. It behoveth every man to blot out the trace of every idle word from the tablet of his heart, and to gaze, with an open and unbiased mind, on the signs of His Revelation, the proofs of His Mission, and the tokens of His glory.

Great indeed is this Day! The allusions made to it in all the sacred Scriptures as the Day of God attest its greatness. The soul of every Prophet of God, of every Divine Messenger, hath thirsted for this wondrous Day. All the divers kindreds of the earth have, likewise, yearned to attain it. No sooner, however, had the Day Star of His Revelation manifested itself in the heaven of God's Will, than all, except those whom the Almighty was pleased to guide, were found dumbfounded and heedless. (Bahá'u'lláh)[74]

There are two aspects to this specific issue of the 'Seal of the Prophets', first whether or not the word translated as 'seal' refers to finality, and second whether the term 'Seal of the Prophets' implies that there will be no more Messengers of Allah. There are numerous pieces of evidence that Bahá'ís have brought forward to explain why the usual interpretation of Muslim scholars is faulty. The following are a few of these:

1. *Textual Reasons.* This line of reasoning concerns itself with the meaning of the two terms *kh͟átam* and *nabí* that constitute the phrase 'Seal of the Prophets (*kh͟átam an-nabiyyin*)'. The first

word in this phrase appears in the Qur'án as *khátam*, which means a signet ring or seal ring which is worn, usually on the finger and which is used when sealing a document; in this context it is best translated as 'ring' or 'ornament'. However, some began to recite the phrase using *khátim*, which conveys the meaning of 'end' or 'finality'. But the fourth caliph, 'Alí ibn Abí Ṭálib, is reported to have specifically corrected the reading of Abú 'Abd ar-Raḥmán as-Salamí and told him to say *khátam an-nabiyyin*, with 'a' after the 't'.[75] This Tradition (*ḥadíth*) is reported by Jalál ad-Dín as-Suyúṭí (1445–1505), the pre-eminent Sunni Islamic scholar of the late 15th century, in his Qur'án commentary *ad-Durr al-Manthúr*, in which he deals at length with this passage of the Qur'án. In the same work by as-Suyúṭi, another Tradition is given in which 'Á'ishah, the wife of the Prophet, is stated to have said:

> Say '*khátam an-nabiyyin*', and do not say 'there is no prophet after him'.[76]

Thus the phrase 'Seal of the Prophets' means Allah giving Muḥammad His seal of approval or regarding Muḥammad as an ornament among the prophets of Allah. Some commentators also state that *khátam an-nabiyyin* means the 'Sealer of the Prophets' in the sense that Muḥammad is the one who gives the seal of approval to the preceding prophets.

> He [Muḥammad] has become like a seal for them [the prophets] by which they are sealed and they are adorned (*yatazayyúna*) by his being from among them.[77]

Even those early authoritative commentators who give a meaning of finality to the word *khátam* point out that this is placed on prophethood only until the Day of Judgement. For example, aṭ-Ṭabarí in his famous commentary says that the phrase *khátam an-nabiyyin* means 'that he [Muḥammad] has sealed prophethood and placed his mark upon it (*ṭaba'a alay-há*) and so this is not open to anyone after him until the coming of the [Last] Hour'.[78] As will be mentioned below, Bahá'ís would agree with this interpretation since they believe that the Day of Judgement has occurred with the advent of the Bahá'í Faith.

Regarding *nabí*, some Bahá'í authors have pointed out that the Qur'án recognizes several different classes of beings between Allah and humankind. Apart from angels, there are two classes that appear as human beings: *nabí* and *rasúl*. These two classes carry out different functions as indeed their names clearly indicate. The word *rasúl* comes from the root meaning 'to send'. It therefore means someone who is sent with a message, a Messenger or apostle. Thus the word *rasúl* applies to those who were sent with a holy book and a new teaching from Allah. The *nabí*, on the other hand, is 'one who prophesies' or 'one who informs' the people about the law and teachings brought by a *rasúl*. Such definitions are given by many authorities in Islam.[79]

These two words are used differently in the Qur'án. Although it is true that some individuals are designated as being both *nabí* and *rasúl* in the Qur'án, this does not always apply. The more important figures, such as Abraham, Moses, Jesus and Muḥammad, are called *rasúls* and *nabís*; this is because they performed the functions of both bringing a new holy book and a new teaching from Allah and also that of prophesying. But lesser figures are known just as *nabí*. They only prophesied and warned the people. For example, Moses is referred to as *rasúl* and *nabí*, while his brother Aaron is only *nabí* (19:53–4). This is because Moses carried out the more important task of bearing a message and a new holy law from Allah (the Torah), while Aaron was only a prophet.

Some Muslim scholars have argued that the term 'Seal of the Prophets' includes Messengers of Allah. They have asserted that *nabí* is the more general inclusive term and *rasúl* is a specific or special form of *nabí*. They assert that every *rasúl* is a *nabí* but not every *nabí* is a *rasúl*. Therefore they argue the assertion that Muḥammad is the 'Seal of the Prophets' includes within it the assertion that he is the 'Seal of the Messengers'. This argument does not accord with what is in the Qur'án, however. Although many figures in the Qur'án are called *nabí* and some of these are also called *rasúl*, there are also some figures such as Húd and Ṣáliḥ who are called *rasúl* but not *nabí*. Thus it is clear that the Qur'án regards *rasúl* and *nabí* as two completely separate and distinct terms and that the word *nabí* does not necessarily include *rasúl*.

It is clear, therefore, that the term 'Seal of the Prophets' (*kh͟átam an-nabiyyin*) refers only to the line of *nabís*. Thus even if the phrase *kh͟átam an-nabiyyin* did mean the 'last of the Prophets', it would not necessarily mean the 'last of the Messengers'. And this is what Bahá'u'lláh claimed to be: the bearer of a new message from Allah.

2. *Contextual Reasons*. The full text of this verse reads 'Muḥammad is not the father of any of your men, but (he is) the Messenger of Allah, and the Seal of the Prophets (*kh͟átam an-nabiyyin*): and Allah has full knowledge of all things' (33:40). The second line of argument advanced by Bahá'ís stems from the context in which this verse was revealed, as recorded in the various books of Islamic history. There are two overlapping explanations of this verse in books of commentary on the Qur'án. The first involves Muḥammad's marriage to the divorced wife of Zayd, his adopted son. The verses leading up to Qur'án 33:40 concern this issue:

> . . . thou didst fear the people but it is more fitting that thou shouldst fear Allah. Then when Zayd had dissolved (his marriage) with her, with the necessary (formality), We joined her in marriage to thee: in order that (in future) there may be no difficulty to the Believers in (the matter of) marriage with the wives of their adopted sons, when the latter have dissolved with the necessary (formality) (their marriage) with them. And Allah's command must be fulfilled.

> There can be no difficulty to the Prophet in what Allah has indicated to him as a duty. It was the practice (approved) of Allah amongst those of old that have passed away. And the command of Allah is a decree determined.
>
> (It is the practice of those) who preach the Messages of Allah, and fear Him, and fear none but Allah: and enough is Allah to call (men) to account.
>
> Muḥammad is not the father of any of your men, but (he is) the Messenger of Allah, and the Seal of the Prophets: and Allah has full knowledge of all things. (33:37–40)

As is clear from these verses in the Qur'án and is confirmed in the books of commentary, the verse 33:40 relates to the episode when Muḥammad married the divorced wife of Zayd, his adopted son. Some of the people objected to this, saying that he had married his daughter-in-law. This verse was revealed to confirm that Muḥammad was not the father of Zayd and therefore there could be no objection to his marrying Zayd's divorced wife. The final part of the verse stating that Muḥammad is the Messenger of Allah and the Seal of the Prophets is there to emphasize the excellence of Muḥammad in defence of the people's criticism of him, and therefore in this context, *khátam an-nabiyyin* means the equivalent of 'the best of the prophets'.

The second explanation also concerns Zayd. While the first explanation elucidates the first part of this verse well, it does not really explain the second part, which is firmly tied in and related to the first part. The word *lákin* (but) in Arabic grammar relates the two halves of a sentence in an oppositional or adversative manner; in other words, the second half of the sentence is intended, in some sense, to have an opposite or opposing meaning to the first half.[80] Some commentators have ignored this link and have just explained the two terms 'the Messenger of Allah and the Seal of the Prophets' in various standard ways. The more careful commentators, such as Abu'l-Qásim Maḥmúd az-Zamakhsharí

(1075–1144) and 'Abd Alláh al-Bayḍáwí (d. *circa* 1291), have, however, sought out explanations that make sense of this linking of the two halves of the sentence. Thus, for example, az-Zamakhsharí, one of the most important of the commentators of the Qur'án, gives the following explanation, which links the second part of the verse to the first; his explanation involves Ibráhím, the son of Muḥammad who died in infancy:

> '*Muḥammad is not the father of any man among you*' – in other words that he is not in reality (i.e. physically) the father of any man among you such that the normal relationship that exists between a father and son would obtain between him and that person with respect to the prohibition on marriage to a daughter-in-law.
>
> '*But*' he is '*the Messenger of Allah*' – and every Messenger is the father of his people in respect of the honour and esteem that is due to him from them and the compassion and friendly admonitions that are due to them from him, but not with regard to the other obligations that pertain between fathers and sons. And Zayd is [the same as] any man among you, who are not in reality (i.e. physically) his sons. His position is the same as your position and his adoption was by way of singling him out and drawing him near and nothing else.
>
> '*And*' he is the '*Seal of the Prophets*' – which means that had he (Muḥammad) had any son who reached the age of manhood, he (the son) would have been a prophet and he (Muḥammad) would not have been the 'Seal of the Prophets'; for it is related of him (Muḥammad) that he said concerning Ibráhím (Muḥammad's son) when he died: 'had he lived, he would have been a prophet.'[81]

Thus az-Zamakhsharí is saying that this verse is intended to state that Muḥammad is not the physical father of any living male child but rather he is the father of his people, in the spiritual sense that every Messenger of Allah is like a father to his people. He is not the physical father of any living male child in that had Muḥammad had any surviving sons they would have succeeded him as a prophet, but as Ibrahím died, Muḥammad would not be succeeded by a prophet.

In explanation of az-Zamak̲h̲s̲h̲arí's commentary, it should be noted that among the Jews there was a tradition that a line of prophets continued the work of each Messenger (see the Tradition quoted below, p. 42). This line of prophets was based on lineal descent, the son of a prophet becoming the next prophet. There are several Traditions that state, as the above passage does, that had Ibráhím, Muḥammad's son, survived, he would have been a prophet.[82] Since Muḥammad had no surviving sons, the Jews of Medina began to say that Muḥammad's adopted son Zayd (who was called by the people 'Zayd son of Muḥammad') would therefore succeed him as prophet. It was in this context that the verse Qur'án 33:40 was revealed, asserting that Muḥammad had no sons and would not be succeeded by a prophet in the Jewish manner.

When later the idea that Muḥammad was the final prophet became a firm doctrine, these Traditions that stated that, had he lived, Ibráhím would have been a prophet, became a problem to Muslim scholars – since they implicitly acknowledge that there is nothing to prevent prophets appearing after Muḥammad. And so we find some of the later scholars denying their authenticity,[83] despite the fact that these Traditions are cited in collections of Traditions that are considered very reliable, such as those of Ibn Májah and Aḥmad ibn Ḥanbal.[84]

Similarly, Fak̲h̲r ad-Dín ar-Rází, who is one of the major classical commentators on the Qur'án, gives the following reason why the two phrases *rasúl Allah* and *k̲h̲átam an-nabiyyín* are inserted at this point in this verse in relation to the statement that 'Muḥammad is not the father of any man among you'.

And so [Allah] Almighty has denied his [Muḥammad] being the father of any son in the proof that He gives establishing certain aspects of fatherhood. And so He says: '*rather he is*

> *the Messenger of Allah*'. For the Messenger of Allah is like a father to his people in his compassion towards them and in the respect that they owe him. No, indeed he is greater than that! For the prophet is dearer to the people than themselves, and a father is not so. Furthermore He informs us about the greater compassion on his part and the greater respect they owe him in His words '*Seal of the Prophets*'. And this is because a prophet is [usually] one who is followed by another prophet, so that if he omits any advice or explanation, this can be rectified by the one who follows him. But the one who does not have a prophet coming after him is more compassionate towards his people, and must guide them better and give them more. Therefore he is as a father is to a son, in that a son also has no one else [after his father].[85]

Thus ar-Rází implies that the intention of the verse is not to preclude any further Messengers of Allah appearing in the future but to assert that Muḥammad's immediate successor would not have the rank of prophet and thereby to exalt Muḥammad's station as being one who would not have a prophet as his successor to guide his people and hence he must give a fuller and more perfect revelation. The interpretations of az-Zamakhsharí and ar-Rází are confirmed in the following Traditions found in the *Ṣaḥíḥs* of al-Bukhárí and Muslim as well as elsewhere:

> The Children of Israel used to be ruled by prophets. Whenever a prophet died another prophet would succeed him. But there will be no prophets after me, rather there will be caliphs (*khulafá*, successors), who will be many.[86]

This Tradition clearly indicates that the phrase 'there will be no prophets after me' relates to the status of the immediate successors of Muḥammad. The statement 'there will be no prophets after me' occurs in many other Traditions with this same meaning; for example, the following Tradition relates to 'Alí's appointment to be in charge of Medina during

Muḥammad's absence on the Tabuk campaign:

> The Apostle of Allah (blessings and peace be upon him) said to 'Alí: 'You are in the same position in relation to me that Aaron (Hárún) was to Moses, except that there will be no prophet after me.'[87]

Here Muḥammad states that just as Aaron was made Moses' deputy as leader of the Israelites during Moses' absence on Mount Sinai, so too was 'Alí made Muḥammad's deputy in Medina during the Tabuk campaign. But Muḥammad, knowing that 'Alí would survive him and that Aaron was a prophet (19:53), hastens to correct anyone who may think that this means that 'Alí will continue on after him with the rank of a prophet, by stating that his immediate successors will not be prophets.

Thus, in summary, the full meaning of verse 33:40 is to assert that Zayd ibn al Ḥáritha should not be considered as the natural son of Muḥammad nor as a potential prophet who would succeed him.

It is worth noting that when these Traditions in which Muḥammad states that 'there will be no prophets after me' are understood in this way, they provide evidence of the concept of progressive revelation that was described above (see pp. 18–24). The revelation of Muḥammad was so much fuller and more complete than those of Moses and Jesus that, as ar-Rází states, there was no need for prophets to follow on after Muḥammad to explain his teachings and ensure that the people kept to these.

3. *Logical Evidence.* The return in the future of Jesus Christ (*al-masíḥ*) to the world is part of Islamic belief. Prophecies of this future occurrence are to be found in the Qur'án and all of the most reliable collections of the Traditions (*ḥadíths*) (see pp. 118, 126–8). Since Jesus is stated in the Qur'án to be a

prophet (*nabí*) and a Messenger (*rasúl*), then his return to the world after the Prophet Muḥammad must be evidence that the phrase 'Seal of the Prophets' does not mean that Muḥammad is the last prophet or Messenger to come to the world. Some Muslim commentators of the Qur'án have tried to get around this problem by stating that although Christ will appear after Muḥammad, he first appeared before Muḥammad; and that in any case, he will keep to the *Sharí'ah* of Muḥammad.[88] This explanation is not in accord with the relevant Traditions, however. According to these Traditions, Christ will come to the earth after Muḥammad as a prophet and he will not keep to the *Sharí'ah* of Muḥammad, since the Traditions specifically state, for example, that he will abolish the *Jizyah* (see p. 126). In other words, he will come as a Messenger of Allah with the authority to abrogate the laws of Islam.

It should also be noted that the verse under discussion (Qur'án 33:40) states that 'Muḥammad . . . is the Messenger of Allah and the Seal of the Prophets'. Thus even if we take *khátam* to mean 'last', it refers only to prophets and not to the Messengers of Allah. If the meaning of the Qur'án had been that the station of both prophet and Messenger of Allah should end with Muḥammad, then the above verse would have been recast as 'Muḥammad . . . is the Seal of the Messengers of Allah and of the Prophets'. The verse as it stands makes a clear distinction between 'Prophet' to which the term 'Seal' applies and the 'Messenger of Allah' to which that term does not apply.

4. *Historical Evidence.* There is much historical evidence that there was no general agreement among the early Muslims that the phrase 'Seal of the Prophets' meant that there would be no prophets after Muḥammad. Certainly up to the middle of the 3rd Islamic century there is a great deal of evidence from literary and historical sources for this. It is thought that the doctrine of Muḥammad being the final prophet was

adopted as official Islamic doctrine in the early years of the 4th Islamic century (late 10th century AD), mainly as a counter to the numerous revolts that had occurred and were still occurring against the caliphate in the name of various persons claiming to be prophets.[89] By making the doctrine of the finality of prophethood in Muḥammad a central tenet in Islam, the Muslim authorities were able to stem the tide of revolts so successfully that in the centuries since that time there have only been a handful of such claimants.

Thus in the literature of the period preceding the formal establishment of this doctrine, we can find evidence of other interpretations of this term *khátam an-nabiyyin*. A literary example would be the 2nd century (8th Christian century) commentary on the *Naqá'iḍ of Jarír and Farazdaq*, which is probably by Abú 'Ubayda. He explains the phrase '*khátam an-nabiyyin*' as meaning the 'best of prophets (*khayr an-nabiyyin*)'. This usage of *khátam*, 'seal', as meaning 'the best' or 'the finest' of a group of people is frequently found in other contexts where it clearly does not mean 'last'.[90] The implication of 'seal' here is the 'seal of perfection' or that the person described is the one who gives the 'seal of approval' to the others in this category. Another example of the usage of *khátam* in early Arabic literature is to be found in the poems of Umayyah ibn Abí aṣ-Ṣalt, who was a contemporary of Muḥammad. He speaks of Muḥammad as being the one through whom 'Allah sealed the prophets before him and after him', thus clearly indicating an expectation of prophets after Muḥammad.[91]

In the realm of writings on Islamic theology, there are the various early attempts to draw up an Islamic creed, *'aqída*. The first such document that is generally accepted as having been a systematic attempt to create a comprehensive official Muslim creed is the *Fiqh Akbar II*, which is thought to have been drawn up by al-Ash'arí (d. 324/935–6) or one of his school at about the end of the 3rd Islamic century (early 10th century AD). In this document, although there is a whole paragraph on the Prophet Muḥammad, there is no mention of him being the last prophet.[92] Other early creeds such as ones attributed to Ibn Ḥanbal, Abú Ḥanífa and to their pupils, also do not refer to Muḥammad as the last prophet or the last Messenger.[93] Such statements do not become standard in this type of text until early in the 4th Islamic century (the middle of the 10th Christian century).

Even Muslim scholars of a later period show some evidence that they are not completely satisfied with the standard Muslim interpretation of the phrase 'Seal of the Prophets'. One of the greatest theologians and mystics that Islam has produced, Muḥammad al-Ghazálí (d. 505/1111), devoted the second book of his most famous work, *Iḥyá' 'Ulúm ad-Dín*, to a consideration of the 'foundations of Islamic belief' (*qawá'id al-'aqá'id*). In this section of his work, al-Ghazálí outlines what he considers to be the essential and necessary beliefs of Muslims. However, at no point in his discussion of prophethood in general or of the prophethood of Muḥammad in particular does al-Ghazálí indicate that he considers the belief that Allah will send no prophets or Messengers of Allah after Muḥammad to be a necessary article of faith for Muslims.[94] Although he refers specifically to the term 'Seal of the Prophets', al-Ghazálí does not say that this means that there will be no future prophets or messengers of Allah. Rather he links the term 'Seal of the Prophets' with the concept that Muḥammad was the 'abrogator of the *Sharí'ahs* of the Jews, Christians and Sabians, which preceded him.' In other words, that 'seal' refers to the abrogation of the previous religions and is not a statement about the future.[95]

Even as late as the 15th century AD, moreover, an author such as as-Suyúṭí, who was the most important Sunni scholar of his generation, found no difficulty in including Traditions which directly contradict the doctrine of the finality of prophethood in Muḥammad in his Qur'án commentary *ad-Durr al-Manthúr* (see above, p. 36).

In summary, the doctrine that Muḥammad was the final prophet and Messenger of Allah, although it is found among some writers from early times, does not appear to have gained general agreement among Muslims until the beginning of the 4th Islamic century (early 10th century AD). Even at much later times, eminent Muslim scholars have indicated that they were not fully convinced of this doctrine.

5. *The Evidence of Other Passages of the Qur'án.* Bahá'ís point out that since the Qur'án is the word of Allah, there can be no contradictions within it. Therefore any single verse must be understood in the context of other verses that relate to the same theme so that an overall understanding of the Qur'án's view on that theme can be built up.

> Then is it only a part of the Book that ye believe in, and do ye reject the rest? (2:85)

There are many proofs advanced by Bahá'í writers that seek to show that the assertion by some that *khátam an-nabiyyin* means that there will be no further Messengers of Allah contradicts other verses of the Qur'án.

A. THE FIXED TERM OF ISLAM AND THE COMING OF A FUTURE MESSENGER OF ALLAH. There are several verses in the Qur'án which imply that the Islamic religious community (*ummah*) will have a fixed term (*ajal*). One passage in particular links this fixed term with the coming of a future Messenger of Allah. We will need to analyze this passage carefully since the translators, influenced by the doctrine that there can be no Messengers of Allah after Muḥammad, have tried to give another interpretation to it. To begin, we give this passage as translated by Yusuf Ali but inserting the Arabic of those words the translation of which is discussed below:

> To every *ummah* is an *ajal*: when their *ajal* is reached not an hour can they cause delay nor (an hour) can they advance (it in anticipation).

> O ye children of Adam! *Immá ya'tiyanna-kum* Messengers from amongst you rehearsing my Signs unto you, – those who are righteous and mend (their lives), – on them shall be no fear nor shall they grieve. (7:34–5)

The term *ummah* is translated 'people' by Yusuf Ali and 'nation' by Pickthall. If we look at the way that this term is used in the Qur'án, we can see, however, that it is used specifically for a religious community. Thus, for example, it is stated that 'for every *ummah* there is a Messenger' (10:47[96], cf. 16:36) and 'unto each *ummah* have We given sacred rites' (22:67).[97] Yusuf Ali agrees with this assessment since, in two places, he also translates *ummah* as 'sect' (45:28). The standard classical Arabic dictionaries give such meanings as 'the people of a particular religion', 'a people to whom a Messenger of Allah is sent' and 'the followers of a prophet'. These meanings are given ahead of such meanings as 'nation' and 'people'.[98] Thus the most accurate translation of the word *ummah* in the Qur'án is 'religious community'.

The term *ajal* is translated 'term' by both Yusuf Ali and Pickthall. It is important to note, however, that, as the next phrase in 7:34 states, it cannot be advanced or postponed (see also 23:43); it is thus a fixed term. The Qur'án also indicates that each *ajal* is linked to a particular sacred scripture: 'For each *ajal* is a Book (revealed)' (13:38). Thus the word *ajal* refers to a religious dispensation that goes on for a specific period of time before being ended. Putting these two terms together, we can see that the phrase 'To every *ummah* is an *ajal*' means 'For every religious community, there is a fixed term.' This is a clear reference to the series of Messengers of Allah that have come to the world, each giving rise to a religious community for a limited period of time and then followed by the next Messenger. This series of Messengers is repeatedly referred to in the Qur'án (Noah, Abraham, Moses, Jesus and Muḥammad; see for example 33:7, 42:13).

Although some Muslim scholars have interpreted the phrase *immá ya'tiyanna-kum* as referring to the past, its grammatical structure is such as to refer to the future. The emphatic form that is used means that 'there shall certainly come to you Messengers . . . ' There would be little point to this verse being in the Qur'án unless it was intended as a warning about the future. One can find other places in the Qur'án where the meaning of this phrase clearly refers to a future event. The following are two passages as translated by Yusuf Ali where the same phrase occurs and where it is clear that the reference is to a future event:

> We said: 'Get ye down all from here; and if, as is sure, there comes to you (*immá ya'tiyanna-kum*) guidance from Me, whosoever follows My guidance, on them shall be no fear, nor shall they grieve. (2:38)

> He said: 'Get ye down, both of you [Adam and Eve], – all together, from the Garden, with enmity one to another: but if, as is sure, there comes to you (*immá ya'tiyanna-kum*) guidance from Me, whosoever follows My guidance, will not lose his way, nor fall into misery.' (20:123)

Thus we can see that *ya'tiyanna-kum* means 'there shall certainly come to you' or 'it is certain that there shall come to you' and the word *immá* makes this a conditional clause: 'If . . .' or 'whenever . . .' In order to contain all of these meanings when the two words are brought together, we would have to translate thus: 'If, as is sure to happen, there shall come to you . . . ' or 'Whenever, as is sure to happen, there shall come to you . . .'

Putting together these two verses (7:34–5) with these explanations, we see that the first verse is a clear reference to a series of Messengers of Allah each coming for a limited period of time to be followed by the next. This is immediately followed by a verse that looks forward to the coming of a future Messenger of Allah. Thus the two verses can be translated as:

> For every religious community there is a fixed term appointed: when their term is reached not an hour can they delay it nor can they advance it.
>
> O children of Adam! Whenever, as is sure to happen, there shall come to you Messengers from among yourselves, rehearsing my signs to you, whoso shall fear Allah and do good works, no fear shall be upon them neither shall they grieve. (7:4–35)

Thus the pattern described in the Qur'án is that of a succession of Messengers of Allah each guiding a people who thereby become a religious community (*ummah*). At the end of the fixed term (*ajal*) of one religious community, a new Messenger of Allah comes and his community takes the place of the previous one, just as the time for the Jewish community ended with the coming of Jesus and the time for the Christian community ended with the coming of Muḥammad. Bahá'ís point out that neither in these verses nor anywhere else in the Qur'án is an exception made for the Islamic *ummah* in this general principle. Therefore the Islamic community also has its fixed term and these two verses point to the future coming of another Messenger of Allah.

And what does the Qur'án describe as happening at the end of the fixed term of each community? A new Messenger of Allah comes with a new holy book and a new teaching, confirming part of the teaching of the previous religion but also abrogating part of it.

> And it was never the part of a Messenger to bring a verse except as Allah permitted. For each fixed term is a Book (revealed). Allah doth blot out or confirm what He pleaseth: with Him is the Mother of the Book [which is the source of all revelation]. (13:38–9)[99]

Indeed Muslims may be said to be in the same position as those who opposed Muḥammad and said that their 'fixed term' had not yet come to an end:

> (Do they not see) that it may well be that their term (*ajal*) is nigh drawing to an end? In what message after this will they then believe? (7:185)

B. THE SERIES OF MESSENGERS. It has already been pointed out that the Qur'án clearly depicts the coming of a series of Messengers from Allah, with Muḥammad as the latest in this series after there had been a break in the succession (5:21). The Qur'án tells of a series of Messengers of Allah coming to the people of the world, each bringing a holy book and establishing a religious community (*ummah*), and each ending the religious dispensation of the previous Messenger. Bahá'ís point out that this pattern is the established pattern of Allah as described in the Qur'án. It is, however, a principle, stated again and again in the Qur'án in relation to various matters, that whatever has been established as the pattern of practice of Allah will not change:

> (Such has been) the practice (approved) of Allah already in the past: no change wilt thou find in the practice (approved) of Allah. (48:23, cf. 17:77, 30:30, 33:62, 35:43)

If this Quranic principle, that the pattern established by Allah in the past will not change, is applied, it means that there will come a future Messenger of Allah after Muḥammad in the same way as there has come a Messenger after all preceding Messengers of Allah.

C. ISLAM AS THE MIDDLE COMMUNITY. It is explicitly stated in the Qur'án that the Muslim community is a middle community. In other words, the Muslim community is between two communities, one that preceded it (the Christian community) and one that is to come after it, when the new Messenger of Allah comes:

> Thus We have appointed you a middle community (*ummatan wasaṭan*), that ye may be witnesses against mankind. (2:143)[100]

Thus it follows that the fixed term for the Islamic community will eventually come and it will be replaced by another community and another holy book.

D. THE INFINITE NATURE OF THE WORD OF ALLAH. Another indication that the revelation of Allah's Word does not end with the Qur'án is its statement regarding the infinite nature of the Word of Allah:

> Say: If the ocean were ink (wherewith to write out) the words of my Lord, sooner would the ocean be exhausted than would the words of my Lord, even if we added another ocean like it, for its aid. (18:109)

> And if all the trees on earth were pens and the Ocean (were ink), with seven Oceans behind it to add to its (supply), yet would not the Words of Allah be exhausted (in the writing): for Allah is Exalted in power, full of Wisdom. (31:27)

These verses indicate that the revealed Word of Allah is potentially limitless. Clearly the vast extent of the Word of Allah envisaged in these and similar verses of the Qur'án is not confined just to a book the size of the Qur'án or even the combined scriptures of the revealed religions such as Judaism and Christianity. Indeed the Qur'án explicitly states that knowledge is sent down through the Messengers of Allah a small part at a time (15:21, 17:85, see p. 22). The Bahá'í scriptures confirm that the word of Allah is inexhaustible and that Messengers of Allah will also appear in the future with additional scriptures from Him (see p. 172).

E. THE COVENANT OF ALLAH. Allah has established a covenant that whenever a Messenger of Allah comes, human beings should accept that Messenger and help him:

> Behold! Allah took the covenant of the Prophets, saying: 'I give you a Book and Wisdom; then comes to you a Messenger confirming what is with you; do ye believe him and render him help.' Allah said: 'Do ye agree and take this My Covenant as binding on you?' They said: 'We agree.' He said: 'Then bear witness and I am with you among the witnesses.' (3:81)

The Qur'án confirms that this covenant was taken with all of the Messengers, including Muḥammad:

> And remember We took from the Prophets their Covenant: as (We did) from thee [Muḥammad]: from Noah, Abraham, Moses and Jesus the son of Mary: We took from them a solemn Covenant. (33:7)

Therefore the Muslims are also under a covenant to accept a new Messenger of Allah whenever he should appear. There would be no point in the covenant being established with Muḥammad if no future Messengers of Allah were expected.

F. THERE WILL ALWAYS BE A NEED FOR MESSENGERS OF ALLAH. The Qur'án indicates that at no time and under no conditions will there be no need for Allah to send down Messengers. Even if circumstances were to change radically and the earth were to be peopled by angels and conditions were those of perfect peace and tranquillity, there would still be a need for Messengers to come from Allah for guidance.

> Say, 'If there were settled on earth angels walking about in peace and quiet, We should certainly have sent them down from the heavens an angel for a Messenger.' (17:95)

G. WARNINGS ABOUT FOLLOWING ONE'S ANCESTRAL FAITH. Furthermore, there are verses in the Qur'án that warn that when a new Messenger of Allah comes, the excuse that one is following the religion of one's forefathers is not acceptable to Allah (see p. 80). Bahá'ís ask: what would be the point of including such verses in the Qur'án if they were not intended to warn Muslims not to reject the new Messenger of Allah when He comes nor to reject the new religion that he brings?

As stated at the beginning of this section, the Qur'án must be understood as a coherent whole: 'Then is it only a part of the Book that ye believe in, and do ye reject the rest?' (2:85). If the standard way of interpreting one verse, 33:40, to mean that there will be no Messengers of Allah after Muḥammad clashes with the clear meaning of other verses, then it is necessary to re-examine the standard interpretation of that verse.

Further evidence from the Qur'án that the phrase 'Seal of the Prophets' was not intended to mean that no further Messengers of Allah would come to humanity will be found elsewhere in this book: in the section below on 'The Lesson from Religious History in the Qur'án', in chapter 4 where the Traditions prophesying the return of Christ are described (see pp. 118, 126–8), and also in chapter 4, where the Qur'án's references to the Day of Judgement and the Day of Resurrection are discussed (see pp. 87–108).

6. *Spiritual and Metaphorical Interpretations.* Among the lines of reasoning used by Bahá'ís in relation to the doctrine of the 'Seal of the Prophets' perhaps the most important is the

following one that is found in the Bahá'í scriptures themselves. This explanation applies not only to the Quranic phrase 'Seal of the Prophets' but by extension also holds true for the references that one sometimes finds in the Traditions to Muḥammad being the Seal of the Messengers or the last of the Messengers of Allah (see below) or to Traditions that speak of Muḥammad being like the last brick in an otherwise complete building. In the Kitáb-i-Íqán (The Book of Certitude), which is the major book of proofs among the Bahá'í scriptures, the question of the 'Seal of the Prophets' is addressed by arguing from the Quranic verse that states that there is no distinction to be made among the Messengers of Allah (Qur'án 2:136; see also p. 18). It is stated that, if one looks at these Messengers of Allah with spiritual eyes, one sees no difference between them. The spiritual reality of Moses and Jesus is the same as the spiritual reality of Muḥammad. Bahá'u'lláh says:

> It is clear and evident to thee that all the Prophets are the Temples of the Cause of God, Who have appeared clothed in divers attire. If thou wilt observe with discriminating eyes, thou wilt behold them all abiding in the same tabernacle, soaring in the same heaven, seated upon the same throne, uttering the same speech, and proclaiming the same Faith. Such is the unity of those Essences of being, those Luminaries of infinite and immeasurable splendour.[101]

And so, for example, had the Christians looked to Muḥammad with a spiritual vision, instead of merely observing the outer aspects, they would have seen the identity between Muḥammad and Jesus, as Bahá'u'lláh notes:

> Every discerning observer will recognize that in the Dispensation of the Qur'án both the Book and the Cause of Jesus were confirmed. As to the matter of names, Muḥammad, Himself, declared: 'I am Jesus.' He recognized the truth of the signs, prophecies, and words of Jesus, and testified that

> they were all of God. In this sense, neither the person of Jesus nor His writings hath differed from that of Muḥammad and of His holy Book, inasmuch as both have championed the Cause of God, uttered His praise, and revealed His commandments. Thus it is that Jesus, Himself, declared: 'I go away and come again unto you.'[102]

In explaining this further, the Bahá'í scriptures use an analogy of the sun, pointing out that while we may designate the sun by various names in order to mark the passage of time, it itself remains the same undivided reality:

> Consider the sun. Were it to say now, 'I am the sun of yesterday,' it would speak the truth. And should it, bearing the sequence of time in mind, claim to be other than that sun, it still would speak the truth. In like manner, if it be said that all the days are but one and the same, it is correct and true. And if it be said, with respect to their particular names and designations, that they differ, that again is true. For though they are the same, yet one doth recognize in each a separate designation, a specific attribute, a particular character. Conceive accordingly the distinction, variation, and unity characteristic of the various Manifestations of holiness, that thou mayest comprehend the allusions made by the creator of all names and attributes to the mysteries of distinction and unity, and discover the answer to thy question as to why that everlasting Beauty should have, at sundry times, called Himself by different names and titles.[103]

This same analogy of the sun is to be found in the Bahá'í scriptures when discussing such terms as 'First' and 'Last' and 'Seal' when applied to the prophets and Messengers of Allah:

> From these statements therefore it hath been made evident and manifest that should a Soul in the 'End that knoweth no end' be made manifest, and arise to proclaim and uphold a Cause which in 'the Beginning that hath no beginning' another Soul had proclaimed and upheld, it can be truly

> declared of Him Who is the Last and of Him Who was the First that they are one and the same, inasmuch as both are the Exponents of one and the same Cause. For this reason, hath the Point of the Bayán [the Báb] . . . likened the Manifestations of God unto the sun which, though it rise from the 'Beginning that hath no beginning' until the 'End that knoweth no end', is none the less the same sun. Now, wert thou to say, that this sun is the former sun, thou speakest the truth; and if thou sayest that this sun is the 'return' of that sun, thou also speakest the truth. Likewise, from this statement it is made evident that the term 'last' is applicable to the 'first,' and the term 'first' applicable to the 'last'; inasmuch as both the 'first' and the 'last' have risen to proclaim one and the same Faith.
>
> Notwithstanding the obviousness of this theme, in the eyes of those that have quaffed the wine of knowledge and certitude, yet how many are those who, through failure to understand its meaning, have allowed the term 'Seal of the Prophets' to obscure their understanding, and deprive them of the grace of all His manifold bounties! Hath not Muḥammad, Himself, declared: 'I am all the Prophets'? Hath He not said as We have already mentioned: 'I am Adam, Noah, Moses, and Jesus'? Why should Muḥammad, that immortal Beauty, Who hath said: 'I am the first Adam' be incapable of saying also: 'I am the last Adam'? For even as He regarded Himself to be the 'First of the Prophets' – that is Adam – in like manner, the 'Seal of the Prophets' is also applicable unto that Divine Beauty. It is admittedly obvious that being the 'First of the Prophets', He likewise is their 'Seal'.[104]

There is also a Tradition cited by Ibn Kat͟hír in his commentary which similarly points to the timelessness of the designation of 'Seal of the Prophets'. In this Tradition, Muḥammad says:

> I was the Seal of the Prophets in the presence of Allah at a time when Adam was still a clod of clay.[105]

The above explanation found in the Bahá'í scriptures also explains a Tradition from the Prophet Muḥammad which is to be found in the *Ṣaḥíḥ* of Muslim and which would otherwise be puzzling:

> I am the last of the Messengers and my mosque is the last of the mosques.[106]

Obviously, Muḥammad did not mean that no more mosques should be built after he built the mosque in Medina, and indeed thousands more mosques have been built. It is far more satisfactory to explain this Tradition in the same way that the Bahá'í scriptures have interpreted 'Seal of the Prophets': that since their reality is one, then every mosque can be considered the first mosque and the last mosque. Bahá'ís would maintain that the Prophet Muḥammad was in this Tradition giving a valuable clue as to how to interpret such phrases as 'Seal of the Prophets' and 'last of the Messengers'.

Finally, it is necessary to say one more thing about these two words 'Messenger' (*rasúl*) and 'prophet' (*nabí*). In what is written above, I have tried to explain matters from the viewpoint of Muslims and so I have used these two words frequently in explaining the claims of Bahá'u'lláh. It should be noted, however, that Bahá'u'lláh himself never uses either of these two words in describing his own claim. He claims to be neither prophet (*nabí*) nor Messenger (*rasúl*). Instead, he introduces a new term to describe his own station and that of the other Messengers of Allah such as Muḥammad, Jesus and Moses. He refers to these founders of the major world religions as 'Manifestations of Allah' (*ẓuhúr Alláh*). One purpose in using a new word is to distinguish the Bahá'í teaching from that of other religions. Whereas Christians claim that Jesus is God and Muslims believe that Muḥammad was essentially just a human being chosen by Allah, the Bahá'í teaching is that these founders of the world religions occupy a station that is intermediate between Allah and humanity.

This intermediate station has aspects of both the human and the divine. Outwardly, the Manifestations appear to be human beings, subject to the same bodily limitations and needs as other human beings, such that Muḥammad says in the Qur'án 'I am but a man like yourselves' (18:110). Yet inwardly, they manifest perfectly all of the names and attributes of Allah, such that they become the perfect embodiments of all virtues and it is for this reason that both Muḥammad and Abraham are stated in the Qur'án to be an 'excellent example' for human beings to follow (33:21, 60:4).

In summary, the application to Muḥammad of the epithet 'Seal of the Prophets (*kh̲átam an-nabiyyin*)' has many levels of meaning and various explanations. At the purely philological level, the word *khátam* means a seal ring that is worn on the finger and thus the phrase can be considered to mean one who gives the seal of approval to the prophets of Allah or one who is an ornament among the prophets of Allah. Even if it is taken to mean 'last', it applies in this verse only to prophets and not to the Messengers of Allah. Historically, there is much evidence that the early Muslims did not think that this phrase meant that there would be no prophets after Muḥammad. Indeed, within the context that it appears (which is related to the position of Zayd, the adopted son of Muḥammad), the early commentators stressed that it was intended to mean that Zayd should not be considered as the son of Muḥammad, for the sons of previous Messengers had succeeded them as prophets whereas Muḥammad's immediate successor would not be a prophet. Indeed, this verse was, in this sense, an indication of the high station of Muḥammad and the exalted nature of his teaching – that he would not need a prophet to succeed him in order to explain his message. Lastly, even if we allow a meaning of finality to this phrase, the essential spiritual unity of the Messengers of Allah means that any designation that is applied to one of them can be applied to all of them. Thus they are all both first and last.

Islam as the Perfect and Chosen Religion of Allah

There are a number of verses of the Qur'án that Muslims point to as evidence that Islam is the perfect and chosen religion of Allah and that therefore no other choice of religion is acceptable to Him.

> This day have I perfected your religion for you, completed my favour upon you, and have chosen for you Islam as your religion. (5:4)

> If anyone desires a religion other than Islam (submission to Allah), it will never be accepted of him . . . (3:85)

> The Religion before Allah is Islam (submission to His Will). (3:19)

In view of these verses, some Muslims have asked: since Islam is the perfected religion of Allah, how can another religion come to the world after it? If Islam is the only acceptable religion to Allah, how can anyone adopt another?

There are several ways of looking at this question. The first is to ask what exactly the word 'Islam' means in this context. Moses brought to the world the Jewish religion, which was later abrogated by Jesus, who brought the Christian religion. Christianity was in turn abrogated by Muḥammad, who brought Islam. And yet the Holy Qur'án refers to Abraham, who preceded all of these prophets, as following the religion of Islam (2:132); to those who followed Moses as Muslims (10:83 and 7:126); and to the disciples of Christ also as Muslims (5:111). It refers to people who were Muslims before the Qur'án itself was revealed (28:52–3, 22:78). What do 'Islam' and 'Muslim' mean in these contexts? Today the word 'Islam' refers to that vast structure of *'ulamá*, mosques, muftis, religious courts, books and institutions that constitute the religion of Islam. A Muslim today is one who takes part in that structure and follows its teachings. But it is clear that this structure did not exist even in the time of Muḥammad, let alone in the time of the Messengers of Allah before Muḥammad. It is clear that the followers of Moses and of Jesus could not have been following the laws and teachings that we today know as Islam since these were not revealed until centuries after their time. What then is the meaning of this puzzling reference to the terms 'Islam' and 'Muslim' when applied to peoples who lived centuries before Muḥammad? These words must obviously mean something other than adherence to the laws and teachings revealed by Muḥammad.

Abú Bakr al-Jaṣáṣ ar-Rází, a prominent Ḥanafí scholar of the 4th Islamic century, deals with this question in a section of his book *Aḥkám al-Qurán* entitled 'In answer to the difficulty raised by those who say that the Qur'án was revealed after Abraham (peace be upon him) and so how can he be a Muslim?' In answer to this problem, he writes:

> Islam here means obedience to Allah Almighty and submission to His Decree (*amrihi*) and it is correct to call any one of the people of truth thus. We have been taught that the former prophets, Abraham and those before him, were (known) by this designation. Thus it is permissible that Abraham be called 'true in faith (*ḥanífan*) and a Muslim' (Qur'án 3:67), even though the Qur'án was revealed after him, because this designation is not specific to the revelation of the Qur'án alone.[107]

Ibn Kat͟hír, in commentary on this verse of the Qur'án 'Indeed we have been Muslims from before [the coming of the Qur'án]' (28:53), states that Muslims in this context (i.e. before the advent of the religion brought by Muḥammad) means 'those who profess Allah's unity, whose devotion to Allah is pure and who are responsive to Him'.[108]

Thus the answer to this puzzle lies in the meaning of the

words 'Islam' and 'Muslim'. These words come from the Arabic root meaning 'to submit or surrender'. Thus the fundamental meaning of the word 'Islam' is 'surrender to Allah's Will'; and the meaning of 'Muslim' is 'one who has surrendered to Allah's Will'. With this in mind, the meaning of the passages that ascribe the terms 'Islam' and 'Muslim' to the religions before Muḥammad becomes clear. The religion of Allah has always been 'surrender to the Will of Allah'. In the time of Moses, 'surrender to the Will of Allah' meant following the teachings of Moses – because that was Allah's Will in that age. Those who followed Moses at that time (i.e. the Jews) were following the 'Will of Allah' and could rightly therefore be termed Muslims (Qur'án 10:84 and 7:126). In that time, Judaism was true 'surrender to the Will of Allah' (Islam). When Jesus came, his message confirmed some of the teachings of the Torah but he also came to change some of them: 'to make lawful to you part of what was (before) forbidden to you' (3:50). After this, it became Allah's Will that the people should follow Jesus and his teachings. Therefore those that followed Jesus were now 'surrendering to the Will of Allah' and could therefore correctly be called Muslims. Thus in that age, Christianity was the true 'surrender to the Will of Allah'; Christianity was the true Islam. And similarly, the Christians were the true Muslims, as indicated in the Qur'án (5:114), until the time of Muḥammad.

The verses in the Qur'án that refer to peoples who lived many centuries before Muḥammad as Muslims obviously do not refer to what we now call a Muslim but rather to the simple fact that those people were following the Will of Allah for their age. In this sense, the religion of Allah has always been 'surrender to the Will of Allah' (Islam) (3:19) and, as as-Suyúṭí states in *ad-Durr al-Manthúr*, every Messenger of Allah has been sent with Islam.[109] 'Surrender to the Will of Allah' (Islam) has always been and will forever continue to be the final, most complete and most perfect religion of Allah. Yusuf Ali also clearly understood this to be the meaning of Islam in these verses, since in two of the verses cited at the beginning of this section, he adds 'submission to Allah' and 'submission to His Will' in parentheses after the word 'Islam'.

There is proof in the nearby verses of the fact that the general meaning of Islam as 'the religion of Allah in every age' is intended in these verses rather than the specific meaning of 'the religion brought by Muḥammad'. Immediately before the verse that states 'If anyone desires a religion other than Islam, never will it be accepted of him' (3:85), there is a verse that shows that it is the general meaning of Islam that is intended:

> Say: 'We believe in Allah, and in what He has revealed to us and what was revealed to Abraham, Isma'il, Isaac, Jacob, and the Tribes and in (the Books) given to Moses, Jesus, and the Prophets, from their Lord; We make no distinction between one and another among them and we are Muslims (bowed in submission) unto Him (Allah).' (3:84)[110]

In other words, verse 3:85 means that if anyone desires a religion other than the Islam (submission) which is referred to in the previous verse (submission to Allah through what was revealed by His Messengers such as Abraham, Moses and Jesus), then this will not be accepted by Allah.

Thus the term Islam as used in the Qur'án means 'surrender to the Will of Allah in each age' and not necessarily adherence to the specific laws and teachings revealed by Muḥammad. From this, Bahá'ís consider that there is a clear explanation of why the Bahá'í Faith is true despite the verses quoted above. In each age, they are the true Muslims who submit to the Will of Allah and follow the teaching of the Messenger of Allah for that age. Thus the followers of Moses were called Jews but the Qur'án recognizes them as Muslims, at least until the coming of Jesus. But if they failed then to follow Jesus, they ceased to be Muslims because they were no longer in a position of 'surrender to the Will of Allah'. And those who followed Jesus were the true Muslims until the coming of Muḥammad. But after that, if they failed to turn to Muḥammad, they were no longer Muslims because they were no longer in a position of 'surrender to the Will of Allah'.

A similar situation applies in the case of the statement: 'This day have I perfected your religion for you, completed my favour upon you, and have chosen for you Islam as your religion' (5:4). The religion brought by Moses is also, for example, stated to be 'complete' (6:154) when it was revealed to him and yet other Messengers of Allah were sent after him. Bahá'ís believe that the religion of Allah that is brought to the earth by His Messengers in each age is perfect and complete for that age.

It is clear, therefore, that the verses in the Qur'án quoted above referring to Islam as the perfect and chosen religion of Allah do not refer to the specific religion brought by Muḥammad, the laws and teachings of Islam, but rather to the state of being in complete submission to the Will of Allah in whatever age the individual lives. This has always been and will always be the only religion acceptable to Allah, just as the Qur'án states. It is and always has been the perfect religion of Allah, just as the Qur'án states. The duty of the individual is to investigate the truth and find out what the Will of Allah is for the age in which he or she is living. Bahá'ís believe that the Bahá'í Faith is the true religion of Allah for this day and therefore the true Muslims (i.e. those who have truly surrendered to the Will of Allah) today are the Bahá'ís. Thus when, for example, some of the Islamic Traditions (*ḥadíths*) prophesy that when the Mahdi comes and Christ returns (see chapter 4), they will spread the religion of Islam and it will triumph over all religions, Bahá'ís consider that the Islam that is intended by these Traditions is Islam in this general sense of the religion of 'surrender to the Will of Allah' – in other words, the Bahá'í Faith.

'Surrender to the Will of Allah' (*Islám*) remains in this day, as it has always been, the true and most perfect religion of Allah; the only religion acceptable to Allah. But just as the expression of Islam has changed with the coming of Moses and Jesus and Muḥammad, so it has now changed again and to be a true Muslim, to have submitted to the Will of Allah in this age, it is necessary to follow the teachings of Allah which have been revealed by Bahá'u'lláh.

The Lesson from Religious History in the Qur'án

Bahá'ís consider that the whole of the Qur'án tells the religious history of humanity in a such a way as to warn Muslims against making any interpretations of it that exclude the possibility of further revelations coming from Allah. The Qur'án tells the story of the various Messengers that were sent by Allah to the people. In the Súrah of al-A'raf, for example, the stories of Noah, Húd, Ṣáliḥ, Lot, Shu'ayb and Moses are told (7:59–162). In each case it is shown that the people opposed the prophets and Messengers sent to them by Allah and rejected their messages. Because these prophets and Messengers came to the people with things that the people did not like or were not expecting, they were rejected, persecuted and some even killed.

> Is it that whenever there comes to you a Messenger [from Allah] with what ye yourselves desire not, ye are puffed up with pride. – Some ye call impostors, and others ye slay! (2:87)

It was principally the secular and religious leaders of the people who feared the changes that a new Messenger of Allah would bring. They feared for their own positions if the people changed their religion and so they instigated the persecutions of the Messenger and his followers. Thus, for example, it is related in the Qur'án that Pharaoh, who was worshipped in the Egyptian religion, feared that Moses would cause the Egyptians to leave their religion:

> Said Pharaoh: 'Leave me to slay Moses; and let him call on his Lord! What I fear is lest he should change your religion, or lest he should cause mischief to appear in the land!' (40:26)

It is useful to look in detail at a couple of examples of this phenomenon. Jesus came to the Jews as their expected Messiah (*Masíḥ*) and brought them Allah's message. Although the Jews were expecting the coming of the Messiah and indeed prayed daily for Allah to speed his advent, yet the Jews rejected Jesus, he was persecuted and eventually sentenced to death. They stated that the Messiah that they were expecting was to be a military figure who would lead them to victory over the Romans and would sit upon the throne of David, whereas Jesus did not possess even a single weapon and had no power. They said that the law of the Torah would never be superseded and that they were expecting the Messiah to confirm the Torah, whereas in fact Jesus broke the laws of the Sabbath and the law of divorce, two of the most important laws of the Torah. They pointed out that the Torah states that its laws, and especially the law of the Sabbath, are established forever and can never be annulled (see, for example, Exodus 31:13–17).

These were the reasons that the Jews gave for rejecting Jesus. Because of their insistence on a literal interpretation of the text of their scriptures, they missed the fact that Jesus did have a great sovereignty and was seated upon a throne, but this was a spiritual sovereignty and not an earthly one and he was seated upon the divine throne and not upon a worldly one (see pp. 215–20). In criticizing Christ for changing the laws of the Torah, they were blind to the fact that 'Allah doeth what He willeth' (Qur'án 14:27). When a Messenger comes from Allah, he has the power to change the laws and teachings of the previous Messenger – although it is also stated in the Qur'án that whenever Allah does cause a Messenger to cancel a previous law, then Allah 'substitutes something better or similar' (2:106) in its place (see pp. 19–20).

As a further example, we may look at Muḥammad. When he appeared with a new law, a new teaching and a new holy book from Allah, he was also rejected by the followers of the previous religions. The Jews and Christians, especially, opposed him and sought ways to undermine him. The Jews raised the same objections to Muḥammad that they had raised against Jesus, saying that he did not fulfil the prophecies and that he had no right to change the law of the Torah. They stated that Allah would not have authorized such a change as He had specifically stated in the Torah that the laws of the Torah are for ever.[111] Allah's hands are tied in this matter, they asserted to Muḥammad. The reply of the Qur'án to this assertion was:

> The Jews say: 'Allah's hand is tied up.' Be their hands tied up and be they accursed for the (blasphemy) they utter. Nay, both His hands are widely outstretched. (5:67)

The Christians had similar objections. Although Jesus had promised that after him there would come the comforter (Paraclete), Christians interpreted this as being the coming of the Holy Ghost at Pentecost and rejected Muslim claims that Muḥammad had fulfilled this prophecy. Just as the Muslims now assert that Muḥammad is the Seal of the Prophets, the Christians could point to such verses as the following to assert that Allah had finished humanity's spiritual development with Jesus and had set His seal upon the Christian community:

The Proofs of the Messenger of Allah

*The Bahá'í scriptures state that the proofs that each Messenger of Allah brings concerning his station and mission are the same. They are primarily his own person and the teachings contained in his book. This same theme is contained in the following Tradition (*ḥadíth*) which can be found in several of the reliable collections of Traditions. Each of the evidences for the truth of Muḥammad's claim that is given here is also true for both the Báb and Bahá'u'lláh. The following is the version of this Tradition given in the* Ṣaḥíḥ *of al-Bukhárí (narrated by 'Abdu'lláh ibn 'Abbás):*

Abú Sufyán ibn Ḥarb informed me that Heraclius, the Byzantine Emperor, had sent a messenger to him while he had been accompanying a caravan from Quraysh. They were merchants doing business in Sham (Syria, Palestine, Lebanon and Jordan), at the time when Allah's Messenger had a truce with Abú Sufyán and the Quraysh infidels. So Abú Sufyán and his companions went to Heraclius at Ílyá (Jerusalem). Heraclius called them in the court and he had all the senior Roman dignitaries around him. He called for his translator who, translating Heraclius's question, said to them, 'Who amongst you is closely related to that man who claims to be a Prophet?' Abú Sufyán replied, 'I am the nearest relative to him (amongst the group).'

Heraclius said, 'Bring him (Abú Sufyán) close to me and make his companions stand behind him.' Abú Sufyán added, 'Heraclius told his translator to tell my companions that he wanted to put some questions to me regarding that man (the Prophet) and that if I told a lie they (my companions) should contradict me.' Abú Sufyán added, 'By Allah! Had I not been afraid of my companions labelling me a liar, I would not have spoken the truth about the Prophet.'

[Heraclius then asked Abú Sufyán a series of questions, after which Heraclius gave the following explanation.]

Heraclius asked the translator to convey to me the following, 'I asked you about his family and your reply was that he belonged to a very noble family. In fact all the Messengers come from noble families amongst their respective peoples. I questioned you whether anybody else amongst you claimed such a thing, your reply was in the negative. If the answer had been in the affirmative, I would have thought that this man was following the previous man's statement. Then I asked you whether anyone of his ancestors was a king. Your reply was in the negative, and if it had been in the affirmative, I would have thought that this man wanted to take back his ancestral kingdom. I further asked whether he was ever accused of telling lies before he said what he said, and your reply was in the negative. So I wondered how a person who does not tell a lie about others could ever tell a lie about Allah. I then asked you whether the rich people followed him or the poor. You replied that it was the poor who followed him. And in fact all the Messengers have been followed by this very class of people. Then I asked you whether his followers were increasing or decreasing. You replied that they were increasing, and in fact this is the way of true faith, till it is complete in all respects. I further asked you whether there was anybody, who, after embracing his religion, became displeased and discarded his religion. Your reply was in the negative, and in fact this is (the sign of) true faith, when its delight enters the hearts and mixes with them completely. I asked you whether he had ever betrayed. You replied in the negative and likewise the Messengers never betray. Then I asked you what he ordered you to do. You replied that he ordered you to worship Allah and Allah alone and not to worship any thing along with Him and forbade you to worship idols and ordered you to pray, to speak the truth and to be chaste. If what you have said is true, he will very soon occupy this place underneath my feet and I knew it (from the scriptures) that he was going to appear but I did not know that he would be from you, and if I could reach him definitely, I would go immediately to meet him and if I were with him, I would certainly wash his feet.' (Al-Bukhárí)[112]

> But it is God who establishes us with you in Christ, and has commissioned us; he has put his seal upon us and given us his Spirit in our hearts as a guarantee. (2 Corinthians 1:20–2)

Christians also pointed to such verses as:

> Heaven and earth shall pass away, but my words shall not pass away. (Matthew 24:35, Mark 13:31, Luke 21:33)

> For there is none other name under heaven given among men, whereby we must be saved. (Acts 4:12)

> Jesus saith unto him, I am the way, the truth, and the life: no man cometh unto the Father, but by me. (John 14:6)

These verses indicated to Christians that the message brought by Jesus was for all time and would never be superseded.

Therefore they asserted that Muḥammad must be an impostor in claiming to be a Messenger of Allah. Muḥammad was commanded in the Qur'án to rebuke such people and to assert that Allah is always able to send down the bounty of His revelation wherever and whenever He pleases:

> Say: 'True guidance is the guidance of Allah: (fear ye) lest a revelation be sent to someone (else) like unto that which was sent unto you? Or that those (receiving such revelation) should engage you in argument before your Lord?' Say: 'All bounties are in the hand of Allah: He granteth them to whom He pleaseth: and Allah careth for all, and He knoweth all things.' (3:73)

Thus for the same two reasons that the Jews rejected Jesus (that he did not fulfil the prophecies and that he had broken and abrogated the Holy Law which was for all time), the Jews and Christians rejected Muḥammad. Instead of going to Muḥammad and listening to his explanations and teachings and then judging these matters fairly, they prejudged the issue and decided against Muḥammad before they even heard what he had to say.

The Bahá'í scriptures point out that, in rejecting Bahá'u-'lláh, the Muslims are doing exactly what the Jews and Christians did in the past and they are doing it for the same reasons. Muslims who reject Bahá'u'lláh as a Messenger of Allah rely on a literal interpretation of certain prophecies and state that Bahá'u'lláh has not fulfilled these. They cling to their interpretation of passages of the Qur'án such as the 'Seal of the Prophets' and refuse to listen to the interpretation given by Bahá'u'lláh. They point to certain verses in the Qur'án which command the Muslims to obey Muḥammad and make him the judge in all their affairs (3:32, 59:7, 4:65). The judgement of Allah on such people is the same as the judgement given in the Qur'án against those Jews who maintained that Allah's hands are tied. In commenting upon the verse quoted above which begins: ' "Allah's hands are tied," say the Jews,' the Bahá'í scriptures state:

> Although the commentators of the Qur'án have related in divers manners the circumstances attending the revelation of this verse, yet thou shouldst endeavour to apprehend the purpose thereof. He saith: How false is that which the Jews have imagined! How can the hand of Him Who is the King in truth, Who caused the countenance of Moses to be made manifest, and conferred upon Him the robe of Prophethood – how can the hand of such a One be chained and fettered? How can He be conceived as powerless to raise up yet another Messenger after Moses? Behold the absurdity of their saying; how far it hath strayed from the path of knowledge and understanding! Observe how in this day also, all these people have occupied themselves with such foolish absurdities. For over a thousand years they have been reciting this verse, and unwittingly pronouncing their censure against the Jews, utterly unaware that they themselves, openly and privily, are voicing the sentiments and belief of the Jewish people! Thou art surely aware of their idle contention, that all Revelation is ended, that the portals of Divine mercy are closed . . . These people have imagined that the flow of God's all-encompassing grace and plenteous mercies, the cessation of which no mind can contemplate, has been halted. From every side they have risen and girded up the loins of tyranny, and exerted the utmost endeavour to quench with the bitter waters of their vain fancy the flame of God's burning Bush, oblivious that the globe of power shall within its own mighty stronghold protect the Lamp of God.[113]

If we look at the Qur'án as a whole, we see that a very large proportion of it is taken up with retelling stories of past prophets. What is the point of such a large part of the revelation given to Muḥammad being taken up with stories of the past? When Muḥammad revealed these stories in the verses of the Qur'án, the people mocked him and said that he was merely repeating 'tales of the ancients' (25:5). But

Muḥammad was not a story-teller. Bahá'ís believe that every verse of the Qur'án is there for a specific reason, to convey a message that Allah wanted to convey to humanity. What then is the purpose of telling these stories of past events? Bahá'ís believe that in repeating these stories, the purpose of the Holy Qur'án was to be a 'Warning' (or Admonition, 25:1) to the Muslims about their own conduct, lest they make the same mistakes as the people of former times. There are verses in the Qur'án that make it clear that the telling of these stories of the peoples of the past is intended as a warning and an admonition to Muslims regarding the future:

> We have already sent down to you verses making things clear, and an illustration from (the story of) people who passed away before you, and an admonition for those who fear (Allah). (24:34)

In the Suráh of Húd, Suráh 11, the stories of the Messengers of Allah are told one after another – Noah, Húd, Ṣáliḥ, Abraham, Shu'ayb and Moses – how they came to the people with the message of Allah, how they were rejected and how Allah's punishment fell upon the people as a consequence. Later in this chapter (11:103), it is specifically stated that these stories are related here in order to be a Sign for that Day on which humankind will be gathered together (i.e. the Day of Judgement) and it specifically warns Muslims about the dangers, on that Day, of merely following what their forefathers have believed. In other words, the Qur'án is here prophesying that on the Day of Judgement another Messenger of Allah will appear and Muslims will, on that Day, be in danger of repeating the errors of the peoples of the past by rejecting him.

> These are some of the stories of communities which We relate unto thee: of them some are standing and some have been mown down (by the sickle of time). It was not We that

> wronged them: they wronged their own souls: the deities other than Allah, whom they invoked, profited them no whit when there issued the decree of thy Lord: nor did they add aught (to their lot) but perdition!
>
> Such is the chastisement of thy Lord when He chastises communities in the midst of their wrong: grievous, indeed, and severe is His chastisement. In that is a Sign for those who fear the Penalty of the Hereafter: that is a Day for which mankind will be gathered together: that will be a Day of Testimony. Nor shall We delay it but for a term appointed. The day it arrives no soul shall speak except by His leave: of those (gathered) some will be wretched and some will be blessed. Those who are wretched shall be in the Fire: there will be for them therein (nothing but) the heaving of sighs and sobs . . . And those who are blessed shall be in the Garden: they will dwell therein for all the time that the heavens and the earth endure . . . Be not then in doubt as to what these men worship. They worship nothing but what their fathers worshipped before (them): but verily We shall pay them back (in full) their portion without (the least) abatement. (11:100–6, 108–9)

It is for this reason that the Súrah of Húd is specifically mentioned in the Bahá'í scriptures and Muslims are called upon to reflect on the message that it conveys:

> To them that are possessed of true understanding and insight the Súrah of Húd surely sufficeth. Ponder a while those holy words in your heart, and, with utter detachment, strive to grasp their meaning. Examine the wondrous behaviour of the Prophets, and recall the defamations and denials uttered by the children of negation and falsehood, perchance you may cause the bird of the human heart to wing its flight away from the abodes of heedlessness and doubt unto the nest of faith and certainty, and drink deep from the pure waters of ancient wisdom, and partake of the fruit of the tree of divine knowledge. Such is the share of the pure in heart of the bread that hath descended from the realms of eternity and holiness.

> Should you acquaint yourself with the indignities heaped upon the Prophets of God, and apprehend the true causes of the objections voiced by their oppressors, you will surely appreciate the significance of their position. Moreover, the more closely you observe the denials of those who have opposed the Manifestations of the divine attributes, the firmer will be your faith in the Cause of God.[114]

For final confirmation that the Muslims are being warned that they too will face the same test as the peoples before them, that a Messenger of Allah will come to them and that they will reject him, there is the following Tradition, found in the *Ṣaḥíḥ*s of both Muslim and al-Bukhárí, warning that the Muslims will make the same mistakes that Jews and Christians did:

> Abú Sa'íd al-Khudrí reported Allah's Messenger (may blessings and peace be upon him) as saying: 'You would tread the same path as was trodden by those before you inch by inch and step by step so much so that if they had entered into the hole of the lizard, you would follow them in this also.' We said: 'Allah's Messenger, do you mean Jews and Christians (by your words) "those before you"?' He said: 'Who else (than those two religious groups)?'[115]

Of course, there are many ways in which Muslims have copied Jews and Christians in doing things that are displeasing to Allah: the creation of numerous sects, for example. But since this Tradition states that Muslims will copy Jews and Christians in every mistake and error that they have made, then this must also include one of the most important mistakes that they made, the one that is most frequently mentioned in the Qur'án and the one about which Muḥammad was most concerned: their error in rejecting the new Messenger of Allah, Muḥammad, when he came and their saying that it is not possible for a new religion to arise and abrogate their religion. Thus this Tradition indicates that the Muslims will make the same errors: by rejecting the next Messenger of Allah when he comes and by stating that it is not possible for a new religion to be established.

In telling these stories of past peoples and past Messengers of Allah, the Qur'án is also acting as the *al-Furqán* ('the Discriminator', 25:1), separating those who truly believe from those who merely pay lip service to the religion of Allah. The Bible states that the meaning of biblical verses is not clear and evident – rather, the verses are 'sealed up' until the time of the end (Daniel 12:9). And yet despite this, the Jews and Christians imagined that they understood the meaning of the Bible sufficiently to reject Muḥammad. They pointed to various signs in the Bible and protested to Muḥammad that these had not been fulfilled. Instead of turning to Muḥammad and seeking guidance about the meaning of the Bible, they turned their backs on him and caused him much grief and suffering.

The Islamic Traditions also allude to this theme in many places. For example, in one Tradition that is quoted by Ibn Májah, it is stated that:

> The Prophet, peace be upon him, mentioned a matter and said: 'There will come a time when knowledge will disappear.' Ziyád ibn Lubayd asked: 'O Messenger of Allah! How is it that knowledge will disappear, when we read the Qur'án, and our sons will read the Qur'án, and their sons will also read the Qur'án, until the Day of Resurrection?' He answered: 'O Ziyád! If I were to show you the most learned men in Medina, would these not be the Jews and the Christians who read the Torah and the Evangel, while not understanding anything that is in them?'[116]

This Tradition indicates that just as the learned Jews and Christians of the time of Muḥammad read the Bible but did not understand in it the references to the Prophet Muḥammad, so in the future the religious leaders of Islam will read the Qur'án and not understand from it the truth about the next Messenger of Allah.

Those Who Have Denied and Opposed the Messengers of Allah

Just as the Qur'án describes and comments in detail upon the actions of those who have denied and opposed the Messengers of Allah, the Bahá'í scriptures also refer to this phenomenon that has occurred in every age including this one:

The wine of renunciation must needs be quaffed, the lofty heights of detachment must needs be attained, and the meditation referred to in the words 'One hour's reflection is preferable to seventy years of pious worship' must needs be observed, so that the secret of the wretched behaviour of the people might be discovered, those people who, despite the love and yearning for truth which they profess, curse the followers of Truth when once He hath been made manifest . . . It is evident that the reason for such behaviour is none other than the annulment of those rules, customs, habits, and ceremonials to which they have been subjected. Otherwise, were the Beauty of the Merciful to comply with those same rules and customs, which are current amongst the people, and were He to sanction their observances, such conflict and mischief would in no wise be made manifest in the world. This exalted tradition is attested and substantiated by these words which He hath revealed: 'The day when the Summoner shall summon to a stern business.' [Qur'án 54:6]

The divine call of the celestial Herald from beyond the Veil of Glory, summoning mankind to renounce utterly all the things to which they cleave, is repugnant to their desire; and this is the cause of the bitter trials and violent commotions which have occurred. Consider the way of the people. They ignore these well-founded traditions, all of which have been fulfilled, and cling unto those of doubtful validity, and ask why these have not been fulfilled. And yet, those things which to them were inconceivable have been made manifest. The signs and tokens of the Truth shine even as the midday sun, and yet the people are wandering, aimlessly and perplexedly, in the wilderness of ignorance and folly. Notwithstanding all the verses of the Qur'án, and the recognized traditions, which are all indicative of a new Faith, a new Law, and a new Revelation, this generation still waiteth in expectation of beholding the promised One who should uphold the Law of the Muḥammadan Dispensation. The Jews and the Christians in like manner uphold the same contention . . .

Behold, how, notwithstanding these and similar traditions, they idly contend that the laws formerly revealed, must in no wise be altered. And yet, is not the object of every Revelation to effect a transformation in the whole character of mankind, a transformation that shall manifest itself both outwardly and inwardly, that shall affect both its inner life and external conditions? For if the character of mankind be not changed, the futility of God's universal Manifestations would be apparent . . . Notwithstanding all these evident and significant traditions, all these unmistakable and undisputed allusions, the people have rejected the immaculate Essence of knowledge and of holy utterance, and have turned unto the exponents of rebellion and error. Despite these recorded traditions and revealed utterances, they speak only that which is prompted by their own selfish desires. And should the Essence of Truth reveal that which is contrary to their inclinations and desires, they will straightway denounce Him as an infidel, and will protest saying: '. . . No such thing hath been provided by our inviolable Law.' Even so in this day such worthless statements have been and are being made by these poor mortals. (Bahá'u'lláh)[117]

The texts of the holy books of each religion have within them certain abstruse allusions and symbolic terms, the meanings of which are not clear to the followers of that religion and which only become clear with the coming of the next Messenger of Allah. This becomes a test for the people at the coming of the next Messenger, separating those who are true believers from those who follow only blindly because their fathers did (Qur'án 43:21) or with crookedness in their hearts (61:5–10). 'Do men think that they will be left alone on saying "We believe", and that they will not be tested?' (Qur'án 29:2)

This principle, that the text of the holy book contains certain abstruse allusions and symbolic terms, also applies to the Qur'án for in that holy book we read that it consists of some verses that are clear and established in meaning and some that are ambiguous and create doubt and become a test by which those in whose hearts there is some crookedness or perversity are deceived:

> He it is Who has sent down to thee the Book: in it are verses basic or fundamental (of established meaning); they are the

> foundation of the Book: others are allegorical. But those in whose hearts is perversity follow the part thereof that is allegorical, seeking discord, and searching for its hidden meanings. (3:7)

> By it [the Qur'án] He [Allah] causes many to stray, and many He leads into the straight path; but He causes not to stray, except those who forsake (the path). (2:26)

The Bahá'í scriptures provide a similar explanation of the reason the divine scriptures always contain verses that are ambiguous or difficult to understand:

> It is evident unto thee that the Birds of Heaven and Doves of Eternity speak a twofold language. One language, the outward language, is devoid of allusions, is unconcealed and unveiled; that it may be a guiding lamp and a beaconing light whereby wayfarers may attain the heights of holiness, and seekers may advance into the realm of eternal reunion. Such are the unveiled traditions and the evident verses already mentioned. The other language is veiled and concealed, so that whatever lieth hidden in the heart of the malevolent may be made manifest and their innermost being be disclosed.[118]

In the same passage that divides the Qur'án into clear, established verses and ambiguous ones, it is stated with regard to what is ambiguous in the Qur'án that 'None knoweth its explanation (*ta'wílahu*) save Allah' (3:7).[119] Elsewhere, however, it is promised that this explanation will be revealed in the future (I have translated *ta'wílahu* as 'its explanation' again here in order to show up the similarity):

> For We had certainly sent unto them a Book, based on knowledge, which We explained in detail, – a guide and a mercy to all who believe. Do they just wait for its explanation (*ta'wílahu*)? On the day its explanation (*ta'wíluhu*) comes,

> those who disregarded it before will say: 'The Messengers of our Lord did indeed bring true (tidings). Have we no intercessors now to intercede on our behalf? Or could we be sent back? Then should we behave differently from our behaviour in the past.' In fact they will have lost their souls, and the things they invented will leave them in the lurch. (7:52–3)[120]

Bahá'ís believe that this verse refers forward to the coming of the Báb and Bahá'u'lláh, who have revealed scriptures that provide the explanation of the ambiguous verses of the Qur'án; their advent is 'the day its explanation (*ta'wíluhu*) comes'.

Thus the Qur'án clearly states the nature of the problem: that people have always denied what they cannot understand and have charged the Messenger of Allah with falsehood even before listening to his explanation of the abstruse passages of their scriptures. This has been the pattern in the past and the Qur'án warns its readers against repeating the mistake:

> Nay, they charge with falsehood that whose knowledge they cannot compass, even before the elucidation thereof hath reached them: thus did those before them make charges of falsehood: but see what was the end of those who did wrong! (10:39)

With these examples and warnings in the Holy Qur'án, it is clear that Muslims must be careful in their judgement of the claims of the Bahá'í Faith for they may run the danger of repeating the same errors that the Jews and Christians made in rejecting Muḥammad, about which they are warned in the Qur'án.

How Muslims should Approach Bahá'u'lláh's Claim

In the Qur'án there is a great deal of advice as to how Muslims should approach someone such as Bahá'u'lláh who claims to reveal the word of Allah. The first advice that comes from the Qur'án is that any such news, even if it comes from a person who one considers bad, should be investigated by a Muslim:

> O ye who believe! if a wicked person comes to you with any news, ascertain the truth, lest ye harm people unwittingly, and afterwards become full of repentance for what ye have done. (49:6)

The Qur'án encourages Muslims to think about what they believe, to investigate matters carefully for themselves and to come to conclusions based on their own knowledge and not the knowledge of others:

> And pursue not that of which thou hast no knowledge; for every act of hearing, or of seeing, or of (feeling in) the heart will be enquired into (on the Day of Reckoning). (17:36)

In particular the Qur'án warns Muslims more than once against merely following the religion of their fathers or of the notable ones among their people. This is what had led previous people to deny the Messenger of Allah when he came to them. The Qur'án states that this is not an acceptable excuse and warns of the dire consequences of doing so:

> They say: 'We found Our fathers following a certain religion, and we do guide ourselves by their footsteps.' Just in the same way, whenever We sent a Warner before thee to any people, the wealthy ones among them said: 'We found Our fathers following a certain religion, and we will certainly follow in their footsteps.'
>
> He said: 'What! even if I brought you better guidance than that which ye found your fathers following?' They said: 'For us, we deny that ye (prophets) are sent (on a mission at all).'
>
> So We exacted retribution from them: now see what was the end of those who rejected (Truth)! (43:22–5, cf. 2:170, 5:104, 21:52, 33:67)

The Qur'án also indicates that in their quest for the truth, Muslims must not be influenced by their religious leaders. For the Jews and Christians trusted their religious leaders in their assessment of Muḥammad's claim and were deceived by them. Their religious leaders blocked the path of truth for them:

> They have taken as lords beside Allah their [Jewish] rabbis and their [Christian] monks and the Messiah son of Mary, when they were bidden to worship only one Allah . . . Fain would they put out the light of Allah with their mouths, but Allah disdaineth (aught) save that He shall perfect His light, however much the disbelievers are averse . . . O ye who believe! Lo, many of the (Jewish) rabbis and the (Christian) monks devour the wealth of mankind wantonly and debar (men) from the way of Allah. (9:31–2, 34)[121]

Reliable Islamic Traditions prophesy that just as the Jewish and Christian religious leaders began by guiding their communities but eventually misled them into rejecting the Prophet Muḥammad when he came, so also the Muslim religious leaders will in time mislead the Muslims:

> I heard Allah's Messenger saying, 'Allah does not take away the knowledge, by taking it away from (the hearts of) the people, but takes it away by the death of the religious learned men till when none of the (religious learned men) remains, people will take as their leaders ignorant persons who when consulted will give their verdict without knowledge. So they will go astray and will lead the people astray.' (al-Bukhárí) [122]

It is therefore necessary for each individual Muslim to consider and investigate for himself or herself a claim such as that of Bahá'u'lláh, regardless of what distinguished Muslim authorities of the present or the past or their own friends or family may say. Ultimately, they themselves will be responsible before Allah for their decision and Allah will not accept from them any excuse such as: 'Our Lord! We obeyed our chiefs and our great ones and they misled us as to the (right) path' (Qur'án 33:67). Indeed, the Qur'án states that the penalty for a person who presents such an excuse should be doubled (33:68).

Each religion, when it first appears, is rejected and even ridiculed by the majority of the people and the followers of the previous religions. When Jesus appeared he was rejected by the Jews. When Muḥammad appeared he was rejected by the Jews and Christians, who in those early years were far more numerous than Muslims. They asserted that what Muḥammad said was contrary to what had been the interpretation of their holy book by generations of Christians and Jews, including their great scholars.

> Then sent We Our Messengers in succession: every time there came to a people their Messenger, they accused him of falsehood: so We made them follow each other (in punishment): We made them as a tale (that is told): so away with a people that will not believe! (Qur'án 23:44)

> . . . And every People plotted against their prophet, to seize him, and disputed by means of vanities, therewith to condemn the Truth. (40:5)

Thus the fact that many Muslims have opposed Bahá'u'lláh and accused him of falsehood means that Bahá'u'lláh has received the same treatment that the Qur'án states all the Messengers of Allah have received at the hands of the people to whom they have come.

Muslims should, therefore, not allow themselves to be influenced by what the majority of Muslims have thought or how the great authorities in Islam have interpreted the Qur'án. The Qur'án itself states that one should not follow a view just because it is held by a majority of the people; the majority of the people are often in error and will lead one away from the truth (the word *ak<u>th</u>ar* in the following quotation can be translated as 'majority'):

> Wert thou to follow the common run (*akhthar*) of those on earth, they will lead thee away from the Way of Allah. They follow nothing but conjecture: they do nothing but lie. (6:116)

Muslims must, therefore, bear in mind that it is possible that their leaders and authorities may be in error when they make judgements about new things and that each person will be responsible for what he or she does; the following of another will not be acceptable to God as an excuse.

False Religions

One matter that worries Muslims when they investigate the Bahá'í Faith is the fear that it may be one of the false religions and Bahá'u'lláh may be one of the false prophets that are foretold in the Qur'án and in the Traditions. Certainly some Muslims have stated that Bahá'u'lláh is a false prophet. It is, however, nothing new for a Messenger of Allah to be accused thus; Muḥammad himself was charged with being a forger and a liar (Qur'án 16:101).

The Qur'án gives great assistance to Muslims in this matter by asserting Allah's guarantee that that which is good will prosper and spread while that which is bad has no roots and will eventually disappear from the surface of the earth. This assurance is given in the Qur'án in the form of a parable:

> Seest thou not how Allah sets forth a parable? – A goodly Word like a goodly tree, whose root is firmly fixed, and its branches (reach) to the heavens, – It brings forth its fruit at all times, by the leave of its Lord. So Allah sets forth parables for men, in order that they may receive admonition. And the parable of an evil Word is that of an evil tree. It is torn up by the root from the surface of the earth: it has no stability. Allah will establish in strength those who believe, with the Word that stands firm, in this world and in the Hereafter; but Allah will leave, to stray, those who do wrong: Allah doeth what He willeth. (14:24–7)

This is reinforced by a statement elsewhere in the Qur'án promising Muslims that 'Falsehood is (by its nature) bound to perish' (17:81).

Muslims must assess the teachings revealed by Bahá'u'lláh (see chapters 5–7), see what have been the fruits of these teachings and decide for themselves whether these are good fruits or evil. But in any case, the fact that the tree of Bahá'u'lláh has survived and even grown for over a hundred years is, under the Qur'án's criteria, evidence in itself that the tree of Bahá'u'lláh is a 'goodly tree' – for 'an evil tree' would not have survived.

It is worth remembering in this connection that the Qur'án assures us that, while it is possible for a true prophet to be killed, it is not possible for a false prophet to survive.[123] No one can falsely claim to be a Messenger of Allah or to lie about the fact that he was bringing Allah's Word without bringing down upon himself the wrath of Allah:

> And if a person were to invent any sayings in Our name, We should certainly seize him by his right hand, and We should certainly then cut off the artery of his heart. Nor could any of you withhold him (from Our wrath). (69:44–7)[124]

The history of Islam offers several examples of persons who claimed to be prophets, such as Musaylima, and were executed or killed.[125] Indeed, it is an historical fact that in the Muslim world no one has been successful in advancing a claim to bring an independent revelation from Allah from the time of Muḥammad until the beginning of the Bahá'í Faith. No one has advanced such a claim and then either survived to the end of his natural life or been able to establish a religious community based on such a claim. Therefore Bahá'ís consider that the very fact that Bahá'u'lláh has made this bold assertion and survived to the end of a long life is itself evidence of the truth of his claim. The survival and spread of the Bahá'í community is further evidence. Indeed, the Qur'án mocks anyone who states that it is possible for a mere human being to establish a new religion:

> What! Have they partners (in godhead) who have established for them some religion without the permission of Allah? (42:21)

It should be noted that this assertion by the Qur'án that it is not possible for anyone to set up a new religion applies only to those who claim to bring a new religion from Allah, a new revelation, a new book and new laws. It does not apply to the many people in Islamic history who have set up sects of Islam, such as the Aḥmadiyyah, Ismá'ílíyyah and others. Whatever other Muslims may think of them, these look to the Qur'án as their holy book and claim to follow the laws of the Qur'án. They are merely sects of Islam and their claims are thus not at all comparable with the claims of Bahá'u'lláh. The Qur'án does not say that it is impossible for people to set up sects of Islam; indeed, it actually prophesies that this will happen.[126] What the Qur'án says cannot happen is for someone to start a new religion falsely, stating that he is a new Messenger of Allah with a new book and new laws. Since this is exactly what Bahá'u'lláh has done, it would seem that, according to the Qur'án, his cannot be a false religion.

The Qur'án emphasizes this point by asserting that once the claim of someone to be a Messenger of Allah is accepted by a group of people, anyone who subsequently disputes with the claimant is subject to the wrath of Allah:

> But those who dispute concerning Allah after He has been accepted, – futile is their dispute in the sight of their Lord: on them is [the] Wrath [of Allah], and for them will be a Penalty terrible. (42:16)

Only Allah answers those who call upon Him; those who summon people to anything other than the truth will find no one responding to their summons (Qur'án 13:14). The very fact, therefore, that there are today millions of people who have responded to the summons of Bahá'u'lláh is itself Quranic proof of the truth of Bahá'u'lláh's claim. Thus the Qur'án puts those Muslims who oppose the Bahá'í Faith into a quandary. If they claim that the Bahá'í Faith is a false religion, then they are also stating that the Qur'án itself is false because, as we have just seen, it states that no false religion will survive and be accepted by large numbers of people.

In summary, then, all Muslims have the individual responsibility of judging Bahá'u'lláh's claim. In order to guide them in reaching a decision, they have the Qur'án. This book contains accounts of numerous previous Messengers of Allah. Each Muslim can judge whether Bahá'u'lláh matches the same criteria as these Messengers. Each Muslim can also read the scriptures revealed by Bahá'u'lláh and learn of the teachings that he brought and then determine whether these teachings are the fruits of a good tree or not. Finally, each Muslim must ask himself: has the Bahá'í Faith met the test set by the Qur'án that only a good tree will survive? If so, then by the criteria of the Qur'án, it must be a true religion and Bahá'u'lláh's claims must be valid.

4

Islamic Prophecies

In this chapter, the various Islamic prophecies both from the Qur'án and from the Traditions (*ḥadíths*) which Bahá'ís regard as being fulfilled in the Bahá'í Faith will be examined.

The Day of Judgement

One of the Bahá'í teachings that Muslims find most difficult to accept is that the Bahá'í scriptures claim that the coming of Bahá'u'lláh is the Day of Judgement. The Qur'án has many statements about the Day of Judgement, which is also called by several other names including the Day of Resurrection and the Day of Reckoning. The literal meaning of the descriptions of this Day would involve the sun being darkened, the stars falling from heaven and the sky being rent asunder (Qur'án 81:1, 2, 11). Since such dramatic signs have clearly not occurred, Muslims feel that the Day of Judgement cannot have happened. And yet the Qur'án also says that the Day of Judgement will occur and people will remain negligent and unaware of it:

> Forewarn them of that woeful day, when Our decrees shall be fulfilled whilst they heedlessly persist in unbelief. (19:39, cf. 12:107, 30:55–6)[127]

We must therefore look for an explanation of the Day of Judgement that explains all of these verses. Indeed, we are also in need of an explanation of these verses that is possible, for it is physically not possible for all the stars (each one of which is many thousands of times larger than the earth) to fall to the earth. The Bahá'í scriptures state that the coming of each of the Messengers of Allah is a Day of Judgement for the followers of the previous Messenger. It is then that they are judged on whether they have truly been following the spirit of the teachings of the former Messenger or whether they have merely followed the outward form of the religion while their hearts are busied with the things of this world. Thus when Muḥammad (blessings and peace be upon him) appeared, it was the Day of Judgement for the Christians and Jews. Those who had been true followers of both the spirit and the outward forms of the teachings of the previous Messengers recognized that the new Messenger, Muḥammad, brought a new message from the same source as the previous one. Those who had only been following the outward form of the religion felt challenged and threatened by the new Messenger of Allah and rejected him and often even persecuted him and his followers. Thus the people are judged by their own actions. 'Do men think they will be left alone on saying, "We believe", and that they will not be tested?' (Qur'án 29:2)

The Qur'án makes it clear that mere outward assertions of belief and outward following of religious laws are not enough. To pass the test set by Allah, there must also be inner spiritual transformation and progress. During the time of Muḥammad, there was a group of those who outwardly professed Islam and followed its laws. But Muḥammad knew that inwardly their hearts were not with him. In Islamic history they are known as the *Munáfiqún* (the Hypocrites). The judgement of the Qur'án on these people is:

> When they meet you, they say, 'We believe': but when they are alone, they bite off the very tips of their fingers at you in their rage. Say: 'Perish in your rage! Allah knoweth well all the secrets of the heart.' (3:119, cf. 5:44–5)

The Bahá'í scriptures state that whenever a new Messenger of Allah comes, he throws into turmoil the old order of things. All individual human beings who come into contact with the new message are put to the test: do they truly believe in the spiritual reality of the divine teachings or are they merely following the outward form of the previous religion; do they within their hearts truly believe or do they harbour evil. In this way, the coming of each of the Messengers of Allah has been a Day of Judgement.

The Bahá'í scriptures point out, moreover, that each time that a Messenger has come from Allah, it has been the leaders of the previous religious dispensation who have taken the lead in opposing the new Messenger. And so it was the Jewish religious leaders who opposed Jesus most strongly and brought him before the Roman authorities, demanding that he be sentenced to death. For this reason, Jesus strongly and at length denounced the Jewish religious leaders (see Matthew 23:1–39). And when Muḥammad announced that he had brought a new message from Allah, he faced opposition from the Jewish and Christian religious leaders. It is for this that the religious leaders are accused in the Qur'án of trying to put out Allah's light and are strongly condemned (see Qur'án 9:31–2, 34).

The Bahá'í scriptures say it is these facts that point to the real meaning of the terms used in the holy books about the Day of Judgement such as the sky being rent asunder, the sun being darkened and the stars falling to earth. When a new Messenger of Allah comes, it is the Day of Judgement or the Day of Reckoning for those who follow the previous religion. The sky or the heaven being rent asunder refers to the fact that the old order is abrogated, the heaven of the old religion has been torn apart by the coming of the new. The sun has been darkened in the sense that the old religious teachings are no longer the source of spiritual light,[128] a new spiritual sun has arisen. The stars falling to earth refers to the loss of the spiritual position of the religious leaders of the previous religion, who fall from their high station because of their opposition to the new teaching from Allah.[129] These are some of the explanations that the Bahá'í scriptures give of these terms which are among the abstruse verses of the Qur'án (Qur'án 3:7). As discussed previously, Muslims are promised that the explanations of these abstruse verses will come on the Day of Judgement (see pp. 77–9).

The Qur'án itself contains clues to the interpretation of the signs that will accompany the Day of Judgement. For example, the prophecy that the sun is to be folded up and lose its light on that Day (81:1) can be interpreted by reference to other verses. Allah is the light of the heavens (24:35) and so the reference to the sun being folded up refers to the loss of the teachings of Allah. When this happens Allah has always in the past and will in the future lead humanity out of the darkness into the light through sending a new Messenger with a new book (5:16–17, 2:257, 14:1, 14:5, 33:43, 57:9, 65:11). The statement that on that Day the earth will shake (*zalzalah*; 99:1, 22:1) is exactly parallelled by the statement in the Qur'án that during the Siege of Medina and the Battle of the Trench the hearts of the believers were shaken with doubt.

> In that situation were the Believers tried: they were shaken as by a tremendous shaking (*zalzalah*). (33:11)

Thus these events that are predicted to occur on the Day of Judgement are symbolic representations of the spiritual reality of what will occur. They are not meant to represent physical reality alone – otherwise how could people remain unaware of them? Rather they each have a symbolic and spiritual meaning: they represent the loss of power and spiritual strength of religion (sun being darkened, 81:1), the loss of true spiritual leadership among the religious leaders (the stars falling or failing to give their light, 77:8, 81:2) and the hearts of the believers being in turmoil (the earth shaking, 99:1).

The Qur'án depicts a succession of peoples who have

existed in the past. To each of these peoples a Messenger has come with a message from Allah and in each case the people have rejected the Messenger and his message. The Qur'án describes how Allah has punished these people and destroyed them (see p. 72). However, the Muslims themselves are not exempt from this process. The Day of Judgement will be a great and terrible day when all will be in fear:

> O mankind! Fear your Lord! For the convulsion of the Hour (of Judgement) will be a thing terrible! (22:1)

The punishment and destruction that is prophesied to befall the Muslims is clearly detailed in the Traditions:

> Narrated 'Abdu'lláh and Abú Músá: The Prophet said, 'Near the establishment of the Hour there will be days during which religious ignorance will spread, knowledge will be taken away (vanish) and there will be much Al-Harj, and Al-Harj means killing.' (al-Bukhárí) [130]

> Narrated Abú Hurayra: The Prophet said, 'The Hour will not be established till a man passes by a grave of somebody and says, "Would that I were in his place."' (al-Bukhárí) [131]

But Allah has also laid down the principle that He will never punish or destroy a people unless he first sends them a Messenger as a warning:

> . . . nor would We visit with Our Wrath until We had sent a Messenger (to give warning). (17:15)

Therefore the Muslims will also be sent a Messenger of Allah before Allah's punishment falls upon them on the Day of Judgement. In the following passage from the Qur'án this whole theme is summarized and it is even stated that the punishment of Allah will occur in one thousand years. It is then that a new Messenger of Allah will come and that will be the Day of Judgement for the Muslims.

> If they treat thy (mission) as false, so did the peoples before them (with their prophets), – the people of Noah and 'Ád and Thamúd; those of Abraham and Lot; and the Companions of the Madyan people; and Moses was rejected (in the same way). But I granted respite to the Unbelievers and (only) after that did I punish them: but how (terrible) was My rejection (of them)! . . .
>
> Yet they ask thee to hasten on the Punishment! But Allah will not fail in His promise. Verily a Day in the sight of thy Lord is like a thousand years of your reckoning. (22:42–4, 47)

This idea that the coming of each Messenger of Allah is the Day of Judgement for the followers of the previous Messengers is supported by the fact that, in the Qur'án, one of the main features of the Day of Judgement is said to be the setting up of the balances or scales (*mízán*, plural *mawázín*) in which the deeds of each individual are weighed up.

> We shall set up scales (*mawázín*) of justice for the day of Judgement, so that not a soul will be dealt with unjustly in the least. And if there be (no more than) the weight of a mustard seed, We will bring it (to account): and sufficient are We to take account. (21:47)

And yet the Qur'án also states that in fact the balance or scales was sent with every Messenger of Allah – and hence the coming of every Messenger is a Day of Judgement:

> We sent aforetime our Messengers with Clear Signs and sent down with them the Book and the Balance (*mízán*, of Right and Wrong), that men may stand forth in justice . . . (57:25)

The Balance is also stated to have been sent down in the day of Muḥammad:

> It is Allah Who has sent down the Book in truth, and the Balance (*mízán*, by which to weigh conduct). (42:17)

Similarly with the word *Ṣayḥah*, which is variously translated as the awful Cry or the mighty Blast. This is something that is prophesied in several verses of the Qur'án to occur as one of the signs of the Day of Judgement.

> The Day when they will hear a (mighty) Blast (*aṣ-Ṣayḥah*) in (very) truth: that will be the Day of Resurrection. (50:42; see also 36:48–9, 51–4)

But it is also something that is stated in the Qur'án to have happened with the coming of Messengers of Allah such as Ṣáliḥ (11:66–7, 54:23–31), S͟hu'ayb (11:94), Lot (15:61–73), Moses (29:39–40) and other Messengers (15:80–3, 23:32–41, 36:20–32, 38:12–14).

The Day of Judgement is described in the Qur'án as the Day of Gathering (*has͟hr*, see for example 50:44). And yet this same word is stated to have first occurred when the Jews of Banú Naḍír were punished after their rejection and betrayal of Muḥammad, thus indicating that the coming of Muḥammad was also a Day of Judgement:

> It is He Who got out the Unbelievers among the People of the Book from their homes at the first gathering (*al-has͟hr*) . . . (59:2)

This is the reason the Qur'án repeatedly warns the people of Mecca and Medina that the Last Hour or the Day of Judgement is nigh. These warnings come especially in the early, Meccan súrahs:

> The (Judgement) ever approaching draws nigh. (53:57)

> And what will make thee realize that perhaps the Hour is close at hand? (42:17)

> A questioner asked about a Penalty to befall the Unbelievers . . . They see the (Day) indeed as a far-off (event): but We see it (quite) near. The Day that the sky will be like molten brass and the mountains will be like wool . . . (70:1, 6–9)

The warnings were given because it was Muḥammad himself who brought the Day of Judgement with his coming. The Qur'án states that the Last Hour or Day of Judgement had already begun with the coming of Muḥammad:

> Await they aught save the Hour, that it should come upon them unawares? And the beginnings thereof have already come. But how, when it hath come upon them, can they take their warning? (47:18)[132]

In the Súrah of Qáf it is specifically stated that the day of Muḥammad was the threatened Day of Judgement. The following statement is in the present tense and does not refer to a future event, as most translations imply:

> And the trumpet is blown. This is the threatened Day. (50:20)[133]

There are also several verses of the Qur'án that clearly state that the coming of Muḥammad was the Hour or Day of Judgement for the Quraysh of Mecca. The Súrah of al-Qamar, for example, was revealed about five years before the Prophet's emigration from Mecca to Medina and is addressed to those Meccans who had disbelieved and opposed him. Here, the first verse specifically states that 'the Hour (of Judgement) is nigh' and in the rest of the súrah the fate of several other peoples who had rejected their Messengers is described. Towards the end of that súrah, referring back to these previous peoples who rejected their Messengers, Allah asks the Meccan opponents of Muḥammad: 'Are your unbelievers (O Quraysh), better than they? or have ye an immunity in the Sacred Books?' (54:43) The súrah goes on to prophesy that the unbelieving Meccans, the Quraysh, will soon be defeated (as did happen a few years later) and this is specifically stated to be the Day of Judgement for them:

> Soon will their multitude be put to flight, and they will show their backs. Nay, the Hour (of Judgement) is the time promised them (for their full recompense): And that Hour will be most grievous and most bitter . . . The Day they will be dragged through the Fire on their faces (they will hear:) 'Taste ye the touch of Hell!' (54:45–6, 48)

There is also a Tradition which indicates that Muḥammad's coming was identical to the Day of Judgement: 'Anas reported the Messenger of Allah as saying: "I and the Last Hour have been sent like this." And he (while doing it) joined the forefinger to the middle finger.'[134]

The fact that the Day of Judgement is to be a Day in which a new Messenger of Allah comes and the people are tested is stated even more clearly in Súrah 69, the Súrah of the Inevitable or Sure Reality (*al-Ḥaqqah*). In trying to explain what the Inevitable or Sure Reality (*al-Ḥaqqah*) involves, the Qur'án refers us back to the calamity that befell the tribes of Thamúd and 'Ád (69:4–8). We know from elsewhere in the Qur'án (7:65–79) that these calamities befell these tribes because a Messenger of Allah, Ṣáliḥ and Húd respectively, was sent to each of them and they rejected him. Then, in further explanation of *al-Ḥaqqah*, it is stated:

> And Pharaoh and those before him, and the cities overthrown, committed habitual sin. And disobeyed (each) the Messenger of their Lord; so He punished them with an abundant Penalty. We, when the water (of Noah's flood) overflowed beyond its limits, carried you (mankind) in the floating (Ark), that We might make it a message unto you,

> and that ears (that should hear the tale and) retain its memory should bear its (lessons) in remembrance. (69:9–12)

Thus it is made quite clear that *al-Ḥaqqah* is the coming of a Messenger of Allah, his rejection by the majority of the people and the subsequent judgement of Allah against them. Then this súrah goes on to state that the Inevitable or Sure Reality (*al-Ḥaqqah*) is the Day of Judgement and the events of this Day are graphically described (see 69:18–37). Súrah 69 is, therefore, a clear indication that the Day of Judgement will be the coming of a future Messenger of Allah, his rejection by the people in the same way that the Messengers of Allah – Ṣáliḥ, Húd, Moses and Noah – were rejected by the peoples to whom they came and Allah's punishment of them for this.

It is, therefore, clear that by 'the Day of Judgement' the Qur'án means the coming of a new Messenger of Allah. The Bahá'í scriptures state that with the coming of Bahá'u'lláh it is again the Day of Judgement, when all, whether Jews, Christians or Muslims, are again tested. Bahá'u'lláh claims to bring a new message from Allah, a new divine teaching, revealing Allah's Will for our present day. He says that it is the day when the balance is set and the scales will weigh human beings and those who have truly believed in and understood the previous messages from Allah, will recognize that his message is from the same source. They will recognize that Allah has spoken again to humanity. But those who are merely following the outward form of their religion or are blindly following their religious leaders without bothering to investigate for themselves are condemned.

In general then, the message of the Qur'án is that the promises of Allah about a Day of Judgement are in the process of being fulfilled with the coming of Muḥammad. It equally sets up the promise of a further, future Day of Judgement which will be the coming a future Messenger of Allah and this will be a judgement for all peoples, including the Muslims. (Further evidence for this may be found on pp. 108–11.)

Bahá'ís also consider that Bahá'u'lláh is the 'Great Announcement' (*an-Nabá' al-A'ẓam*) which the Qur'án says will be made on the Day of Judgement. If one examines the Qur'án, one sees that the word *an-nabá'* (news, announcement, story) is almost always used to mean the call of a Messenger of Allah, the announcement of his message (see, for example, 10:71, 26:70, 28:3). Sometimes it is used of the call of Messengers of Allah in general (6:34, 6:67). The expression 'Great Announcement' (*an-Nabá' al-A'ẓam*) is even used to describe Muḥammad's own message (38:67–8). Bahá'ís therefore consider it very significant when it is prophesied in the Qur'án that the 'Great Announcement' (*an-Nabá' al-A'ẓam*) will occur on the Day of Judgement, the day of Separation (*Yawm al-Faṣl*). In the Súrat an-Nabá' of the Qur'án, it is stated:

> Concerning what are they disputing? Concerning the Great News [Announcement], about which they cannot agree. Verily, they shall soon (come to) know! Verily, verily, they shall soon (come to) know! . . . Verily the Day of Sorting Out [Separation] is a thing appointed, – the Day that the Trumpet shall be sounded, and ye shall come forth in crowds; and the heavens shall be opened as if there were doors . . . Truly Hell is as a place of ambush. (78:1–5, 17–19, 21)

Thus these verses from the Surat an-Nabá' indicate that what will happen on the Day of Judgement will be occurrence of a 'Great Announcement', the call of a new Messenger of Allah. This passage is also of great importance because it says 'Verily, they shall soon come to know' and then repeats this. This signifies that the event shall occur twice. Bahá'ís consider that, because of its importance as the Day of Judgement, two Messengers of Allah have appeared in this age: the Báb and Bahá'u'lláh.

The Qur'án indicates in another place also that there will be two Messengers of Allah on the Day of Judgement. It says that there will be two blasts on the Trumpet on the Day of Resurrection:

> And the trumpet is blown, and all who are in the heavens and the earth swoon away, save him whom Allah willeth. Then it is blown a second time, and behold them standing waiting![135]
>
> And the Earth will shine with the glory of its Lord: the Record (of Deeds) will be placed (open); the prophets and the witnesses will be brought forward and a just decision pronounced between them; and they will not be wronged (in the least). (39:68–9, cf. 79:6–7)

These two Messengers of Allah, the Báb and Bahá'u'lláh, came so close to one another that the Qur'án indicates that although there will be two trumpet blasts, they will seem as one call (79:6–7, 13; see translations of both Yusuf Ali and Pickthall).

It is also possible to see a prophecy of the advent of two Messengers of Allah in the following verse:

> O ye that believe! Fear Allah, and believe in His Messenger, and He will bestow on you the *kiflayn*. (57:28)

There are several ways of interpreting the dual noun *kiflayn* but since there is general agreement that where *kifl* occurs elsewhere in the Qur'án (21:85, 38:48), it refers to a prophet or Messenger of Allah, then a possible translation of this phrase is: 'He (Allah) will send to you two Messengers of Allah.'

One phrase that is used of the Day of Judgement in the Qur'án is *Yawm ad-Dín* (37:20), which is often translated as Day of Judgement but when the word *dín* appears by itself in the Qur'án, it is most commonly translated by both Yusuf Ali and Pickthall as a 'religion' or 'faith' (e.g. 2:132, 256; 3:19). That a new religion will appear on the Day of Judgement is shown by another verse, which if *ad-dín* is translated as 'religion' becomes:

> Verily that which ye are promised is true; and verily the Religion (*ad-Dín*) must indeed come. (51:5–6)

Bahá'ís believe that the Qur'án contains a remarkable prediction of the events that occurred with the coming of the Báb and Bahá'u'lláh – a prophecy that the Muslims would reject the coming of a new Messenger of Allah with the assertion that their own Messenger was the last one and that Allah would not raise up another. This passage begins by making it clear that it refers forward to the events of the Day of Judgement or the Day of Mutual Calling, as it is named here:

> 'And O my People! I fear for you a Day when there will be mutual calling (and wailing), – a day when ye shall turn your backs and flee: no defender shall ye have from Allah: any whom Allah leaves to stray, there is none to guide . . .' (40:32–3)

Then in the very next verse there is the explanation of why Muḥammad fears for his people. In clarifying this, Muḥammad refers back to what happened after the Messenger of Allah Joseph came:

> And to you there came Joseph in times gone by, with Clear Signs but ye ceased not to doubt of the (mission) for which he had come: at length, when he died, ye said: 'No Messenger will Allah send after him.' Thus doth Allah leave to stray such as transgress and live in doubt . . . (40:34)

And in the verse following this one, the Qur'án describes Allah's extreme displeasure at those who follow such a course and of Allah's punishment of them:

> '(Such) as dispute about the Signs of Allah without any authority that hath reached them. Grievous and odious (is

The Day of Judgement

Bahá'u'lláh claims that all of the numerous prophecies in the Qur'án regarding the Day of Judgement have been fulfilled spiritually by his coming. He specifically refers to many of these prophecies in the following passage, which is set out in the form of a series of questions about whether the prophecies of the Qur'án concerning the Day of Judgement have been fulfilled:

O thou who hast set thy face towards the splendours of My Countenance! Vague fancies have encompassed the dwellers of the earth and debarred them from turning towards the Horizon of Certitude, and its brightness, and its manifestations and its lights. Vain imaginings have withheld them from Him Who is the Self-Subsisting. They speak as prompted by their own caprices, and understand not.

Among them are those who have said: 'Have the verses been sent down?' Say: 'Yea, by Him Who is the Lord of the heavens!'

'Hath the Hour (*as-Sá'ah*, 18:21, 40:59, 7:187) come?' 'Nay, more; it hath passed, by Him Who is the Revealer of clear tokens!

Verily, the Inevitable (*al-Ḥáqqah*, 69:1–3) is come, and He, the True One, hath appeared with proof and testimony.

The Plain (*as-Sáhirah*, 79:14) is disclosed, and mankind is sore vexed and fearful . . .'

Say: 'The stunning trumpet-blast (*aṣ-Ṣákhah*, 80:33) hath been loudly raised, and the Day (*al-Yawm*, 2:48 etc.) is God's, the One, the Unconstrained.'

'Hath the Catastrophe (*aṭ-Ṭámah*, 79:34) come to pass?' Say: 'Yea, by the Lord of Lords!'

'Is the Resurrection (*al-Qiyámah*, 75:1, etc.) come?' 'Nay, more; He Who is the Self-Subsisting hath appeared with the Kingdom of His signs.'

'Seest thou men laid low (*ṣar'an*, 69:7)?' 'Yea, by my Lord, the Exalted, the Most High!'

'Have the tree-stumps (*a'jáz*, 54:20) been uprooted?' 'Yea, more; the mountains have been scattered in dust (*al-jabál nusifat*, 77:10); by Him the Lord of attributes!'

They say: 'Where is Paradise (*al-Jannah*), and where is Hell (*an-Nár*, 47:15, etc.)?' Say: 'The one is reunion with Me; the other thine own self, O thou who dost associate a partner with God and doubtest.'

They say: 'We see not the Balance (*al-Mízán*, 42:17).' Say: 'Surely, by my Lord, the God of Mercy! None can see it except such as are endued with insight.'

> 'Have the stars fallen (*an-nujúm*, 81:2)?' Say: 'Yea, when He Who is the Self-Subsisting dwelt in the Land of Mystery (Adrianople). Take heed, ye who are endued with discernment!'
>
> All the signs appeared when We drew forth the Hand of Power from the bosom of majesty and might (27:12).
>
> Verily, the Crier (*al-Munád*, 50:41) hath cried out, when the promised time (*al-mí'ád*, 34:30) came, and they that have recognized the splendours of Sinai have swooned away (4:153–4) in the wilderness of hesitation, before the awful majesty of thy Lord, the Lord of creation.
>
> The trumpet (*an-náqúr*, 74:8) asketh: 'Hath the Bugle (*aṣ-Ṣúr*, 78:18) been sounded?' Say: 'Yea, by the King of Revelation!, when He mounted the throne of His Name, the All-Merciful' . . .
>
> They that have gone astray have said: 'When were the heavens (*as-sama*, 73:18) cleft asunder?' Say: 'While ye lay in the graves of waywardness and error' . . .
>
> And among them is he who saith: 'Have men been gathered together (67:24, etc.)?' Say: 'Yea, by My Lord!, whilst thou didst lie in the cradle of idle fancies' . . .
>
> And among them is he who saith: 'Have I been assembled with others, blind (20:124)?' Say: 'Yea, by Him that rideth upon the clouds!' . . .
>
> Say: 'The light hath shone forth from the horizon of Revelation, and the whole earth hath been illumined at the coming of Him Who is the Lord of the Day of the Covenant!'
>
> The doubters have perished, whilst he that turned, guided by the light of assurance, unto the Dayspring of Certitude hath prospered. (Bahá'u'lláh)[136]

such conduct) in the sight of Allah and of the Believers. Thus doth Allah seal up every heart – of arrogant and obstinate transgressors.' (40:35)

Thus in four short verses, the Qur'án has prophesied that on the Day of Judgement many Muslims would deny the new Messenger of Allah and would say of their own prophet, Muḥammad, what the followers of Joseph said about theirs, that 'no Messenger will Allah send after him' and that this would be the cause of Allah's condemnation of them.

One of the signs of the Day of Judgement that is frequently

mentioned in the Qur'án and the Islamic Traditions is that of smoke (*dukhán*),[137] or sometimes clouds (*ghamám*).[138] The Bahá'í scriptures explain the meanings of these words thus:

> By the term 'clouds' is meant those things that are contrary to the ways and desires of men. Even as He hath revealed in the verse already quoted: 'As oft as an Apostle [a Messenger] cometh unto you with that which your souls desire not, ye swell with pride, accusing some of being impostors and slaying others.' [Qur'án 2:87] These 'clouds' signify, in one sense, the annulment of laws, the abrogation of former Dispensations, the repeal of rituals and customs current amongst men, the exalting of the illiterate faithful above the learned opposers of the Faith. In another sense, they mean the appearance of that immortal Beauty in the image of mortal man, with such human limitations as eating and drinking, poverty and riches, glory and abasement, sleeping and waking, and such other things as cast doubt in the minds of men, and cause them to turn away. All such veils are symbolically referred to as 'clouds' . . .
>
> It is evident that the changes brought about in every Dispensation constitute the dark clouds that intervene between the eye of man's understanding and the divine Luminary which shineth forth from the dayspring of the divine Essence. Consider how men for generations have been blindly imitating their fathers, and have been trained according to such ways and manners as have been laid down by the dictates of their Faith. Were these men, therefore, to discover suddenly that a Man, Who hath been living in their midst, Who, with respect to every human limitation, hath been their equal, had risen to abolish every established principle imposed by their Faith – principles by which for centuries they have been disciplined, and every opposer and denier of which they have come to regard as infidel, profligate and wicked, – they would of a certainty be veiled and hindered from acknowledging His truth.[139]

The symbolic term 'smoke' denotes grave dissensions, the

> abrogation and demolition of recognized standards, and the utter destruction of their narrow-minded exponents. What smoke more dense and overpowering than the one which hath now enshrouded all the peoples of the world, which hath become a torment unto them, and from which they hopelessly fail to deliver themselves, however much they strive?[140]

The Day of Resurrection

Some Muslims may object to the Bahá'í interpretation of the Day of Judgement by saying that the Day of Judgement is also the Day of Resurrection and yet the dead have not risen from their graves. Bahá'ís would respond by saying that just as the Day of Judgement has a metaphorical meaning and a spiritual fulfilment, so also does the Day of Resurrection. Those who are spiritually dead are raised to a new spiritual life with the coming of each Messenger of Allah. According to the Islamic tradition, the Arabs were in the depths of spiritual degradation before the coming of Muḥammad. According to the Qur'án, they had such practices as burying their infant daughters alive. They were as ones who were spiritually dead. The coming of Muḥammad brought them back to spiritual life; it resurrected them. This understanding of spiritual death and spiritual life is in accordance with the following verse of the Qur'án, which tells the Muslims that they were dead and Allah gave them life:

> How disbelieve ye in Allah when ye were dead and He gave life to you! (2:28)[141]

This verse is in the past tense and so clearly refers to the fact that Muḥammad had brought spiritual life to the Arabs, who had not been physically dead but spiritually. Similarly, the Qur'án refers to the conversion of Muḥammad's uncle, Hamzah, to Islam in a way that makes it clear that when death and life are referred to, it is spiritual death and spiritual life that is meant:

> Can he who was dead, to whom We gave life, and a light whereby he can walk amongst men, be like him who is in the depths of darkness from which he can never come out? (6:122)

From these examples and others,[142] it is clear that the Qur'án is mainly concerned with spiritual life and death. And so when it speaks of the Day of Resurrection, it is the spiritual raising up of the spiritually dead to life that is meant. This is what happens whenever a new Messenger of Allah comes. The Qur'án describes a cycle of destruction and regeneration. But this destruction is not a literal physical destruction; it is a spiritual destruction, a spiritual death. When they reject the new Messenger of Allah, the people become spiritually dead. But from among the people a small number recognize the Messenger. This group is thus said to have been raised to life by Allah. This is, of course, a spiritual life.

> See they not how many of those before them We did destroy? – Generations We had established on the earth, in strength such as We have not given to you – for whom We poured out rain from the skies in abundance, and gave (fertile) streams flowing beneath their (feet): yet for their sins We destroyed them, and raised in their wake fresh generations (to succeed them). (6:6)

This raising to life of the new people is achieved through the influence and guidance of the new Messenger of Allah and his book. Thus for example, regarding Moses, it is stated in the Qur'án that:

> We did reveal to Moses the Book after We had destroyed the earlier generations, (to give) insight to men and guidance and mercy that they might receive admonition. (28:43)

It is this pattern of the eventual spiritual death of each people followed by the raising up by Allah of a new generation through a new Messenger of Allah that is the meaning of the Day of Resurrection (*Qiyámah*). The Muslims are also part of this process. They were also raised up as a new generation from the posterity of other peoples through the coming of the Prophet Muḥammad:

> Thy Lord is Self-sufficient full of Mercy: if it were His Will, He could destroy you, and in your place appoint whom He will as your successors, even as he raised you up from the posterity of other people. (6:133)

Just as with statements about the Day of Judgement (see pp. 93–4), the people are warned by Muḥammad in an early, Meccan súrah that their resurrection is close at hand:

> They say: 'What! When we are reduced to bones and dust, should we really be raised up (to be) a new creation?' . . . Then will they say: 'Who will cause us to return?' Say: 'He Who created you first!' Then will they wag their heads towards thee, and say, 'When will that be?' Say, 'May be it will be quite soon!' (17:49, 51)

The Qur'án also prophesies a future Day of Resurrection, which will occur with the coming of another Messenger of Allah. For example, the Qur'án speaks of a series of deaths and resurrections that have and will happen to the Muslims. It states that they had been (spiritually) dead before Islam but through it had been brought to life again (resurrected). Then it states that at some stage in the future they will die again and be brought to life again. Since the Qur'án uses exactly the same words within the same verse about what had happened in the past and what will happen in the future, it is clear that what will occur in the future will be the same as what happened in the past – in other words, that the Muslims will in the future again be spiritually dead and will, through the coming of a new Messenger and a new religion from Allah, be raised to life again.

> How can ye reject the faith in Allah? – Seeing that ye were without life, and He gave you life; then will He cause you to die, and will again bring you to life; and again to Him will ye return. (2:28)

Bahá'ís have interpreted many other passages of the Qur'án as referring to Bahá'u'lláh's coming. For example, there is the following verse:

> And listen for the Day when the Caller (*al-munádí*) will call out from a place quite near . . . (50:41)

The Caller (*al-munádí*) is identified elsewhere in the Qur'án as one who calls people to Faith (*ímán*, 3:193), in other words a Messenger of Allah. This verse is followed by one that clearly connects the coming of this Messenger of Allah with the Day of Resurrection:

> The day when they will hear a (mighty) Blast in (very) truth: that will be the Day of Resurrection. (50:42)

Indeed, as we have seen, elsewhere in the Qur'án the Day of Resurrection is called 'the Day of Mutual Calling' (see p. 99).[143] Thus this verse (50:41) is prophesying the coming of a Messenger of Allah on the Day of Resurrection. Furthermore, this passage of the Qur'án also points to the place of his coming. Almost every important Muslim scholar and commentator has stated that the 'place quite near' to Medina, where Muḥammad revealed this verse of the Qur'án, is in fact the area of the Holy Land or Palestine. Thus, for example, az-Zamakhsharí, in commentary on this verse, states that the 'place quite near' refers to: 'the rock of the Bayt al-Muqaddas (or Bayt al-Maqdis, the Holy Land, referring to Palestine and Jerusalem) for it is the nearest place on earth to heaven by twelve miles and it is the centre of the world'. Az-Zamakhsharí also confirms that this whole verse concerns the events of the Day of Resurrection.[144] Similarly Ibn Májah cites a Tradition confirming that Jerusalem and Palestine is the place where the Gathering (*al-Maḥshar*) will occur on the Day of Judgement:

> I said: O Apostle of Allah! Tell me about the Holy Land (Bayt al-Maqdis).
>
> He said: It is the Land of Gathering (*al-Maḥshar*) . . . and so go there and pray, for one prayer there is the equivalent of a thousand prayers elsewhere.[145]

In summary, then, these two verses: 'And listen for the Day when the Caller will call out from a place quite near; the day when they will hear a (mighty) Blast in (very) truth: that will be the Day of Resurrection' (50:41–2), mean: be attentive for a day when a Messenger of Allah will issue a summons from the land of Palestine and that will be the Day of Resurrection. Bahá'ís believe of course that this refers to the appearance of Bahá'u'lláh in 'Akká, from where he addressed his call to humankind.

Similar to the word *al-munádí* is the word *ad-dá'í*, which also appears in the Qur'án and can also be translated as 'the caller' or 'one who invites'. This word is also used to describe the Messengers of Allah. Thus, for example, Muḥammad is addressed:

> O Prophet! Truly We have sent thee as a Witness, a Bearer of Glad Tidings, and a Warner, – and as one who invites (*ad-dá'í*) to Allah's (Grace) by His leave, and as a Lamp spreading light. (33:45–6)[146]

In the Qur'án it is clearly prophesied that on the Day of Judgement (20:100), another Caller (*ad-dá'í*) – in other words, another Messenger of Allah – will appear and: 'On that Day will they follow the Caller (*ad-dá'í*).' (20:108)

This promise of the appearance of a Caller (*ad-dá'í*) on the Day of Judgement is made even more clearly in the Súrah of al-Qamar. This súrah begins by stating that 'the Hour (of Judgement) is nigh' (54:1). It goes on to say that the people will ignore the signs that come to them of the Day of Judgement and advises Muḥammad that, since they will not listen, he should turn away from them until:

> The day that the Caller will call (them) to a terrible affair. They will come forth, – their eyes humbled – from (their) graves, (torpid) like locusts scattered abroad, hastening, with eyes transfixed, towards the Caller! – 'Hard is this Day!' the Unbelievers will say. (54:6–8)

Then as if to emphasize the point that the Caller who will appear on the Day of Judgement will be a Messenger of Allah, the súrah goes on to say that this will be like the days of Noah when the people rejected their Messenger and Allah punished them with a severe penalty as a warning. The súrah continues by giving similar accounts of the coming of several Messengers of Allah such as Húd, who was sent as a warner to the people of 'Ád; Ṣáliḥ, who was sent as a warner to the people of Thamúd; Lot and Moses. The message of the súrah to Muslims is clear: Messengers of Allah came to these other people and they were punished by Allah when they rejected them; a Messenger of Allah (a Caller) will also come to the Muslims on the Day of Judgement (the day that the Caller will call them to a terrible affair) and they should be warned by this súrah not to reject him.

The Universal Day of Judgement

We have seen above that Bahá'ís consider that the coming of every Messenger of Allah has been a Day of Judgement, a Day of Resurrection. Why then, it may be asked, does the Qur'án place such great emphasis on its prophecies of the future Day of Judgement? The majority of the súrahs that come towards the end of the Qur'án are on this subject and it is a recurrent important theme in the súrahs at the beginning too. If, as Bahá'ís claim, each coming of a Messenger of Allah is a Day of Judgement, then surely the coming of Bahá'u'lláh would be no different to the coming of other Messengers of Allah and there would be no need for such a great emphasis on this Day in the Qur'án. What difference is there about Bahá'u'lláh's coming compared to the other Messengers that warrants such an emphasis?

As has been mentioned earlier, Muslims can understand Bahá'u'lláh to be a further Messenger from Allah sent in a succession of Messengers that Allah has decreed should come to earth to guide humanity. Although it has been mentioned that the station of each of these Messengers is equal,[147] nevertheless the importance to humanity of some of these Messengers is greater than others ('Some of the Messengers We have caused to excel others,' 2:253).[148] The Bahá'í scriptures explain that throughout the ages Allah has sent Messengers to all the peoples of the world. This is confirmed in the Qur'án which states that 'To every people (was sent) a Messenger' (10:47). All of these Messengers who have founded the great religions have taught of the coming of a great Universal Day of Judgement that would affect the whole world. Each of the founders of the world religions has also taught about the coming of a future saviour. Thus the Buddha taught of the coming of the fifth Buddha, Krishna taught that he would one day return, the Jews are expecting their Messiah, the Christians are expecting the return of Christ and the Muslims are expecting the Mahdi and also the coming of Jesus Christ (*al-masíḥ*). (Regarding the concept of Return, see pp. 128–31.)

The Bahá'í scriptures explain that the reason for the importance of this Day, the reason why it has been so extensively spoken of in the Qur'án and in the other scriptures of the world's religions, is that on this Day there will appear a single, universal figure who will represent the fulfilment of all of these prophecies.

> The time foreordained unto the peoples and kindreds of the earth is now come. The promises of God, as recorded in the holy Scriptures, have all been fulfilled.[149]

> Say, God is my witness! The Promised One Himself hath come down from heaven, seated upon the crimson cloud with the hosts of revelation on His right, and the angels of inspiration on His left, and the Decree hath been fulfilled at the behest of God, the Omnipotent, the Almighty.[150]

Bahá'ís consider that this is foretold in the Qur'án where it is stated that the Messenger of each community will come to them on the Day of Judgement:

> To every people (was sent) a Messenger: when their Messenger comes (before them), the matter will be judged between them with justice, and they will not be wronged. (10:47)

Thus, in summary, each of the founders of the great world religions has prophesied a Day when he or his spirit will return. The Qur'án predicts a Day when all peoples will be called together in the presence of their Messenger. Bahá'ís believe that Bahá'u'lláh's coming is the simultaneous fulfilment of all of these prophecies. The coming of Bahá'u'lláh is the return of the Promised One of each religion, the Day when the followers of each religion are gathered together with their returned Messenger. It thus becomes the Universal Day of Judgement.

The Messenger of Allah is also sometimes called an Imám in the Qur'án.[151] Thus Bahá'ís believe that the following verse also bears witness to this theme of a future Day when the different peoples of the world are gathered together before their Messenger of Allah – a prophecy that Bahá'ís believe was fulfilled by Bahá'u'lláh:

> One day We shall call together all human beings with their Imám: those who are given their record in their right hand will read it (with pleasure), and they will not be dealt with unjustly in the least. (17:71)[152]

This then is the importance of the Universal Day of Judgement, which Bahá'ís believe to have been fulfilled through the coming of Bahá'u'lláh. It is the coming together of all the strands of the religious history of humanity with the advent of a single, universal figure who is the Promised One of all of the religions of the world. This gathering together of all the peoples of the world in unity is the primary purpose of the mission of Bahá'u'lláh (see pp. 154–60). This is why this Day has been emphasized so much in the Qur'án and in the scriptures of all the religions.

The Meeting with Allah

As we have seen, Bahá'ís consider that we are now living in the Day of Judgement prophesied in the Qur'án. The Qur'án makes it very clear just how important this Day is compared to other days as it explicitly states that on this Day of Judgement humanity will meet with Allah. This meeting with Allah (*liqá*)[153] is an important theme in the Qur'án and there are many verses referring to it, for example:

> Allah is He Who raised the heavens without any pillars that ye can see; is firmly established on the Throne (of Authority) . . . He doth regulate all affairs, explaining the Signs in detail, that ye may believe with certainty in the meeting with your Lord. (13:2, cf. 75:22–3, 29:5, 41:54)

> Do they not reflect in their own minds? Not but for just ends and for a term appointed, did Allah create the heavens and the earth, and all between them: yet are there truly many among men who deny the meeting with their Lord (at the Resurrection)! (30:8)

This is also stated in the Traditions. For example, Muḥammad is recorded as pointing on one occasion to the full moon and saying:

> You will see your Lord on the Day of Resurrection as you see this (full moon) and you will have no difficulty in seeing Him. (al-Bukhárí, Muslim, Ibn Ḥanbal)[154]

Indeed, the Qur'án, in several places, specifically foretells a grievous punishment for those who do not believe in the meeting with Allah; for example:

> One day He will gather them together: (it will be) as if they had tarried but an hour of a day: they will recognize each other: assuredly those will be lost who denied the meeting with Allah and refused to receive true guidance. (10:45, cf. 6:31, 7:147, 10:7, 10:11, 10:15, 18:105, 29:23)

And yet we are told that Allah is closer to us than our main jugular vein (Qur'án 50:16). If He is so close to us, why do we not see Him now? What is the difference that occurs on the Day of Judgement? How will the situation be different so that Allah will become visible on that Day when we are told that the attributes of Allah are unchanging and one of these is that He cannot be seen; we are told in the Qur'án that no vision is able to take Him in.

> No vision can grasp Him, but His grasp is over all vision: He is above all comprehension, yet is acquainted with all things. (6:103)

Indeed, according to reliable Traditions, even Muḥammad himself was not able to see Allah.[155] Similarly, we are told in the Qur'án that when Moses asked to see Allah, the impossibility of this request was demonstrated to him when only a part of Allah was shown to a mountain and it was turned into dust (7:143; see p. 14).

Thus we are in a quandary: on the one hand we are told that humanity will see Allah on the Day of Judgement; on the other, we are told that it is not possible to see Allah and even to try would lead to destruction. In the Bahá'í scriptures, this enigma is resolved by reference to the Messengers of Allah. These Messengers appear to outward seeming to be ordinary human beings but, in reality, they are far more. They speak for Allah and act for Him; they are the representatives of Allah; it can be said that they are 'as Allah' for human beings. Thus for example, when, at the time of the Treaty of Ḥudaybiya, the Muslims one by one placed their hands on Muḥammad's hand and pledged their loyalty to him, the following verse was revealed in the Qur'án: 'Those who swear allegiance unto thee (Muḥammad), [in reality] swear allegiance only unto Allah' (48:10).[156] Similarly, in many places in the Qur'án we find the Messenger of Allah linked together with Allah as though they were, for humans, indistinguishable. Time and again the Qur'án refers to 'Allah and His Messenger' as one unit. It is 'Allah and His Messenger' that human beings must obey (3:32, 4:59, 8:20, 8:46); it is in 'Allah and His Messenger' that human beings must believe (3:179, 4:136, 4:152); it is to both that the believers are summoned (24:51); to reject or wage war upon one is to reject or wage war upon both (5:36, 8:13, 9:54, 9:84, 9:107); that which is forbidden by one is forbidden by both (9:29); that which has been decided by one has been decided by both (33:36). Some actions that must refer to the Messenger of Allah are stated to refer to 'Allah and His Messenger'. For example, the Muslims are told that if they differ among themselves over anything, they should refer it to 'Allah and His Messenger' (4:59). Since it is not possible to refer anything directly to Allah, the phrase 'Allah and His Messenger' here must refer to the Messenger of Allah acting 'as Allah'. When Muḥammad acted to cancel the treaty with the idolators of Mecca, this action is stated in the Qur'án to have been done by 'Allah and His Messenger' (9:3). Similarly, Bahá'u'lláh, referring to the

Messengers of Allah, states that they are 'as Allah' to the world of humanity:

> Whoso recognizeth them hath recognized God. Whoso hearkeneth to their call, hath hearkened to the Voice of God, and whoso testifieth to the truth of their Revelation, hath testified to the truth of God Himself. Whoso turneth away from them, hath turned away from God, and whoso disbelieveth in them, hath disbelieved in God. Every one of them is the Way of God that connecteth this world with the realms above, and the Standard of His Truth unto every one in the kingdoms of earth and heaven. They are the Manifestations of God amidst men, the evidences of His Truth, and the signs of His glory.[157]

It is for this reason that these Messengers of Allah are often referred to in the Bahá'í scriptures as Manifestations of Allah. Thus the Messengers of Allah, such as Muḥammad, have been 'as Allah' for human beings. What is meant by the 'meeting with Allah' on the Day of Judgement, then, is that another Messenger of Allah will come to the world who will be 'as Allah' for human beings and the 'meeting with Allah' referred to in the Qur'án, which cannot for the above reasons occur literally, will occur through the presence of this Messenger of Allah. For those who see him, it will be as though they have seen Allah, just as the Prophet Muḥammad said that those who had seen him had seen Allah.[158]

This interpretation is made clear in Traditions that indicate that the meeting with Allah that is prophesied to occur on the Day of Resurrection will be a meeting with a man who looks like any other man (but who will in reality be 'as Allah'). In one Tradition, for example, advice is given on how to distinguish Allah from the Dajjál, the evil figure who will also appear in that Day (see pp. 203–4).

> Narrated by 'Abdu'lláh bin 'Umar: The Messenger of Allah stood up amongst the people and then praised and glorified

> Allah as He deserved and then he mentioned the Dajjál, saying, 'I warn you of him, and there was no prophet who did not warn his followers of him; but I will tell you something about him which no prophet has told his followers: the Dajjál is one-eyed whereas Allah is not.' (Al-Buk͟hárí)[159]

This Tradition makes it clear that what is meant by the 'meeting with Allah' on the Day of Judgement is that a man will appear who will to outward seeming be just an ordinary human being with no outward distinguishing marks (so ordinary will he seem that Muḥammad felt it necessary to give his followers some guidance on how to distinguish him from the Dajjál), but in his inward reality this man will be the representative of Allah, he will be 'as Allah' to humanity. This is what Bahá'ís believe has happened with the coming of Bahá'u'lláh. Although some have stated that the Last Hour, when the Mahdi, Christ and the Dajjál will appear, is something that will occur before the 'meeting with Allah' and the Day of Judgement, this Tradition also explains that the coming of the Dajjál and the 'meeting with Allah' will all be part of the events of the Last Hour. Similarly, a verse in the Qur'án makes it clear that the 'meeting with Allah' is associated with the 'appointed time' or 'fixed term' (*ajal*) that Allah has set for the Muslim community (see p. 48).

> For those whose hopes are in the meeting with Allah (let them strive); for the Term (appointed) by Allah is surely coming: and He hears and knows (all things). (29:5)

Interestingly, there is a Tradition in the *Ṣaḥíḥ* of al-Buk͟hárí which links this theme of the meeting with Allah to the fact that, on the Day of Resurrection, Allah will appear twice. On the first occasion He will not be recognized and will be rejected. It is only on His second appearance that He will be accepted. Bahá'ís believe that this refers to the coming of the Báb, who was rejected, and the subsequent coming of Bahá'u'lláh. This Tradition again shows that the appearance of Allah on the Day of Judgement will not occur, as most Muslims expect, with trumpets blowing and Allah descending from heaven in a literal sense. For if that were to occur, who would deny Allah then? And yet, this Tradition clearly states that on the first occasion of His coming, He will not be recognized and He will be rejected.

> On the authority of Abú Hurayra: The people said, 'O Messenger of Allah! Shall we see our Lord on the Day of Resurrection?' The Prophet said, 'Do you have any difficulty in seeing the moon on a full moon night?' They said, 'No, O Messenger of Allah.' He said, 'Do you have any difficulty in seeing the sun when there are no clouds?' They said, 'No, O Messenger of Allah.' He said, 'So you will see Him, like that. Allah will gather all the people on the Day of Resurrection, and say, "Whoever worshipped something (in the world) should follow (that thing)." So, whoever worshipped the sun will follow the sun, and whoever worshipped the moon will follow the moon, and whoever used to worship certain (other false) deities, he will follow those deities. And there will remain only this nation . . . Allah will come to them and say, "I am your Lord". They will (deny Him and) say, "We will stay here till our Lord comes, for when our Lord comes, we will recognize Him." So Allah will come to them in His appearance which they know, and will say, "I am your Lord." They will say, "You are our Lord", so they will follow Him.' (Al-Bukhárí)[160]

The Bahá'í scriptures refer to this theme of the 'meeting with Allah' in connection with the verse containing the phrase 'Seal of the Prophets'. They point out that Muslims have allowed the phrase 'Seal of the Prophets' to become a barrier between them and the truth, despite the fact that a mere four verses after this one comes the promise that they will 'meet Him' (or 'attain to the Divine Presence'). They have allowed the first phrase to blind them to the implications of the second. The passage in the Qur'án is as follows:

> 40. Muḥammad is not the father of any of your men but (he is) the Messenger of Allah and the Seal of the Prophets: and Allah has full knowledge of all things.
> 41. O ye who believe! celebrate the praises of Allah and do this often;
> 42. And glorify Him morning and evening.
> 43. He it is Who sends blessings on you, as do His angels, that He may bring you out from the depths of Darkness into Light: and He is Full of Mercy to the Believers.
> 44. Their salutation on the Day they meet Him [attain the Divine Presence] will be 'Peace!'; and He has prepared for them a generous Reward.
> 45. O Prophet! Truly We have sent thee as a Witness, a Bearer of Glad Tidings and a Warner . . . (33:40–5)

Bahá'u'lláh comments on this passage:

> How strange! These people with one hand cling to those verses of the Qur'án and those traditions of the people of certitude which they have found to accord with their inclinations and interests, and with the other reject those which are contrary to their selfish desires. 'Believe ye then part of the Book, and deny part?'[Qur'án 2:85] How could ye judge that which ye understand not? Even as the Lord of being hath in His unerring Book, after speaking of the 'Seal' in His exalted utterance: 'Muḥammad is the Apostle of God and the Seal of the Prophets' [33:40], hath revealed unto all people the promise of 'attainment unto the divine Presence'. [33:44] To this attainment to the presence of the immortal King testify the verses of the Book . . .
>
> And yet, through the mystery of the former verse, they have turned away from the grace promised by the latter, despite the fact that 'attainment unto the divine Presence' in the 'Day of Resurrection' is explicitly stated in the Book. It hath been demonstrated and definitely established, through clear evidences, that by 'Resurrection' is meant the

rise of the Manifestation of God to proclaim His Cause, and by 'attainment unto the divine Presence' is meant attainment unto the presence of His Beauty in the person of His Manifestation. For verily, 'No vision taketh in Him, but He taketh in all vision.'[Qur'án 6:103] Notwithstanding all these indubitable facts and lucid statements, they have foolishly clung to the term 'seal', and remained utterly deprived of the recognition of Him Who is the Revealer of both the Seal and the Beginning, in the day of His presence. 'If God should chastise men for their perverse doings, He would not leave upon the earth a moving thing! But to an appointed time doth He respite them.' [Qur'án 16:61] But apart from all these things, had this people attained unto a drop of the crystal streams flowing from the words: 'God doeth whatsoever He willeth, and ordaineth whatsoever He pleaseth', they would not have raised any unseemly cavils, such as these, against the focal Centre of His Revelation.[161]

The Coming of the Mahdi and the Return of Jesus Christ

Among the many signs that the Qur'án gives relating to the Day of Judgement is the return of Jesus Christ (al-Masíḥ ibn Maryam):

> And (Jesus) shall be a Sign (for the coming of) the Hour (of Judgment): therefore have no doubt about the (Hour), but follow ye Me: this is a Straight Way. (43:61)

In the Traditions relating the words of the Prophet Muḥammad, there are many prophecies both about the coming of the Mahdi and the return of Jesus. These are to be found in the most reliable of the collections of the Traditions.[162] Bahá'ís believe that Bahá'u'lláh was the return of Jesus prophesied in these Islamic Traditions and that Bahá'u'lláh's predecessor, the Báb, was the Mahdi. They believe that the prophecies in the Sunni collections of Traditions about these events were fulfilled by the coming of the Báb and Bahá'u'lláh.

As indicated previously (see pp. 47–8), the Qur'án states that each religious community (*ummah*) has a fixed term and suggests that after this fixed term a new Messenger comes with a new message from Allah. Bahá'ís maintain moreover that there is in the Qur'án an indication of how long the fixed term of the Islamic *ummah* will be. To understand this allusion, however, it is necessary to understand the meaning of the word *al-amr* as it is used in the Qur'án.

The word *al-amr*, when it is used in the Qur'án in relation to Allah, refers to Allah's ordering of the affairs of the world (see, for example, 2:117, 10:3, 10:31). But more frequently it refers to Allah's decree to punish those who, after they have been called by one of Allah's Messengers to the truth, turn away from Him (see 7:150, 9:48, 9:106, 15:66, 16:33, 19:39, 46:25, 51:44, 57:14, 65:8). There are many examples of this usage of the word *al-amr*. In the Súrah of Húd, for example, Noah calls the people to Allah and warns them but when they fail to respond the decree of Allah (*al-amr*) falls upon them and they are destroyed (11:43–4); Abraham calls the people to Allah and warns them, but when they fail to respond, the decree of Allah (*al-amr*) falls upon them (11:76); Moses calls Pharaoh and his people to Allah and warns them, but when they fail to respond, the decree of Allah (*al-amr*) falls upon them (11:101). This pattern is repeated throughout the whole súrah (see also 11:58 and 11:66). The last verse in this súrah states that '*al-amr* returns to Allah' (11:123).

In other súrahs we find that this decree of Allah (*al-amr*) was also imminent in the time of Muḥammad. He was charged with calling the people to Allah but the Qur'án warns the people that the decree of Allah (*al-amr*) is at hand if they do not listen to Muḥammad (16:1). In other places in the Qur'án *al-amr* also refers to the holy book (44:2–5, 54:3), the path laid down by Muḥammad (45:18) and is the authority given to the Messengers of Allah (28:44).

And so *al-amr*, as it is used in the Qur'án, refers to the appearance of a Messenger of Allah, his calling the people to Him and then if they disobey (as usually they do), the decree

Prophecies Related to the Báb (the Mahdi) in the Traditions

The following are prophecies about the Mahdi from the major books of Sunni *ḥadíth*. Bahá'ís believe that the Báb fulfilled the prophecies about the Mahdi (see also chapter 8):

The Mahdi will be a Descendant of Muḥammad

From the *Sunan* of Abú Dáwud:
Narrated by Umm Salamah, Ummu'l-Mu'minín: The Prophet (peace be upon him) said: The Mahdi will be of my family, of the descendants of Fáṭimah.[163]

The Báb belonged to a family that was well known to be descendants of the Prophet Muḥammad through Fáṭimah.

The Mahdi will Fill the Earth with Justice

From the *Sunan* of Abú Dáwud:
Narrated by 'Abdu'lláh ibn Mas'úd: The Prophet (peace be upon him) said: If only one day of this world remained, Allah would lengthen that day, till He raised up in it a man who belongs to me or to my family . . . who will fill the earth with equity and justice as it has been filled with oppression and tyranny.[164]

The Báb gives great priority to the concept of justice in his writings. The Bahá'í teachings are also centred on the concept of justice. The Bahá'í institutions are called by Bahá'u'lláh the Houses of Justice because it is Bahá'u'lláh's intention that the people should be able to turn to them for justice. He instructs that there should be one in every locality in the world.

The Mahdi will Rule for Seven Years

From the *Sunan* of Abú Dáwud:
Narrated Abú Sa'íd al-Khudrí: The Prophet (peace be upon him) said: The Mahdi will be of my stock . . . he will rule for seven years.[165]

The ministry of the Báb ended in its seventh year. (Regarding the word 'rule', see section on 'The Sovereignty of the Mahdi', pp. 215–20.)

Black Flags will Proceed from Khurasan in the Time of the Mahdi

From the *Musnad* of Ibn Ḥanbal:
Thawbán reported that the Messenger of Allah said: When you see black standards coming from Khurasan go to them for Allah's caliph the Mahdi will be among them.[166]

During the ministry of the Báb, some of his followers proceeded from Khurasan with a black standard (see p. 195).

of Allah comes to pass and they are punished. It also refers to the authority of the Messenger of Allah, the holy book which he brings and the path laid down by the Messenger of Allah. All of these meanings are of relevance when the following verse of the Qur'án (the translation of which I have adjusted in accordance with the explanations given in the paragraphs immediately above) is considered:

> He establishes His decree (*al-amr*) from the heavens unto the earth and it will go up to Him in a Day, the length of which is one thousand years in your reckoning. (32:5)

The coming of Muḥammad was, as has already been demonstrated, the coming from Allah of *al-amr*. Those who believed in Muḥammad were saved and those who rejected Him faced Allah's punishment. Bahá'ís state that this verse prophesies that the decree (*al-amr*) that was given to Muḥammad would return to Allah after a period of one thousand years. This indicates that after one thousand years the authority given to Muḥammad would be ended and would return to Allah. The cycle would then be repeated and another Messenger of Allah would come, call the people to Him and renew His decree. If there were to be no further revelation from Allah after Muḥammad, the fixed term of one thousand years would not be specified. As the term of one thousand years is fixed in the Qur'án, this indicates that at the end of this time the decree of Allah (*al-amr*) would be renewed and would come down to earth again. The following *ḥadíth*, which is found in almost all of the major collections of Traditions in this or similar forms, states that at the end of the Islamic dispensation, after the *amr* given to Muḥammad has returned to Allah, the *amr* of Allah will return to this world. (This Tradition is further examined on pp. 123–4.)

> 'Umar ibn al-Khaṭṭáb (may Allah be pleased with him) gave the oration on Friday and said: I heard the Messenger of Allah (peace be upon him) saying: 'A party of my people will continue victorious upon the right path until the Cause of Allah (*amr Alláh*) shall come.'[167]

The return of *al-amr* (the divine cause) can only, according to the usage of the Qur'án, be through the coming of another Messenger of Allah, which is, of course, exactly what Bahá'ís believe has happened with the coming of Bahá'u'lláh.

A second interpretation of the word *al-amr* in this verse (32:5) may be obtained by studying the authors of the great commentaries on the Qur'án. According to az-Zamakhsharí commenting on this verse, *al-amr* means those 'acts of obedience and pious deeds which are ordained' by Allah and are sent down with the angel Gabriel as revelation (*al-wahy*). Since al-Bayḍáwí's commentary is based on az-Zamakhsharí, it is not surprising that al-Bayḍáwí concurs with this. Both of these great Islamic scholars then identify the 'Day' which is mentioned in this verse as being the Last Hour (*as-sá'ah*) and as the Day of Resurrection (*yawm al-qiyámah*).[168]

Putting these two interpretations together, we can come to the conclusion that the Last Hour or Day of Resurrection is to be identified with the coming of a new revelation sent down from Allah. This interpretation is confirmed in the opening chapter of the *Sunan* of Ibn Májah. Here there is a Tradition which states:

> A party of my people will be aided upon the right path, and those who oppose them shall not harm them, until the Cause of Allah (*amr Alláh*) shall come.[169]

What is interesting is that four Traditions earlier in this same book there is a parallel Tradition relating to the Last Hour or Day of Judgement that states:

> A party of my people will be aided, and those who desert them shall not harm them, until the [Last] Hour arises.[170]

These two Traditions are so similar to one another in structure and meaning that it seems most likely that they refer to the same event. Similarly, in the *Ṣaḥíḥ* of Muslim, there are Traditions similar to the one above that says that 'A party of my people will continue victorious upon the right path until the Cause of Allah (*amr Alláh*) shall come' and these are placed side by side with Traditions that say that 'A party of my people will continue victorious upon the right path until the Day of Judgement (or Last Hour) shall come'.[171] Thus these two Traditions placed side by side in these two great collections of *ḥadíths* indicate to us that the coming of the Cause of Allah, which as we have seen is the coming of a Messenger of Allah, will occur on the Day of Judgement. All of this is evidence for the Bahá'í assertion that these three things (the coming of a new Messenger with a new revelation, the coming of the Cause of Allah and the Day of Judgement or Last Hour) are equated with one another in these verses and Traditions precisely because all refer to the same future event, the coming of Bahá'u'lláh. Another version of this same *ḥadíth*, given by Ibn Ḥanbal, ties this Tradition closely to the events of the life of Bahá'u'lláh in that it gives the place where these events will occur as being in the land of Palestine:

> The Messenger of Allah said: 'A party of my people will be following the [true] religion, victorious over their enemies (and those who oppose them will be unable to harm them except

> for whatever misfortunes may afflict them) until the Cause of Allah (*amr Alláh*) shall come to them while they are in this state.' And they said 'O Messenger of Allah! Where shall they be?' He said: 'In Jerusalem and the lands around it.'[172]

Another passage of the Qur'án that Bahá'ís believe refers to Bahá'u'lláh's coming are the opening words of Súrah al-Bayyinah:

> Those who reject (Truth) among the People of the Book and among the Polytheists were not going to depart (from their ways) until there come to them Clear Evidence (*ḥattá ta'tiya-hum al-bayyinah*) . . . (98:1)

The next two verses from this passage of the Qur'án go on to say what the Clear Evidence (*al-bayyinah*) is: it is 'a Messenger (*rasúl*) from Allah, rehearsing scriptures kept pure and holy: wherein are laws [books] right and straight' (98:2–3). Now, because of their interpretation of the 'Seal of the Prophets', Muslims have regarded this passage as referring to Muḥammad but the Arabic is in fact phrased in such a way as to refer to a future event: the coming of a Messenger of Allah in the future. There are numerous examples of the same phrasing (*ḥattá ta'tiya-hum*) in the Qur'án and the Traditions that show that this phrase in this context always refers to the future.[173] The meaning of the verse is thus that the People of the Book (Jews and Christians) and the polytheists will not desist from their rejection of Muḥammad and Islam until there shall come to them a future Messenger of Allah. There is further evidence that this Messenger is not Muḥammad himself in that it is stated that this future Messenger would do two things that Muḥammad did not do: he would bring the People of the Book to the truth (this did not happen in the time of Muḥammad, as he was rejected by Jews and Christians) and he would bring books and scriptures (this does not apply to Muḥammad who brought only one holy book, the Qur'án). These conditions were fulfilled by Bahá'u'lláh.

One Tradition that clearly prophesies that a Messenger of Allah will bring a new religion and a new Holy Law (*Sharí'ah*) and that he will be opposed by the Muslim religious leaders is recorded by Shaykh 'Abd al-Wahháb ash-Sha'rání (d. 1565) in his book, *al-Yawáqít wa'l-Jawáhir*:

> He will cause to appear a religion that he holds within himself which even were the Messenger of Allah (Muḥammad) to be alive, he would judge according to it. And in his time, there will only remain this religion, purified from personal opinion. The schools (*madháhib*) of the *'ulamá* will oppose most of his ordinances (*aḥkámihi*). And they will be dismayed at him on account of this for they will consider that, after their leadership, Allah will not allow a single mujtahid to remain.[174]

Another event that is prophesied in the Qur'án and the Traditions is that the tribes of Ya'júj and Ma'júj (Gog and Magog), who had been contained to the north, would be freed and come down from the mountains. The Qur'án states that this will be a sign that the promised day is near:

> Until the Gog and Magog (people) are let through (their barrier) and they swiftly swarm from every hill. Then will the True Promise draw nigh (of fulfilment). (21:96–7)

Bahá'ís consider that this prophecy was fulfilled at the beginning of the 19th century when Russia came down from the north attacking and conquering the realms of Islam. They defeated the Ottomans repeatedly, annexing the Crimea and much of the European part of the Ottoman Empire and advancing as far as Adrianople (Edirne) in 1829. At the same time, Iran lost all of its Caucasian provinces to Russia in two wars (1804–13 and 1826–8). Russia also began at this time to conquer the area of Central Asia, which had been an important centre of Islamic civilization. All these events occurred shortly before the Báb declared his mission in 1844.

Prophecies Related to Bahá'u'lláh (the Return of Christ) in the Traditions

The following are prophecies from the major books of Sunni *ḥadíth* which Bahá'ís believe were fulfilled by Bahá'u'lláh (see also chapter 8). Bahá'ís believe that Bahá'u'lláh was the return of Christ (al-Masíḥ):

The Descent of Jesus

From the *Ṣaḥíḥ* of al-Bukhárí:
Narrated by Abú Hurayra: Allah's Messenger said, 'The Hour will not be established until the son of Mary (i.e. Jesus) descends amongst you as a just ruler, he will break the cross, kill the pigs, and abolish the *Jizyah* tax. Money will be in abundance so that nobody will accept it (as charitable gifts).'[175]

Bahá'ís interpret this as meaning that on his return Jesus will have the full authority of a Messenger of Allah. He will supersede the previous religions and abrogate and replace their laws. This is expressed symbolically in this Tradition as he will 'break the cross' (superseding Christianity), 'kill the pigs' (for food, abrogating the laws of Judaism) and 'abolish the *Jizyah*' (superseding the Islamic *Sharí'ah*). Bahá'u'lláh did all of this both symbolically and, in the case of abolishing the prohibition on eating pork and the *Jizyah* tax, literally also.

His Ministry will be for 40 Years

From the *Sunan* of Abú Dáwud:
Narrated by Abú Hurayra: The Prophet (peace be upon him) said: . . . He (Jesus) will descend (to the earth) . . . He will destroy the Antichrist (the Dajjál) and will live on the earth for 40 years and then he will die.[176]

Bahá'u'lláh's ministry lasted 40 years (1852–92). (Concerning the Dajjál, see pp. 203–4.)

Allah will Change the Arab People for Persians

From the *Ṣaḥíḥ* of at-Tirmidhí:

Abú Hurayra said: Some of the companions of the Messenger of Allah (upon him be greetings and praise) said: 'O Messenger of Allah! Who are those people about whom Allah has said that if we turn back (from the Path), He will substitute in our stead another people and they would not be like us (i.e. Qur'án 47:38)?' And Salman (the Persian) was beside the Messenger of Allah and the Messenger of Allah struck him (on the thigh) and took Salman and said: 'This man and his people. By the One in whose hand is my soul! Were faith to be suspended in the Pleiades men from among the Persians would attain unto it.'[177]

The majority of the early followers of the Báb and Bahá'u'lláh were Persians.

The Last Remaining Supporter of the Mahdi will come to 'Akká

In *al-Futuḥát al-Makkiyyah*, S͟hayk͟h Muḥyi ad-Dín ibn al-'Arabí records the following *ḥadít͟h* concerning the Mahdi and his supporters or ministers (*wuzará*):

He (the Mahdi) will emerge at a time of decline in religion. Allah will constrain through him what was not constrained though the Qur'án, such that a man who is ignorant, cowardly and miserly one evening will be transformed to being learned, brave and generous on the morrow . . . He will witness the most mighty battle (Armageddon), the banquet of Allah, upon the plain of 'Akká. He will banish tyranny and those who espouse it and he will revive religion . . . His martyrs will be the best of martyrs and his trusted ones the most excellent of trustees. In order to help him, Allah has kept hidden in a secret place a people whom He has made aware of the concealed and revealed realities of things and of whatever Allah has ordained for His servants. And they will make their decisions through their consultations . . . And his supporters whom Allah has caused to help him – in accordance with His words 'It is incumbent upon Us to help the believers (Qur'án 30:47)' – they will follow in the footsteps of those of the companions (of the Prophet) who held true to the covenant that they had made with Allah. And they will all be Persians, there being no Arabs among them, but they will speak Arabic . . . They are the most favoured of the supporters and the most excellent of the trustees . . . And all of them will be killed except one who will be upon the plain of 'Akká, the divine table that Allah has laid out for all creatures.[178]

The Báb (the Mahdi) emerged at the time of the decline of the religion of Islam and ordained new laws and teachings to revive religion.

Concerning his leading followers (the text uses the word *vazír*, plural *wuzará*, which can be translated as 'supporters' or 'ministers' but which I have rendered here as 'leading followers'), they were mostly Persians but being of the religious class they spoke Arabic. All of the leading disciples of the Báb were martyred in Iran and, of the rest, the most prominent was Bahá'u'lláh, who was exiled to 'Akká in Syria. This Tradition mentions making decisions through consultation, which is what the Bahá'ís do (see pp. 169–70). The table with food laid out is also referred to in the Qur'án (5:112–15) as being a miracle of Christ, here mentioned in relation to the returned Christ. Bahá'ís consider that it refers to a heavenly feast of spiritual food.

The Concept of Return

Many Muslims are expecting that the return of Jesus Christ which is prophesied in the Muslim Traditions will be the return of the self-same person who was alive on earth two thousand years ago. It will therefore surprise them to learn that Bahá'ís believe that Bahá'u'lláh, who was born in Iran in AD 1817, is the return of Christ. According to Bahá'í teachings, when the holy scriptures speak of return, they are referring to the return of the attributes and characteristics of one individual or group of people in another individual or group of people living at a later time. The Bahá'í scriptures give proof of this from the Qur'án:

> And it came to pass that on a certain day a number of the opponents of that peerless Beauty, those that had strayed far from God's imperishable Sanctuary, scornfully spoke these words unto Muḥammad: 'Verily, God hath entered into a covenant with us that we are not to credit an apostle until he present us a sacrifice which fire out of heaven shall devour.' [Qur'án 3:183] The purport of this verse is that God hath covenanted with them that they should not believe in any messenger unless he work the miracle of Abel and Cain, that is, offer a sacrifice, and the fire from heaven consume it; even as they had heard it recounted in the story of Abel, which story is recorded in the scriptures. To this,

> Muḥammad, answering, said: 'Already have Apostles before me come to you with sure testimonies, and with that of which ye speak. Wherefore slew ye them? Tell me, if ye are men of truth.' [Qur'án 3:183] And now, be fair; How could those people living in the days of Muḥammad have existed, thousands of years before, in the age of Adam or other Prophets? Why should Muḥammad, that Essence of truthfulness, have charged the people of His day with the murder of Abel or other Prophets? Thou hast none other alternative except to regard Muḥammad as an impostor or a fool – which God forbid! – or to maintain that those people of wickedness were the self-same people who in every age opposed and cavilled at the Prophets and Messengers of God, till they finally caused them all to suffer martyrdom.[179]

In summary, the Qur'án indicates that it considers the people who spoke such scornful words to Muḥammad as being the same as those who had persecuted and martyred prophets in former times. In this same passage, the Bahá'í scriptures point to another verse of the Qur'án:

> Likewise, Muḥammad, in another verse, uttereth His protest against the people of that age. He saith: 'Although they had before prayed for victory over those who believed not, yet when there came unto them, He of Whom they had knowledge, they disbelieved in Him. The curse of God on the infidels!'[Qur'án 2:89] Reflect how this verse also implieth that the people living in the days of Muḥammad were the same people who in the days of the Prophets of old contended and fought in order to promote the Faith, and teach the Cause, of God. And yet, how could the generations living at the time of Jesus and Moses, and those who lived in the days of Muḥammad, be regarded as being actually one and the same people? Moreover, those whom they had formerly known were Moses, the Revealer of the Pentateuch, and Jesus, the Author of the Gospel. Notwithstanding, why did Muḥammad say: 'When He of Whom they had knowledge came unto them' – that is Jesus or Moses – 'they disbelieved in Him'? Was not Muḥammad to outward seeming called

> by a different name? Did He not come forth out of a different city? Did He not speak a different language, and reveal a different Law? How then can the truth of this verse be established, and its meaning be made clear?[180]

Thus the Bahá'í scriptures establish, with proofs from the Holy Qur'án, that each Messenger of Allah who comes to humanity is, in this sense, a return of the previous Messengers, his followers are the return of those who followed the previous Messengers and even his opponents are the return of those who opposed the former Messengers.

> Strive therefore to comprehend the meaning of 'return' which hath been so explicitly revealed in the Qur'án itself, and which none hath as yet understood. What sayest thou? If thou sayest that Muḥammad was the 'return' of the Prophets of old, as is witnessed by this verse, His Companions must likewise be the 'return' of the bygone Companions, even as the 'return' of the former people is clearly attested by the text of the above-mentioned verses. And if thou deniest this, thou hast surely repudiated the truth of the Qur'án, the surest testimony of God unto men. In like manner, endeavour to grasp the significance of 'return', 'revelation', and 'resurrection', as witnessed in the days of the Manifestations of the divine Essence, that thou mayest behold with thine own eyes the 'return' of the holy souls into sanctified and illumined bodies, and mayest wash away the dust of ignorance, and cleanse the darkened self with the waters of mercy flowing from the Source of divine Knowledge; that perchance thou mayest, through the power of God and the light of divine guidance, distinguish the Morn of everlasting splendour from the darksome night of error.[181]

The Bahá'í scriptures go on in this passage to give a second meaning to this concept of 'return'. Given the oneness of the Messengers of Allah (see pp. 18–19), any one of them can be regarded as identical to any other. Thus, in this sense, Bahá'u-'lláh can be regarded as identical to Christ and therefore the return of Christ:

> Furthermore, it is evident to thee that the Bearers of the trust of God are made manifest unto the peoples of the earth as the Exponents of a new Cause and the Bearers of a new Message. Inasmuch as these Birds of the Celestial Throne are all sent down from the heaven of the Will of God, and as they all arise to proclaim His irresistible Faith, they therefore are regarded as one soul and the same person. For they all drink from the one Cup of the love of God, and all partake of the fruit of the same Tree of Oneness . . . In this respect, if thou callest them all by one name, and dost ascribe to them the same attribute, thou hast not erred from the truth. Even as He hath revealed: 'No distinction do We make between any of His Messengers!' [Qur'án 2:285] . . . Thus hath Muḥammad, the Point of the Qur'án, revealed: 'I am all the Prophets.' Likewise, He saith: 'I am the first Adam, Noah, Moses, and Jesus' . . . Sayings such as this, which indicate the essential unity of those Exponents of Oneness, have also emanated from the Channels of God's immortal utterance, and the Treasuries of the gems of divine knowledge, and have been recorded in the scriptures. These Countenances are the recipients of the Divine Command, and the day-springs of His Revelation. This Revelation is exalted above the veils of plurality and the exigencies of number. Thus He saith: 'Our Cause is but one.' [Qur'án 54:50] Inasmuch as the Cause is one and the same, the Exponents thereof also must needs be one and the same.[182]

In summary, then, the Bahá'í scriptures state that when 'return' is spoken of by any of the Messengers of Allah, the meaning is that there will come a time when a person will appear with the same station as that Messenger and there will also be peoples with the same characteristics of supporting or opposing the Messenger of Allah. Spiritually, given the Messengers of Allah are one, any of them can claim to be identical to any other. It is in these senses that Bahá'u'lláh claims to be the return of Christ that is prophesied in the Qur'án and the reliable books of Traditions.

Syria and 'Akká

The land of Syria and the city of 'Akká were Bahá'u'lláh's final place of exile. His shrine near 'Akká is considered by Bahá'ís the most holy place on earth and is the direction in which prayers are said (*qiblah*). The twin cities of Haifa and 'Akká are where the World Centre of the Bahá'í Faith is located (see p. 170).

There are many Islamic Traditions about Syria in general and the city of 'Akká in particular. The land of Syria is greatly praised in compilations of Traditions which are considered among the most reliable. There are several Traditions in which Muḥammad urges his followers to go to the land of Syria at the time of the End, for example:

> Ibn Hawála said: 'Choose for me (a place to go), O Messenger of Allah, if I should reach that time.' He said: 'Get thee to Syria for it is Allah's chosen land and for it He has selected His most favoured servants . . . for Allah has taken special charge of Syria and its inhabitants on my account.'[183]

> There will come a time for the people when there will not be a believer upon the earth except those who cleave to Syria.[184]

> The Messenger of Allah said: 'Before the day of Resurrection, a fire will issue from Ḥaḍramawt (or from the direction of Ḥaḍramawt), and will assemble humankind.' They said: 'O Messenger of Allah! What do you command us to do?' He said: 'Get thee to Syria!'[185]

More specifically, 'Akká itself is mentioned in several Traditions of the Prophet Muḥammad. The famous Muslim geographer Yáqút in his *Mu'jam al-Buldán* mentions in his entry on 'Akká the Tradition 'Well is it with him who has seen 'Akká'.[186]

The eminent scholar Abu'l-Ḥasan 'Alí ar-Raba'í al-Málikí,

known as Ibn Abí Hawl (who died in 444 AH/1052 AD and whose work is used by many later scholars) in his book *Faḍá'il ash-Shám wa Dimashq* has a whole chapter on Traditions of the Prophet about 'Akká and Askalon. Among the Traditions that he cites are the following:

> The Messenger of Allah said: I give you news of a city, set on the shore of the sea, white and pleasing in the eyes of Allah; it is called 'Akká.

> The Messenger of Allah said: Verily the best of shores is the shore of Askalon and better than that is 'Akká. And the excellence of 'Akká over other shores is as my excellence is over the prophets.

> The Messenger of Allah said: There is a city between two mountains and upon the sea called 'Akká. He who enters therein longing for it, his sins both of the past and the future will be forgiven him, and he who leaves it, loathing it, his departure will not be blessed. And in it is a spring called the Spring of the Cow. He who drinks from it, Allah will fill his heart with light and he who pours forth its waters upon himself, will remain pure until the Day of Resurrection.

> There is a city suspended beneath the throne of Allah (may He be glorified and exalted) called 'Akká. He who goes to it to defend it, anticipating a reward (from Allah), (Allah) will write down for him the reward of one who has fasted and prayed, bowing and prostrating, until the Day of Resurrection.

> The Messenger of Allah said: There is a city, set on the shore of the sea, white and pleasing in the eyes of Allah; it is called 'Akká. The bite of a flea in that place is the equivalent of a spear wound (received while fighting) in the path of Allah Almighty. He who glorifies Allah in it, Allah will reinforce his voice. And he who takes up a sword, aiming it at the vainglory of the enemy, Allah Almighty will gather him up

with his brother al-Khiḍr (upon him be peace) and will protect him from the most great terror (on the Day of Judgement).

Allah will build a house of light for the one who has seen the site of the martyrs of 'Akká.

'Umar ibn al-Khaṭṭáb addressed Ka'b al-Aḥbar (a leading Jewish convert to Islam), saying to him: O Abú Isḥáq! When you enter Syria and meet the people of 'Akká, help them for they are the ones who will be looked to on the Day of Resurrection. O Abú Isḥáq! I heard the Messenger of Allah (may the peace and blessings of Allah be upon him) say that there will be kings and princes at the Last Days, and the poor of 'Akká and Askalon will be the kings and princes of the Last Days.

'Uthmán ibn 'Afán (may Allah be pleased with him) said: To keep watch for one night in 'Akká is better than one thousand nights of waking and days of fasting (elsewhere).

'Á'ishah (may Allah be pleased with her) said: I heard the Messenger of Allah saying that the houris of the spring scatter the camphor of paradise upon the spring which is called the Spring of the Cow, which is in 'Akká. And she said: I heard the Messenger of Allah saying that he who drinks from the Spring of the Cow and he who washes (in water) from it and from the Spring of Salwán which is in Jerusalem and from the Spring of Zamzam which is in Mecca, Allah will protect his body from (Hell-)fire. And she said: I heard the Messenger of Allah saying well is it with him from my community who has seen 'Akká and with him who has seen the one who has seen 'Akká.[187]

Other Traditions mentioning 'Akká are quoted elsewhere in this book (see p. 127). Bahá'ís also believe that it was 'Akká, which is in the vicinity (or precincts) of Jerusalem, which is mentioned in the verse of the Night-Journey in the Qur'án:

> Glory to (Allah) Who did take His Servant for a Journey by night from the Sacred Mosque [Mecca] to the Farthest Mosque [Jerusalem] whose precincts We did bless, – in order that We might show him some of Our Signs: for He is the One Who heareth and seeth (all things). (17:1)

'Akká has several other claims to religious importance. At 'Akká is to be found a shrine which is said to be the grave of the Prophet Ṣáliḥ and a spring just outside 'Akká is called the Spring of the Cow ('Ayn al-Baqar, see above) because Adam is said to have found there a cow which became the ancestor of all of humanity's domesticated cattle.

Some scholars have tended to discount the Traditions that extol Syria and its towns saying that these were forged either during the Umayyad caliphate when Syria was being defended against the Byzantines or during the Crusades when people were being encouraged to go to Syria to defend Islam against the Crusaders. It is perhaps natural that scholars should be puzzled by the fact that great importance is given to Syria and its towns (when, for example, there are not nearly as many Traditions about other great early centres of Islam such as Iraq and Egypt) and should try to explain this by asserting that there was forgery of these Traditions. The town of 'Akká, for example, had no importance in Islamic sacred history and so it was strange that it should have been treated in this way. It should be noted, however, that the Traditions about Syria quoted above are from such compilers of Traditions as Ibn Ḥanbal and at-Tirmidhí, which are accounted as being among the most reliable. Furthermore, most of the great collections of Traditions containing the Traditions about Syria and 'Akká were compiled during the 'Abbasid caliphate which had its capital in Baghdad. During this period, there was a great reaction to the Umayyad caliphate based in Damascus. There was therefore some pressure not to record Traditions that praised and glorified Syria and its towns. Nor can these Traditions have been forged in relation to the Crusades. All of the Traditions quoted above about Syria and 'Akká are from books that were compiled before the era of the Crusades.

Conclusion

The subject of prophecies is a difficult one since each person will read a prophecy and understand something different from it. It is a sad fact that the peoples of the world have generally misunderstood and misinterpreted the prophecies of their holy books. The Jews misinterpreted the prophecies that were in their scriptures and rejected Jesus when he came to them. They were expecting a military leader as their Messiah, one who would lead them to victory. Had the Jews gone to Jesus and asked what the correct interpretation of their prophecies was, they would have heard from him the truth. Similarly, the Christians misinterpreted the prophecies that were in their scriptures and rejected Muḥammad when he came instead of asking him the true meaning of their prophecies. History, therefore, shows that Muslims need to be very cautious in relation to their own prophecies. It seems that rather than assuming that they know what their prophecies mean, it would be better if they looked with an open mind at the interpretations that Bahá'u'lláh has revealed and see whether these are not reasonable and coherent explanations.

5

Bahá'í Spirituality

For those of us who live in the more developed world, science has led to a great increase in our physical comfort and convenience; it has given us the freedom and time to develop ourselves. Yet people in the modern world are just as, if not more, unhappy and unfulfilled than their predecessors at any time in the past. Many feel themselves to be wandering through their lives aimlessly not knowing what to do with the freedom that science and technology has given them. Many have thought that the answer is to fill this vacuum by pursuing what they think will give them happiness, whether this be power, wealth or sex, while an increasing number seek to escape the emptiness and despair of their lives by turning to alcohol and drugs. Yet all of these answers turn out to be no answer at all. They lead to dissatisfaction, greater despair and alienation. This fragmentation and aimlessness in our lives is reflected in our societies in a failure of interpersonal relationships: marital breakdown, loneliness, violent inhuman crimes, a rising suicide rate and so on.

Just over a hundred years ago, Allah, who in the Bahá'í scriptures likens Himself to a doctor healing the spiritual disease with which our present-day world is afflicted, states that He has examined the condition of the world, made His diagnosis and prescribed, through the revelation of Bahá'u-'lláh, the remedy:

> The All-Knowing Physician hath His finger on the pulse of mankind. He perceiveth the disease, and prescribeth, in His

> unerring wisdom, the remedy. Every age hath its own problem, and every soul its particular aspiration. The remedy the world needeth in its present-day afflictions can never be the same as that which a subsequent age may require. Be anxiously concerned with the needs of the age ye live in, and centre your deliberations on its exigencies and requirements.[188]

As part of the diagnosis, the Divine Physician, through the Bahá'í scriptures, surveys the human world and perceives that we have lost sight of our true nature: we do not realize who we truly are and, as a result, we have become enslaved to our passions and desires, have lost our orientation and are wandering aimlessly, trusting to the prescriptions and instructions of unskilled doctors while ignoring the remedies of the True Physician. And so, in the Bahá'í scriptures, Allah issues His call, summoning us to a realization of our true selves, urging us to free ourselves from the illusions of the world and to turn ourselves towards the divine, the transcendent reality that is the true orientation of our lives. Only in this way will we find what will give us peace, contentment and lasting happiness.

> O Son of Spirit! I created thee rich, why dost thou bring thyself down to poverty? Noble I made thee, wherewith dost thou abase thyself?
> Out of the essence of knowledge I gave thee being, why seekest thou enlightenment from anyone beside Me?
> Out of the clay of love I moulded thee, how dost thou busy thyself with another?[189]

The Bahá'í scriptures state that we as human beings are enmeshed in the snare of materialism. We are so engrossed in the drive to acquire the things of this world that we do not realize that although we think that we possess things, in reality we are often possessed by them. The larger and more expensive a possession is, the greater the tyranny it exercises over our lives. The more we have, the greater our greed becomes and so that greed will never be satisfied.

> O Son of Man! Thou dost wish for gold and I desire thy freedom from it. Thou thinkest thyself rich in its possession, and I recognize thy wealth in thy sanctity therefrom.
> By My life! This is My knowledge, and that is thy fancy; how can My way accord with thine?[190]

And even those who are not trapped by material things are often dominated by what the Bahá'í scriptures call the 'idle fancies and vain imaginings' of our minds.

> O Son of Man! Many a day hath passed over thee whilst thou hast busied thyself with thy fancies and idle imaginings.
> How long art thou to slumber on thy bed?
> Lift up thy head from slumber, for the Sun hath risen to the zenith, haply it may shine upon thee with the light of beauty.[191]

Looking at the condition of the human world, then, Allah condemns the materialism and self-delusion on which it is based:

> Alas! Alas! O Lovers of Worldly Desire!
> Even as the swiftness of lightning ye have passed by the Beloved One, and have set your hearts on satanic fancies.
> Ye bow the knee before your vain imagining, and call it truth.
> Ye turn your eyes towards the thorn, and name it a flower.
> Not a pure breath have ye breathed, nor hath the breeze of detachment been wafted from the meadows of your hearts.
> Ye have cast to the winds the loving counsels of the Beloved and have effaced them utterly from the tablet of your hearts,
> and even as the beasts of the field, ye move and have your being within the pastures of desire and passion.[192]

Allah reminds us that the days of our lives are swiftly passing while we remain enmeshed in this lamentable condition:

> O Ye that are Lying as Dead on the Couch of Heedlessness!
> Ages have passed and your precious lives are well-nigh ended, yet not a single breath of purity hath reached Our court of holiness from you . . .
> Him whom I abhor ye have loved, and of My foe ye have made a friend.
> Notwithstanding, ye walk on My earth complacent and self-satisfied, heedless that My earth is weary of you and everything within it shunneth you.
> Were ye but to open your eyes, ye would, in truth, prefer a myriad griefs unto this joy, and would count death itself better than this life.[193]

> O My Children! I fear lest, bereft of the melody of the dove of heaven,
> ye will sink back to the shades of utter loss, and,
> never having gazed upon the beauty of the rose,
> return to water and clay.[194]

Allah urges us during our brief, ephemeral lives upon this earth to seize our chance:

> O My Servant!
> Free thyself from the fetters of this world,
> and loose thy soul from the prison of self.
> Seize thy chance,
> for it will come to thee no more.[195]

Everything in this world will return to dust, so if we want something that will last, that will be of enduring value, Allah says that we must turn to the spiritual world, to eternal values and goals:

O Friends!
Abandon not the everlasting beauty
for a beauty that must die,
and set not your affections
on this mortal world of dust.[196]

And so Allah states that the answer, the prescription that will give human beings the inner peace that they want, is to turn towards the divine, to turn towards the spiritual and away from the material:

O Son of Utterance!
Turn thy face unto Mine and renounce all save Me;
for My sovereignty endureth
and My dominion perisheth not.
If thou seekest another than Me,
yea, if thou searchest the universe for evermore,
thy quest will be in vain.[197]

Bahá'u'lláh has revealed a great deal about the path of spiritual development that the individual must take. In a brief introductory book, it is only possible to focus on a few points.

Taking the First Step

In travelling the path of spirituality, it is clear from the Bahá'í scriptures and indeed from the scriptures of other religions that it is up to human beings to take the first step on the path. Thus in the Bible, Jesus says: 'Knock, and it shall be opened unto you' (Luke 11:9). We must make the first movement and knock. In the Qur'án, we find the words: 'Whoso maketh efforts for us, in our ways shall we assuredly guide them' (29:69).[198] We have to make the initial effort and then Allah will guide us. Similarly the Bahá'í scriptures say that we must take the first step:

O Son of Love!
Thou art but one step away from the glorious heights above and from the celestial tree of love.
Take thou one pace and with the next advance into the immortal realm and enter the pavilion of eternity.[199]

In the Bahá'í scriptures we find the analogy of the human heart as a mirror – it reflects whatever it is turned towards. If it is turned towards heaven, it reflects heavenly things and if it is turned towards earth, it reflects earthly concerns. And so we must make the effort to turn our hearts towards the divine and away from the perishable and evanescent attractions of the world. It is we ourselves who must make that initial effort to move the mirror of our hearts. If we are not turned towards Allah, His light cannot shine in our mirror, His love cannot be reflected in our soul:

O Son of Being!
Love Me, that I may love thee.
If thou lovest Me not,
My love can in no wise reach thee.
Know this, O servant.[200]

Detachment

After we have taken the first step and made the initial effort, we need to try to detach ourselves from this world. We must try to cleanse our heart from its attachment to the things of this world, which Bahá'u'lláh likens to dust which he urges us to clean from off the mirror of our hearts. He tells us to:

. . . cleanse thine heart from the world and all its vanities, and suffer not the love of any stranger to enter and dwell therein. Not until thou dost purify thine heart from every trace of such love can the brightness of the light of God shed its radiance upon it, for to none hath God given more than one heart . . . And as the human heart . . . is one and undivided, it behoveth thee to take heed that its affections be, also, one and undivided. Cleave thou, therefore, with the whole affection of thine heart, unto His love, and withdraw it from the love of any one besides Him . . . My sole purpose in revealing to thee these words is to sanctify thee from the transitory things of the earth, and aid thee to enter the realm of everlasting glory . . .[201]

Bahá'u'lláh asserts that there is only room in our hearts for one love and so we must choose – will we choose Allah or the world?

O My Friend in Word! Ponder awhile.
Hast thou ever heard that friend and foe should abide in one heart?
Cast out then the stranger, that the Friend may enter His home.[202]

Bahá'u'lláh reveals that if we truly seek for spiritual development we must first be prepared to detach ourselves from the things of this world. In outlining the requirements of the spiritual quest, the Bahá'í scriptures state:

. . . O My brother! When a true seeker determineth to take the step of search in the path leading unto the knowledge of the Ancient of Days, he must, before all else, cleanse and purify his heart, which is the seat of the revelation of the inner mysteries of God, from the obscuring dust of all acquired knowledge, and the allusions of the embodiments of satanic fancy. He must purge his breast, which is the sanctuary of the abiding love of the Beloved, of every defilement, and sanctify his soul from all that pertaineth to water and clay, from all shadowy and ephemeral attachments. He must so cleanse his heart that no remnant of either love or hate may linger therein, lest that love blindly incline him to error, or that hate repel him away from the truth . . . That seeker must at all times put his trust in God, must renounce the peoples of the earth, must detach himself from the world of dust, and cleave unto Him Who is the Lord of Lords.[203]

And so the Bahá'í scriptures enumerate one by one the requirements of the true seeker upon the spiritual path. Their description of spirituality involves the acquisition of virtues.

Virtues

The passage from the Bahá'í scriptures that is quoted above goes on to describe the virtues that must be acquired upon the path to spirituality:

> He must never seek to exalt himself above any one,
> must wash away from the tablet of his heart every trace of pride and vain-glory,
> must cling unto patience and resignation, observe silence, and refrain from idle talk . . .
> That seeker should, also, regard backbiting as grievous error . . .
> He should be content with little, and be freed from all inordinate desire.
> He should treasure the companionship of those that have renounced the world,
> and regard avoidance of boastful and worldly people a precious benefit.
> At the dawn of every day he should commune with God,
> and, with all his soul, persevere in the quest of his Beloved.
> He should consume every wayward thought with the flame of His loving mention, and,
> with the swiftness of lightning, pass by all else save Him.
> He should succour the dispossessed,
> and never withhold his favour from the destitute.
> He should show kindness to animals,
> how much more unto his fellow-man . . .
> He should not hesitate to offer up his life for his Beloved,
> nor allow the censure of the people to turn him away from the Truth.[204]

The Bahá'í scriptures teach that we must seek to acquire such virtues as love, justice, patience, trustworthiness, truthfulness, etc. There is not room to list and describe all of these but some are described elsewhere in this book (see pp. 27–31).

Troubles and Difficulties

Bahá'u'lláh reveals to those who are seeking to follow the path of spirituality that it is inevitable that they will meet with troubles and trials and difficulties. The very act of breaking the ties of materialism, greed and desire that bind us to this world is a painful one. Bahá'u'lláh states that pain is our constant companion, our ever-present steed, as we travel along the valley in our spiritual quest:

> The steed of this Valley is pain; and if there be no pain this journey will never end. In this station the lover hath no thought save the Beloved, and seeketh no refuge save the Friend . . .
>
> Wherefore must the veils of the satanic self be burned away at the fire of love, that the spirit may be purified and cleansed and thus may know the station of the Lord of the Worlds.[205]

If there be no pain, there will be no progress. 'Abdu'l-Bahá, the son of Bahá'u'lláh, has described the way that pain and suffering functions in our lives. He was asked the question: 'Does the soul progress more through sorrow or through the joy in this world?' He replied:

> The mind and spirit of man advance when he is tried by suffering. The more the ground is ploughed the better the seed will grow, the better the harvest will be. Just as the plough furrows the earth deeply, purifying it of weeds and thistles, so suffering and tribulation free man from the petty affairs of this worldly life until he arrives at a state of

Prayer in Times of Hardship and Difficulties

O my Lord! Thou knowest that the people are encircled with pain and calamities and are environed with hardships and trouble. Every trial doth attack man and every dire adversity doth assail him like unto the assault of a serpent. There is no shelter and asylum for him except under the wing of Thy protection, preservation, guard and custody.

O Thou the Merciful One! O my Lord! Make Thy protection my armour, Thy preservation my shield, humbleness before the door of Thy oneness my guard, and Thy custody and defence my fortress and my abode. Preserve me from the suggestions of self and desire, and guard me from every sickness, trial, difficulty and ordeal.

Verily, Thou art the Protector, the Guardian, the Preserver, the Sufficer, and verily, Thou art the Merciful of the Most Merciful. ('Abdu'l-Bahá)[206]

> complete detachment. His attitude in this world will be that of divine happiness. Man is, so to speak, unripe: the heat of the fire of suffering will mature him. Look back to the times past and you will find that the greatest men have suffered most.[207]

Thus suffering is necessary for our spiritual advancement and therefore if we understood its true nature, we would welcome it.

> O Son of Man! My calamity is My providence, outwardly it is fire and vengeance, but inwardly it is light and mercy. Hasten thereunto that thou mayest become an eternal light and an immortal spirit. This is My command unto thee, do thou observe it.[208]

The Purpose of the Physical World

All that has been written thus far in this chapter is very close to what may be found in Islam and in other religions. Many of the great Sufi masters have written in a similar way about the need for detachment and the virtues of the spiritual path. Some of the holy Traditions (*al-ḥadíth al-qudsí*) are parallel to the quotations from the Bahá'í scriptures given above. Where the Bahá'í teachings do differ is in the practical details and structures that are given for ascending the spiritual path.

In many other spiritual traditions the practical aspects of the spiritual path have been put in the hands of a spiritual guide: the priest of a community, the guru, the shaykh or murshid of a Sufi order, the abbot of a monastery. In many spiritual traditions, because the world has been recognized as being the source of our distraction from the spiritual path, the adherents of that tradition have been advised to remove themselves from the world, either as ascetics or in a monastic community. The Bahá'í teachings advise against both of these aspects of the path.

Bahá'u'lláh reveals that the use of a human spiritual guide is a dangerous practice. While undoubtedly genuine spiritual leaders do exist, many are also fraudulent or lead people into error. Allah has ordained that the day of the religious leader or professional – whether shaykh, molla, priest, guru or monk – is over. Each individual now has the obligation to read the scriptures for himself or herself and to understand the spiritual path.

> Leaders of religion, in every age, have hindered their people from attaining the shores of eternal salvation, inasmuch as they held the reins of authority in their mighty grasp. Some for the lust of leadership, others through want of knowledge and understanding, have been the cause of the deprivation of the people. By their sanction and authority, every Prophet of God hath drunk from the chalice of sacrifice, and winged His flight unto the heights of glory. What unspeakable cruelties they that have occupied the seats of authority and learning have inflicted upon the true Monarchs of the world, those Gems of divine virtue! Content with a transitory dominion, they have deprived themselves of an everlasting sovereignty. Thus, their eyes beheld not the light of the

countenance of the Well-Beloved, nor did their ears hearken unto the sweet melodies of the Bird of Desire. For this reason, in all sacred books mention hath been made of the divines of every age.[209]

This is similar to the Qur'án's statement addressed to the religious leaders of the Christians and Jews:

> Ye People of the Book! Why reject ye the Signs of Allah of which ye are (yourselves) witnesses? Ye People of the Book! Why do ye clothe truth with falsehood and conceal the Truth while ye have knowledge? . . .
>
> Say: 'O ye People of the Book! Why obstruct ye those who believe, from the path of Allah, seeking to make it crooked, while ye were yourselves witnesses (to Allah's Covenant)? But Allah is not unmindful of all that ye do.' (3:70–1, 99)

Bahá'u'lláh reveals that while monasteries and spiritual asceticism may have had some role to play in the past, these are no longer appropriate today.

> The pious deeds of the monks and priests among the followers of the Spirit [Jesus] – upon Him be the peace of God – are remembered in His presence. In this Day, however, let them give up the life of seclusion and direct their steps towards the open world and busy themselves with that which will profit themselves and others.[210]

Allah states that this physical world, far from obstructing us in our spiritual quest, has, in fact, been created specifically to help us:

> O Son of Bounty! Out of the wastes of nothingness, with the clay of My command I made thee to appear, and have ordained for thy training every atom in existence and the essence of all created things. Thus, ere thou didst issue from thy mother's womb, I destined for thee two founts of gleaming milk, eyes to watch over thee, and hearts to love

> thee. Out of My loving-kindness, 'neath the shade of My mercy I nurtured thee, and guarded thee by the essence of My grace and favour. And My purpose in all this was that thou mightest attain My everlasting dominion and become worthy of My invisible bestowals. And yet heedless thou didst remain, and when fully grown, thou didst neglect all My bounties and occupied thyself with thine idle imaginings, in such wise that thou didst become wholly forgetful, and, turning away from the portals of the Friend didst abide within the courts of My enemy.[211]

The Bahá'í scriptures thus picture this physical world as a giant classroom where human beings obtain spiritual education. We have not, however, been left to our own devices but have had spiritual educators, the founders of the world religions, who give us the instructions we need to progress spiritually. Bahá'u'lláh reveals that we can best achieve this progress by living in the world, not seeking to cut ourselves off from it. While a certain degree of removal from the world may be necessary in order to pray and meditate, which all religions tell us is important, we must also engage in the world so that the spiritual qualities we are seeking to acquire may be perfected. How will we know if we have acquired such spiritual qualities as love, justice, trustworthiness and truthfulness unless we live in the world and put ourselves to the test in the concrete situations of daily life?

Part of our spiritual progress is the spiritual discipline of saying daily prayers and meditating, observing an annual fast and obeying other laws. This pattern of life keeps us in touch with our true spiritual reality and connects us with the spiritual world which is the source of our strength. Such laws have been given in every religion. Bahá'u'lláh has revealed similar laws (see pp. 175–86).

Lastly, Bahá'u'lláh has given us a substitute for the spiritual communities of other religions, to take the place of monasteries and communities led by abbots, shaykhs and gurus. He has created the Bahá'í community, a structure that involves everyone in such activities as consultation and united action in service to others, activities which help us to acquire the virtues that we should seek (see pp. 27–31). The ideal of unity and the mechanisms of consultation (see pp. 169–70) in the Bahá'í community compel us to recognize faults of egotism and arrogance within ourselves and to try to remedy these. The ideal of consultation requires us to perfect within ourselves the qualities of patience, forbearance, justice and other virtues. Within the Bahá'í community, spiritual development becomes the responsibility and prerogative of everyone, not a select group of monks or religious professionals.

Within the Bahá'í community structure, authority and obedience do not go to individuals such as mollas, shaykhs, priests and gurus; they go to elected institutions. For spiritual guidance, Bahá'ís are advised to take advantage of the mechanisms of consultation so as to obtain the collective wisdom of a group of people and not rely on the whims and comparatively limited knowledge of a single individual.

6

Social Teachings and Bahá'í Community Life

The teachings and laws given by the Messengers of Allah can be considered to consist of two parts: those which are eternal and unchanging and those which vary with time. In the first category are such teachings as ethics, morality and the spiritual development of the individual. The second category relates to laws and social teachings and these are altered by the Messengers of Allah in accordance with the requirements of each age. The Qur'án itself testifies to the fact that Allah has revealed a different Holy Law to each people in the past:

> To each among you have We prescribed a Law and an Open Way. If Allah had so willed, He would have made you a single People but (His plan is) to test you in what He hath given you . . . (5:51, cf. 22:67)

Few would deny that the world has changed enormously from its condition only two hundred years ago. Some of the laws that the Prophet Muḥammad (blessings and peace be upon him) brought to humanity are no longer suitable in the modern world and are therefore ignored even by pious Muslims. For example, Islam decrees that polytheists should be considered unclean (9:28) and should be killed (9:5), but in today's multi-cultural societies, we find Muslims living side by side with Hindus and Buddhists in situations that would make the application of this law an impossible burden. Similarly, the majority of Muslim states no longer find it possible to apply the law that requires the cutting off of the hand of a thief (5:41) or to allow the owning of slaves (2:178, 2:221, 24:31–2, 33:55) and no Muslim state since the 18th century has carried out the injunction to wage *jihád* against the unbelievers (9:123). The Qur'án states that whenever any of the laws of Allah become forgotten, Allah reveals new laws, better adapted to the times, to take their place:

> None of Our revelations do We abrogate or cause to be forgotten, but We substitute something better or similar: knowest thou not that Allah hath power over all things? (2:106)

Although Muslim commentators have traditionally regarded this verse as applying to those verses that Muḥammad revealed and then later abrogated, logic would suggest that, in addition to this, there is no reason why the verse should not refer to those commands of previous Messengers of Allah which Muḥammad abrogated and changed for other commands. This is because the verse states that it deals with both 'Our revelations' that 'We abrogate' and ones 'We . . . cause to be forgotten'. There is no compelling reason to assume that even the first group, the abrogated verses, refers exclusively to those verses which Muḥammad revealed and later abrogated. It could equally refer to revelations of previous Messengers which Muḥammad also abrogated. Even if we assume that the abrogated verses refer only to those verses that Muḥammad revealed and later abrogated, it would be difficult to maintain that the second group, the verses 'We . . . cause to be forgotten', also only refers to verses which Muḥammad revealed and later abrogated. It seems unlikely that verses Muḥammad had revealed only a few years earlier had already been forgotten. It seems logical that this second phrase refers to the revelations of previous Messengers. Yusuf Ali believed this to be the case, as he writes in commentary on this verse in his translation of the Qur'án:

> The word which I have translated by the word 'revelations' is *Áyát* . . . It is not only used for verses of the Qur'án, but in a general sense for Allah's revelations, as in ii. 39, and for other Signs of Allah in history or nature, or miracles, as in ii. 61. It has even been used for human signs and tokens of wonder, as, for example, monuments or landmarks built by the ancient people of 'Ád (xxvi. 128). What is the meaning here? If we take it in a general sense, it means that Allah's Message from age to age is always the same, but that its form may differ according to the needs and exigencies of the time. That form was different as given to Moses and then to Jesus and then to Muḥammad. Some commentators apply it also to the *Áyát* of the Qur'án. There is nothing derogatory in this if we believe in progressive revelation.[212]

Bahá'u'lláh claims that this is precisely what has happened in this age. The laws of the Qur'án have been forgotten and he has come to reveal a new law from Allah. Just as the Prophet Muḥammad gave humanity laws and teachings that were right for bringing into being a just society in his time, so Bahá'u'lláh teaches that his purpose is to bring new teachings that are designed to achieve the same aim, a just society, but are adapted for the needs of the present day. Bahá'ís also call this 'progressive revelation' (see pp. 18–24). Bahá'u'lláh states that the teachings of the Messenger of Allah change in order to suit the conditions of the time:

> Little wonder, then, if the treatment prescribed by the physician in this day should not be found to be identical with that which he prescribed before. How could it be otherwise when the ills affecting the sufferer necessitate at every stage of his sickness a special remedy? In like manner, every time the Prophets of God have illumined the world with the resplendent radiance of the Day Star of Divine knowledge, they have invariably summoned its peoples to embrace the light of God through such means as best befitted the exigencies of the age in which they appeared. They were thus able to scatter the darkness of ignorance, and to shed upon the world the glory of their own knowledge.[213]

The Unity of Humankind

While Muḥammad emphasized in his teaching the unity of the Muslim community (*ummah*) and allowed a place within that community for the Jews and Christians (People of the Book), he decreed that other unbelievers, such as polytheists, should be excluded from it. Such people are unclean (*nájis*, Qur'án 9:28) and therefore no Muslim community should include them.

The Bahá'í scriptures reveal that the time has now come for the unity of the whole of the world of humanity. Therefore Allah has abrogated the concept of impurity, whether of people or of things:

> God hath, likewise, as a bounty from His presence, abolished the concept of 'uncleanness', whereby divers things and peoples have been held to be impure. He, of a certainty, is the Ever-Forgiving, the Most Generous. Verily, all created things were immersed in the sea of purification when, on that first day of Riḍván (see p. 202), We shed upon the whole of creation the splendours of Our most excellent Names and Our most exalted Attributes. This, verily, is a token of My loving providence, which hath encompassed all the worlds.[214]

Apart from abolishing the legal basis for any discrimination, the Bahá'í scriptures positively instruct the Bahá'ís to consort with all peoples and call for unity among the people of the world:

> It is permitted that the peoples and kindreds of the world associate with one another with joy and radiance. O people! Consort with the followers of all religions in a spirit of friendliness and fellowship.[215]

> The Great Being saith: O well-beloved ones! The tabernacle of unity hath been raised; regard ye not one another as strangers. Ye are the fruits of one tree, and the leaves of one branch.[216]

This unity brought by the teachings revealed by Bahá'u'lláh is, Bahá'ís believe, the gathering together on the Day of Judgement that is prophesied in the Qur'án:

> Allah! there is no god but He: of a surety He will gather you together against the Day of Judgement, about which there is no doubt. And whose word can be truer than Allah's? (4:87)

Universal Peace and World Order

Alongside the teaching of the unity of humankind, the Bahá'í scriptures also emphasize the importance of peace and state that the inauguration of peace is a major feature of Bahá'u-'lláh's mission. Indeed, this inauguration of an age of peace is what is prophesied in the Islamic Traditions (*ḥadí<u>th</u>s*):

> And the earth will be filled with peace, just as water fills a jug. And the word will be one, and only Allah will be worshipped, and war will lay down its burdens. (Ibn Májah)[217]

To the kings and rulers of the world Bahá'u'lláh addressed himself, urging them to make efforts to achieve the lesser (political) peace:

> We pray God – exalted be His glory – and cherish the hope that He may graciously assist the manifestations of affluence and power and the daysprings of sovereignty and glory, the kings of the earth . . . to establish the Lesser Peace. This, indeed, is the greatest means for insuring the tranquillity of the nations. It is incumbent upon the Sovereigns of the world – may God assist them – unitedly to hold fast unto this Peace, which is the chief instrument for the protection of all mankind. It is Our hope that they will arise to achieve what will be conducive to the well-being of man.[218]

In order to achieve this, Bahá'u'lláh introduced the concept of collective security. Addressing the kings and rulers, he wrote:

> It is their duty to convene an all-inclusive assembly, which either they themselves or their ministers will attend, and to enforce whatever measures are required to establish unity and concord amongst men. They must put away the weapons of war, and turn to the instruments of universal reconstruction. Should one king rise up against another, all the other kings must arise to deter him. Arms and armaments will, then, be no more needed beyond that which is necessary to insure the internal security of their respective countries. If they attain unto this all-surpassing blessing, the people of each nation will pursue, with tranquillity and contentment, their own occupations, and the groanings and lamentations of most men would be silenced.[219]

The ultimate goal, however, is the Most Great Peace, which will result from the true unity and the spiritualization of the human world. Shoghi Effendi describes its nature thus:

> The Most Great Peace, on the other hand, as conceived by Bahá'u'lláh – a peace that must inevitably follow as the practical consequence of the spiritualization of the world and the fusion of all its races, creeds, classes and nations – can rest on no other basis, and can be preserved through no other agency, except the divinely appointed ordinances that are implicit in the World Order that stands associated with His Holy Name. In His Tablet, revealed . . . to Queen Victoria, Bahá'u'lláh, alluding to this Most Great Peace, has declared: 'That which the Lord hath ordained as the sovereign remedy and mightiest instrument for the healing of all the world is the union of all its peoples in one universal Cause, one common Faith. This can in no wise be achieved except through the power of a skilled, an all-powerful and inspired Physician. This, verily, is the truth, and all else naught but error . . .'[220]

Since the problems that the world faces (environmental pollution, global poverty, the arms race and so on) are international in nature, they must be tackled at the international level by global institutions. Shoghi Effendi describes the main features of the world that must evolve to meet the criteria that Bahá'u'lláh has set for peace:

> This commonwealth must, as far as we can visualize it, consist of:
>
> - A world legislature, whose members will, as the trustees of the whole of mankind, ultimately control the entire resources of all the component nations, and will enact such laws as shall be required to regulate the life, satisfy the needs and adjust the relationships of all races and peoples.
>
> - A world executive, backed by an international Force, will carry out the decisions arrived at, and apply the laws enacted by, this world legislature, and will safeguard the organic unity of the whole commonwealth.
>
> - A world tribunal will adjudicate and deliver its compulsory and final verdict in all and any disputes that may arise between the various elements constituting this universal system.
>
> - A mechanism of world inter-communication will be devised, embracing the whole planet, freed from national hindrances and restrictions, and functioning with marvellous swiftness and perfect regularity.
>
> - A world metropolis will act as the nerve centre of a world civilization, the focus towards which the unifying forces of life will converge and from which its energizing influences will radiate.
>
> - A world language will either be invented or chosen from among the existing languages and will be taught in the schools of all the federated nations as an auxiliary to their mother tongue.

- A world script, a world literature, a uniform and universal system of currency, of weights and measures, will simplify and facilitate intercourse and understanding among the nations and races of mankind.[221]

Other features of this world commonwealth envisioned by Shoghi Effendi include:

> In such a world society, science and religion, the two most potent forces in human life, will be reconciled, will cooperate, and will harmoniously develop. The press will, under such a system, while giving full scope to the expression of the diversified views and convictions of mankind, cease to be mischievously manipulated by vested interests, whether private or public, and will be liberated from the influence of contending governments and peoples. The economic resources of the world will be organized, its sources of raw materials will be tapped and fully utilized, its markets will be coordinated and developed, and the distribution of its products will be equitably regulated.[222]

As the result of such a development, the Bahá'í writings envisage that the whole picture of the planet will be changed:

> National rivalries, hatreds, and intrigues will cease, and racial animosity and prejudice will be replaced by racial amity, understanding and cooperation. The causes of religious strife will be permanently removed, economic barriers and restrictions will be completely abolished, and the inordinate distinction between classes will be obliterated. Destitution on the one hand, and gross accumulation of ownership on the other, will disappear. The enormous energy dissipated and wasted on war, whether economic or political, will be consecrated to such ends as will extend the range of human inventions and technical development, to the increase of the productivity of mankind, to the extermination of disease, to the extension of scientific research, to the raising of the standard of physical health, to the sharpening and refine-

> ment of the human brain, to the exploitation of the unused and unsuspected resources of the planet, to the prolongation of human life, and to the furtherance of any other agency that can stimulate the intellectual, the moral, and spiritual life of the entire human race.[223]

As can be seen from these quotations, the vision of the future of the world that the Bahá'ís have rejects much of the political structure and international order that we have experienced in the last one hundred years. It rejects the emphasis placed on the national will and national interests of powerful nations (usually at the expense of smaller nations). It rejects the idea that the balance of terror that existed during the Cold War is a sustainable mechanism for peace. It also rejects the present situation where a single super-power dominates the world and imposes its will. It rejects the extremes of both communism and capitalism as an adequate basis on which to build the future. Firm foundations for the future of the world can only be built on the basis of justice, equity and mutual respect among the peoples of the world and regard for the rights of the individual. Peace must be based upon multilateral collective arrangements where the security of each state is assured by treaties that are guaranteed by strong international institutions. These international institutions must be able, if necessary, to override the wishes of even the most powerful states and to control the activities of the most influential of multi-national companies. Humanity's future must be determined through cooperation and consultation rather than confrontation and the attempt by one nation to dominate another. Bahá'ís believe that they are building the foundations of this future world order as they build the Bahá'í administrative order (see pp. 167–9), since this is the embryo of that future world. Bahá'ís believe that only on the basis of these principles can the world be filled with peace as the Islamic prophecy cited above demands and only through the establishment of the Bahá'í administrative order and its

Houses of Justice can the era of divine justice be instituted, as Islamic prophecy foretells happening at the time of the Mahdi (see p. 120).

Freedom from Prejudice

One of the main causes of disunity and conflict in the world is people harbouring prejudices against other human beings. Such prejudices include racial and ethnic prejudices, national prejudices, religious and sectarian prejudices and even prejudices against others because of their age, gender, disabilities or class. 'Abdu'l-Bahá has stated:

> Other sources of human dissension are political, racial and patriotic prejudices. These have been removed by Bahá'u-'lláh. He has said, and has guarded His statement by rational proofs from the Holy Books, that the world of humanity is one race, the surface of the earth one place of residence and that these imaginary racial barriers and political boundaries are without right or foundation. Man is degraded in becoming the captive of his own illusions and suppositions. The earth is one earth, and the same atmosphere surrounds it. No difference or preference has been made by God for its human inhabitants; but man has laid the foundation of prejudice, hatred and discord with his fellowman by considering nationalities separate in importance and races different in rights and privileges.[224]

The Bahá'í teachings condemn all such prejudices not only for being destructive of the cohesion of society but also for preventing every individual in that society from achieving his or her full potential:

> Therefore it is imperative that we should renounce our own particular prejudices and superstitions if we earnestly desire to seek the truth. Unless we make a distinction in our minds between dogma, superstition and prejudice on the one hand,

and truth on the other, we cannot succeed. When we are in earnest in our search for anything we look for it everywhere.[225]

Equality of the Sexes

The largest group of people in the world suffering the effects of prejudice is women. Both Islam and the Bahá'í Faith are agreed that women and men are equal in status and spiritual capacity:

Islam	Bahá'í
For Muslim men and women, – for believing men and women, for devout men and women, for true men and women, for men and women who are patient and constant, for men and women who humble themselves, for men and women who give in charity, for men and women who fast (and deny themselves), for men and women who guard their chastity, and for men and women who engage much in Allah's praise, – for them has Allah prepared forgiveness and great reward. (Qur'án 33:35)	Exalted, immensely exalted is He Who hath removed differences and established harmony . . . Praised be God, the Pen of the Most High hath lifted distinctions from between His servants and handmaidens, and, through His consummate favours and all-encompassing mercy, hath conferred upon all a station and rank of the same plane. He hath broken the back of vain imaginings with the sword of utterance and hath obliterated the perils of idle fancies through the pervasive power of His might. (Bahá'u'lláh)[226]

Although the teachings of the Prophet Muḥammad brought about great advances in the position of women in the society to which he came, nevertheless inequalities have remained and women continue to hold a lower position than men in most societies. Bahá'u'lláh has stated that this must cease. The main cause for any perceived deficiency in women is the lack of education. Women must therefore be educated and must take their position in society. On this issue, 'Abdu'l-Bahá has said:

> It has been objected by some that woman is not equally capable with man and that she is deficient by creation. This is pure imagination. The difference in capability between man and woman is due entirely to opportunity and education. Heretofore woman has been denied the right and privilege of equal development. If equal opportunity be granted her, there is no doubt she would be the peer of man . . .
>
> The purpose, in brief, is this: that if woman be fully educated and granted her rights, she will attain the capacity for wonderful accomplishments and prove herself the equal of man. She is the coadjutor of man, his complement and helpmeet. Both are human; both are endowed with potentialities of intelligence and embody the virtues of humanity. In all human powers and functions they are partners and coequals. At present in spheres of human activity woman does not manifest her natal prerogatives, owing to lack of education and opportunity. Without doubt education will establish her equality with men.[227]

Moreover, 'Abdu'l-Bahá has stated that women playing a greater role in society will in itself be a major contribution to bringing peace to the world.

> Another fact of equal importance in bringing about international peace is woman's suffrage. That is to say, when perfect equality shall be established between men and women, peace may be realized for the simple reason that womankind in general will never favour warfare. Women will not be willing to allow those whom they have so tenderly cared for to go to the battlefield. When they shall have a vote, they will oppose any cause of warfare.[228]

Science and Religion

The assumption has grown in the modern world that science is necessarily opposed to religion. In the Bahá'í view, however, the human mind and its reasoning ability are among the distinguishing marks of humanity, and science, which is the fruit of this, is regarded as a divine gift. In particular, the conflict that has occurred between science and religion over such concepts as evolution is considered to have been wrong. Science and religion should instead be seen as complementary aspects of human progress and development. 'Abdu'l-Bahá says:

> Religion and science are the two wings upon which man's intelligence can soar into the heights, with which the human soul can progress. It is not possible to fly with one wing alone! Should a man try to fly with the wing of religion alone he would quickly fall into the quagmire of superstition, whilst on the other hand, with the wing of science alone he would also make no progress, but fall into the despairing slough of materialism.[229]

Education

One of the most important ways of achieving the changes that will bring peace, freedom from prejudice and the consciousness of the oneness of humanity is education. Therefore the need for education has been given an important place in the range of Bahá'í teachings:

> Man is the supreme Talisman. Lack of a proper education hath, however, deprived him of that which he doth inherently possess . . . The Great Being saith: Regard man as a mine rich in gems of inestimable value. Education can, alone, cause it to reveal its treasures, and enable mankind to benefit therefrom.[230]

The responsibility for the education of children rests primarily with the parents and then on teachers. So important is this task that Bahá'u'lláh raises it to the status of the worship of Allah:

... know ye that in God's sight, the best of all ways to worship Him is to educate the children and train them in all the perfections of humankind; and no nobler deed than this can be imagined.[231]

The Importance of Education

The root cause of wrongdoing is ignorance ... Good character must be taught. Light must be spread afar, so that, in the school of humanity, all may acquire the heavenly characteristics of the spirit, and see for themselves beyond any doubt that there is no fiercer hell, no more fiery abyss, than to possess a character that is evil and unsound ... The individual must be educated to such a high degree that he would rather have his throat cut than tell a lie ... Thus will be kindled the sense of human dignity and pride ... It followeth that the children's school must be a place of utmost discipline and order, that instruction must be thorough, and provision must be made for the rectification and refinement of character; so that, in his earliest years, within the very essence of the child, the divine foundation will be laid and the structure of holiness raised up.

Know that this matter of instruction, of character rectification and refinement, of heartening and encouraging the child, is of the utmost importance, for such are basic principles of God ...

It is extremely difficult to teach the individual and refine his character once puberty is passed. By then, as experience has shown, even if every effort be exerted to modify some tendency of his, it all availeth nothing. He may, perhaps, improve somewhat today; but let a few days pass and he forgetteth, and turneth backward to his habitual condition and accustomed ways. Therefore it is in early childhood that a firm foundation must be laid. While the branch is green and tender it can easily be made straight. ('Abdu'l-Bahá)[232]

Marriage and Family Life

According to the Bahá'í teachings, marriage and a strong healthy family life are the basis of society. It is only on such a basis that the rest of society can function and prosper (for the marriage laws, see pp. 180–1). It is within the family that the children get their earliest training and it is therefore important for the structure and stability of society itself that the family is strong and well-supported. If a husband and wife are truly united in a spiritual and physical marriage, then great results can come from that marriage. The most important of these is the raising of children:

> Thus the husband and wife are brought into affinity, are united and harmonized, even as though they were one person. Through their mutual union, companionship and love great results are produced in the world, both material and spiritual. The spiritual result is the appearance of divine bounties. The material result is the children who are born in the cradle of the love of God.[233]

Each person in the family must be respected as an individual and must be given both the love and the space to develop and grow. The parents should be mindful of their responsibilities and should carry these out in a loving and caring manner, without violence or injustice. Children, for their part, are instructed to be respectful and obedient towards their parents and also to appreciate and be grateful for what has been done for them.

> The integrity of the family bond must be constantly considered, and the rights of the individual members must not be transgressed. The rights of the son, the father, the mother – none of them must be transgressed, none of them must be arbitrary. Just as the son has certain obligations to his father, the father, likewise, has certain obligations to his son. The mother, the sister and other members of the household have their certain prerogatives. All these rights and prerogatives must be conserved, yet the unity of the family must be sustained. The injury of one shall be considered the injury of all; the comfort of each, the comfort of all; the honour of one, the honour of all.[234]

Bahá'í Community Life

The basis of the Bahá'í community is a gathering of all the Bahá'ís in an area that takes place on the first day of every Bahá'í month (see Bahá'í calendar, pp. 181–2). Called the Nineteen Day Feast, the gathering comprises a devotional portion (prayers and readings from the scripture), an administrative portion (consultation on the affairs of the community) and a social portion (refreshments, singing, conversation, etc.).

The Bahá'í community also gathers on other occasions such as on holy days (see pp. 182–3), for study sessions and children's classes, and at meetings called to introduce the Bahá'í Faith to those who are not Bahá'ís (these latter meetings are often called firesides).

The aim of the Bahá'í community is to bring together people from every race and religious and social background in order to achieve a 'blending of these highly differentiated elements of the human race, harmoniously interwoven into the fabric of an all-embracing Bahá'í fraternity, and assimilated through the dynamic processes of a divinely appointed Administrative Order, and contributing each its share to the enrichment and glory of Bahá'í community life'.[235] In this way are the circumstances created that enable each individual to develop his or her intellectual, artistic and spiritual potential.

> . . . when divers shades of thought, temperament and character, are brought together under the power and influence of one central agency, the beauty and glory of human perfection will be revealed and made manifest.[236]

The House of Worship (Mashriqu'l-Adhkár)

At present, Bahá'ís in most local communities have no special place of worship. They meet either in each other's homes or at a Bahá'í centre. It is envisaged, however, that in the future in each town there will be built a house of worship (*Mashriqu'l-*

Adhkár). Around it will be built schools, universities, libraries, medical facilities, orphanages and so on. This will become the spiritual and social centre of the community. At present, there are only seven of these houses of worship around the world, built as a token of future intentions. These seven are: near Chicago, USA; near Kampala, Uganda; near Sydney, Australia; near Frankfurt, Germany; near Panama City, Panama; near Apia, Samoa; and in New Delhi, India.

The Administration of the Bahá'í Community

The structure and organization of the Bahá'í community is different in many ways from that of Islam or any other religious community. The first point of difference arises from the fact that there are no priests or any other form of religious professional class in the Bahá'í community. In place of individual religious leaders, the Bahá'í Faith has a unique structure of elected administrative bodies. All authority in the Bahá'í community rests with these elected bodies and not with individuals. At the local level, all of the adult Bahá'ís in the community elect nine people, men or women, to a body called the Local Spiritual Assembly, which administers the affairs of the Bahá'í community in each area. Bahá'ís also elect delegates to a national convention at which nine people are elected to the National Spiritual Assembly, which administers the affairs of the Bahá'í Faith at the national level. The members of the National Spiritual Assemblies elect the Universal House of Justice, which is the supreme administrative body of the Bahá'í Faith.

Elections for these Bahá'í institutions are carried out in a spirit of prayer and quiet reflection. There are no nominations, no electioneering and no political parties. The process of election is considered to be a vehicle for choosing individuals who have the necessary moral, spiritual and administrative capabilities to consult together and cooperate to promote the common good. Those elected do not represent any particular interest or faction. They must see themselves as chosen for a service to the whole community, a service which they must perform prayerfully and conscientiously.

In parallel to the elected institutions, there are also certain individuals who are appointed for limited terms to membership of the Continental Boards of Counsellors and the Auxiliary Boards. These individuals have no authority but have the responsibility of encouraging and protecting the Bahá'í community.

The key institutions and guiding principles of the Bahá'í administration are based on the writings of the central figures of the Bahá'í Faith. Bahá'ís therefore regard their administration as sacred in nature and as an integral part of the religion. The Bahá'í teachings would remain, Bahá'ís believe, just ideas without the Bahá'í administration to give them form:

> To accept the Cause without the administration is like to accept the teachings without acknowledging the divine station of Bahá'u'lláh. To be a Bahá'í is to accept the Cause in its entirety. To take exception to one basic principle is to deny the authority and sovereignty of Bahá'u'lláh, and therefore is to deny the Cause. The administration is the social order of Bahá'u'lláh. Without it all the principles of the Cause will remain abortive.[237]

On the other hand, Bahá'ís are also warned not to allow the Bahá'í administration to become an end in itself:

> The friends must never mistake the Bahá'í administration for an end in itself. It is merely the instrument of the spirit of the Faith. This Cause is a Cause which God has revealed to humanity as a whole. It is designed to benefit the entire human race, and the only way it can do this is to re-form the community life of mankind, as well as seeking to regenerate the individual. The Bahá'í Administration is only the first shaping of what in future will come to be the social life and laws of community living. As yet the believers are only just

beginning to grasp and practise it properly. So we must have patience if at times it seems a little self-conscious and rigid in its workings.[238]

Consultation

The Qur'án instructs Muslims to conduct their affairs by mutual consultation (*shúrá*, 42:38). The mechanism for this was not, however, clearly laid out by Muḥammad and indeed has been the cause of much disagreement in the Islamic world down to the present day. Bahá'u'lláh also stressed the importance of consultation:

> In all things it is necessary to consult. This matter should be forcibly stressed by thee, so that consultation may be observed by all. The intent of what hath been revealed from the Pen of the Most High is that consultation may be fully carried out among the friends, inasmuch as it is and will always be a cause of awareness and of awakening and a source of good and well-being.[239]

In the Bahá'í scriptures the principles and procedures for this consultative process are clearly laid out. Consultation is the mechanism for discussing matters and making decisions in the Bahá'í community, whether in the Nineteen Day Feast or by the Local or National Spiritual Assembly. The aim of the consultative process is to encourage all present to express their opinions openly and frankly so that the ideas that emerge build upon each other and the final result represents the best of the collective wisdom of all present. It is therefore necessary for all who take part in this process to do so with humility and an openness to the ideas of others. 'Abdu'l-Bahá also recommends this method of consultation for the purpose of obtaining guidance in personal matters. Consultation thus replaces the spiritual guidance given by religious leaders in other religions.

Consultation

The prime requisites for them that take counsel together are purity of motive, radiance of spirit, detachment from all else save God, attraction to His Divine Fragrances, humility and lowliness amongst His loved ones, patience and long-suffering in difficulties and servitude to His exalted Threshold. Should they be graciously aided to acquire these attributes, victory from the unseen Kingdom of Bahá shall be vouchsafed to them . . . The members [of a spiritual assembly] must take counsel together in such wise that no occasion for ill-feeling or discord may arise. This can be attained when every member expresseth with absolute freedom his own opinion and setteth forth his argument. Should any one oppose, he must on no account feel hurt for not until matters are fully discussed can the right way be revealed. The shining spark of truth cometh forth only after the clash of differing opinions. If after discussion, a decision be carried unanimously, well and good; but if the Lord forbid, differences of opinion should arise, a majority of voices must prevail. ('Abdu'l-Bahá)[240]

The Bahá'í World Centre

Bahá'u'lláh was exiled in 1868 by the Ottoman Turkish authorities to the city of 'Akká which was at that time part of the province of Syria. Bahá'u'lláh passed away there in 1892 and his shrine located at Bahjí, just outside 'Akká, is considered the holiest place in the world by Bahá'ís. It is the *qiblah*, the point to which Bahá'ís turn in prayer. During his lifetime Bahá'u'lláh gave instructions for the building of the shrine of the Báb on Mount Carmel on the opposite side of the bay from 'Akká, a spot that is now part of the city of Haifa.

'Akká and Haifa are now cities in the state of Israel. The shrine of Bahá'u'lláh is the spiritual centre of the Bahá'í world, while around the shrine of the Báb in Haifa the buildings for the world administrative centre of the Bahá'í Faith have been built. These buildings include the seat of the Universal House of Justice, the elected body which is the supreme authority of the Bahá'í world.

The Covenant

We have previously mentioned Allah's covenant (promise or agreement) with human beings: that whenever Allah sends a new Messenger with guidance, the people will follow him. In addition to this general covenant, the Bahá'í Faith teaches that there is a second, specific covenant made by Bahá'u'lláh with his followers that they will follow the guidance of 'Abdu'l-Bahá in his interpretations of the Bahá'í scriptures. 'Abdu'l-Bahá continued this covenant by stating in his Will and Testament that Bahá'ís should follow the guidance of Shoghi Effendi and the Universal House of Justice. Shoghi Effendi was appointed as the authorized interpreter of the Bahá'í scriptures and the Universal House of Justice was authorized to legislate on any matters not specifically covered in the texts. Thus in the Bahá'í Faith all matters connected with authoritative interpretation and legislation to deal with new problems that may arise are covered by these provisions.

These provisions of the covenant are considered very important, even central to the Bahá'í Faith. Since one of the main purposes of Bahá'u'lláh's mission is to achieve unity in the world, it is of great importance that there be no disunity in the Bahá'í Faith. Thus 'Abdu'l-Bahá, for example, states that:

> The Bahá'ís are commanded to establish the oneness of mankind; if they cannot unite around one point how will they be able to bring about the unity of mankind?
>
> The purpose of the Blessed Beauty [Bahá'u'lláh] in entering into this Covenant and Testament was to gather all existent beings around one point so that the thoughtless souls, who in every cycle and generation have been the cause of dissension, may not undermine the Cause. He hath, therefore, commanded that whatever emanateth from the Centre of the Covenant is right and is under His protection and favour, while all else is error.[241]

This unity within the Bahá'í Faith is maintained by the fact that every Bahá'í enters into a covenant that he or she will turn to and obey the centre of the covenant. The centre of the covenant now in the Bahá'í world is the Universal House of Justice, an institution whose authority is founded in explicit provisions made in the writings of both Bahá'u'lláh and 'Abdu'l-Bahá. All disputes and disagreements not settled at lower levels of the Bahá'í administration are referred to this body and its decisions are final.

Future Revelations

It is an essential part of the Bahá'í teachings that Allah's guidance has come to humanity through a series of individuals who are the Messengers of Allah and the Manifestations of Allah's name and attributes. These individuals will continue to come to humanity whenever it is in need of further guidance from Allah. The revelation of Bahá'u'lláh is thus not the last revelation of Allah's Will. The Bahá'í scriptures state that in the future a further revelation will come from Allah but that this will not happen for at least a thousand years.[242]

Scripture and Tradition

Bahá'ís regard everything written by the Báb and Bahá'u'lláh as scripture. They regard it as authoritative and of equal stature to the Qur'án – in other words, they consider all of these to be the Word of Allah. The works of 'Abdu'l-Bahá and Shoghi Effendi are regarded as authoritative interpretations of that scripture. All Bahá'ís are encouraged to read the Bahá'í scriptures and to gain their own understanding of them. No Bahá'í is permitted, however, to state that his or her interpretation is the only correct one and that the interpretations of others are wrong. This provision, which is part of the doctrine of the covenant, prevents Bahá'ís from setting up sectarian divisions based upon their own interpretations of the scriptures.

In Islam, a great deal of authority is also given to the Traditions and much of the Holy Law (*Sharí'ah*) of Islam is in fact based on them. These Traditions are the reported sayings and actions of the Prophet Muḥammad which were transmitted orally and written down more than a century, sometimes several centuries, later. Muslims acknowledge that there are some problems with the reliability of some of these Traditions and have devised ways of checking their authenticity, since it is known that there were some individuals who forged Traditions while the memory of others was not dependable. A very elaborate system was developed to classify these Traditions in terms of their reliability. In addition to the many factors that went into this work was one general rule that no Tradition was accepted if it contradicted the Qur'án in any way.

For Bahá'ís, on the other hand, only the written scriptures of the Báb and Bahá'u'lláh and the written interpretations of those scriptures by 'Abdu'l-Bahá and Shoghi Effendi are authoritative. This provides such a wealth of original material, in the handwriting of its authors or of approved scribes and secretaries, that there is no need to rely on material that is orally transmitted and may therefore be unreliable. The words and actions of the central figures of the Bahá'í Faith, as recorded in the Bahá'í histories, in the notes taken by those who accompanied Bahá'u'lláh and in the records of pilgrims who came to visit him, are therefore not considered authoritative. Since 'Abdu'l-Bahá is the Perfect Exemplar of the Bahá'í teachings – in other words, Bahá'ís are encouraged to follow his example in their lives – stories of 'Abdu'l-Bahá are often told and many Bahá'ís find them uplifting and educative, but they too are not authoritative.

> [Shoghi Effendi] would also urge you to attach no importance to the stories told about 'Abdu'l-Bahá or to those attributed

to Him by the friends. These should be regarded in the same light as the notes and impressions of visiting pilgrims. They need not be suppressed, but they should not also be given prominence or official recognition.[243]

7

Bahá'í Law

Each Messenger of Allah that has come has revealed the laws of his religion and these have usually been different to those of the previous religion. Indeed, it is often the change in the law that is one of the greatest tests for the followers of the Messenger. The Messengers of Allah have brought new laws in relation to such personal matters as prayer and fasting as well as certain social matters such as marriage, divorce and inheritance. Moses (peace be upon him) brought the laws contained in the Torah; Jesus (peace be upon him) established a new prayer and altered some of the Jewish laws, such as those of the Sabbath and of divorce; Muḥammad (blessings and peace be upon him) established a new set of laws, as revealed in the Qur'án; and Bahá'u'lláh has also brought new laws, most of which were revealed in Bahá'u'lláh's major work, the Kitáb-i-Aqdas. Each of the Messengers of Allah has also brought a new calendar and each religion has its own set of holy days. While the Bahá'ís of the Middle East have followed all of these laws, they have been applied in the West in a gradual manner, according to the instructions of the head of the Faith.

Prayer

The Bahá'í scriptures have established the obligation to say a ritual prayer (*ṣalát*). Bahá'ís have been given, however, the choice of three such prayers: a long prayer to be said once

Obligatory Prayer

The following is the medium obligatory prayer, to be recited daily, in the morning, at noon, and in the evening. It includes the instructions for the ablutions (*wuḍú'*).

Whoso wisheth to pray, let him wash his hands, and while he washeth, let him say:

Strengthen my hand, O my God, that it may take hold of Thy Book with such steadfastness that the hosts of the world shall have no power over it. Guard it, then, from meddling with whatsoever doth not belong unto it. Thou art, verily, the Almighty, the Most Powerful.

And while washing his face, let him say:

I have turned my face unto Thee, O my Lord! Illumine it with the light of Thy countenance. Protect it, then, from turning to anyone but Thee.

Then let him stand up, and facing the Qiblih [Point of Adoration, i.e. Bahjí, see p. 170], let him say:

God testifieth that there is none other God but Him. His are the kingdoms of Revelation and of creation. He, in truth, hath manifested Him Who is the Day-Spring of Revelation, Who conversed on Sinai, through Whom the Supreme Horizon hath been made to shine, and the Lote-Tree beyond which there is no passing hath spoken, and through Whom the call hath been proclaimed unto all who are in heaven and on earth: 'Lo, the All-Possessing is come. Earth and heaven, glory and dominion are God's, the Lord of all men, and the Possessor of the Throne on high and of earth below!'

Let him, then, bend down, with hands resting on the knees, and say:

Exalted art Thou above my praise and the praise of anyone beside me, above my description and the description of all who are in heaven and all who are on earth!

Then, standing with open hands, palms upward toward the face, let him say:

Disappoint not, O my God, him that hath, with beseeching fingers, clung to the hem of Thy mercy and Thy grace, O Thou Who of those who show mercy art the Most Merciful!

Let him, then, be seated and say:

I bear witness to Thy unity and Thy oneness, and that Thou art God, and that there is none other God beside Thee. Thou hast, verily, revealed Thy Cause, fulfilled Thy Covenant, and opened wide the door of Thy grace to all that dwell in heaven and on earth. Blessing and peace, salutation and glory, rest upon Thy loved ones, whom the changes and chances of the world have not deterred from turning unto Thee, and who have given their all, in the hope of obtaining that which is with Thee. Thou art, in truth, the Ever-Forgiving, the All-Bountiful.

(If anyone choose to recite instead of the long verse these words: 'God testifieth that there is none other God but Him, the Help in Peril, the Self-Subsisting', it would be sufficient. And likewise, it would suffice were he, while seated, to choose to recite these words: 'I bear witness to Thy unity and Thy oneness, and that Thou art God, and that there is none other God beside Thee.')[244]

a day at any time; a medium-length prayer to be said three times a day; or a short prayer that must be said once between noon and sunset. The prayer is preceded by ablutions (*wuḍú'*). The Bahá'í scriptures instruct that these prayers should be said individually and not communally.

In addition to these obligatory prayers, Bahá'u'lláh has revealed many other prayers and supplications (*du'á*, *munáját*) which can be said at any time. These are said in times of trouble or ill-health, in order to beseech Allah for spiritual qualities, in thanks to and praise of Allah, and at any other time that a person may wish to commune with Him. Bahá'ís are also commanded to read the scriptures every morning and evening and to meditate upon them. When asked why human beings should pray, 'Abdu'l-Bahá wrote:

> The wisdom of prayer is this: That it causeth a connection between the servant and the True One, because in that state man with all heart and soul turneth his face towards His Highness the Almighty, seeking His association and desiring

His love and compassion. The greatest happiness for a lover is to converse with his beloved, and the greatest gift for a seeker is to become familiar with the object of his longing; that is why with every soul who is attracted to the Kingdom of God, his greatest hope is to find an opportunity to entreat and supplicate before his Beloved, appeal for His mercy and grace and be immersed in the ocean of His utterance, goodness and generosity.[245]

Prayers Revealed by Bahá'u'lláh

The following are two prayers revealed by Bahá'u'lláh, the first for spiritual qualities and contentment, the second for healing.

Create in me a pure heart, O my God, and renew a tranquil conscience within me, O my Hope! Through the spirit of power confirm Thou me in Thy Cause, O my Best-Beloved, and by the light of Thy glory reveal unto me Thy path, O Thou the Goal of my desire! Through the power of Thy transcendent might lift me up unto the heaven of Thy holiness, O Source of my being, and by the breezes of Thine eternity gladden me, O Thou Who art my God! Let Thine everlasting melodies breathe tranquillity on me, O my Companion, and let the riches of Thine ancient countenance deliver me from all except Thee, O my Master, and let the tidings of the revelation of Thine incorruptible Essence bring me joy, O Thou Who art the most manifest of the manifest and the most hidden of the hidden![246]

Thy name is my healing, O my God, and remembrance of Thee is my remedy. Nearness to Thee is my hope, and love for Thee is my companion. Thy mercy to me is my healing and my succour in both this world and the world to come. Thou, verily, art the All-Bountiful, the All-Knowing, the All-Wise.[247]

Fasting

The last month of the Bahá'í year (the month of 'Alá, Loftiness, 2–20 March, see p. 182) is set aside for fasting. Bahá'ís fast from sunrise to sunset. Travellers, pregnant and breast-feeding mothers and the sick are exempt from fasting.

> The fasting period, which lasts nineteen days starting as a rule from the second of March every year and ending on the twentieth of the same month, involves complete abstention from food and drink from sunrise till sunset. It is essentially a period of meditation and prayer, of spiritual recuperation, during which the believer must strive to make the necessary readjustments in his inner life, and to refresh and reinvigorate the spiritual forces latent in his soul. Its significance and purpose are, therefore, fundamentally spiritual in character. Fasting is symbolic, and a reminder of abstinence from selfish and carnal desires.[248]

Religious Taxes

In Islam the laws of *zakát* (a tax for the benefit of the poor and other classes, Qur'án 9:60) and the *khums* (a one-fifth tax payable to the Prophet and to certain people such as the poor and orphans, Qur'án 8:41) were established in the Qur'án. In the Bahá'í Faith the *khums* is replaced by a religious tax called the Ḥuqúqu'lláh (the rights of Allah). This is a 19 per cent tax on most classes of capital gains above a certain minimum threshold. It is payable to the Centre of the Faith, which is at present the Universal House of Justice, and can be used for any purpose it determines. In practice much of it is used to support the poorer Bahá'í communities in the world. There are also provisions for the *zakát* to be paid. Concerning the Ḥuqúqu'lláh, Bahá'u'lláh writes:

> It is incumbent upon everyone to discharge the obligation of Ḥuqúq. The advantages gained from this deed revert to the persons themselves. However the acceptance of the offerings dependeth on the spirit of joy, fellowship and contentment that the righteous souls who fulfil this injunction

> will manifest. If such is the attitude acceptance is permissible, and not otherwise. Verify thy Lord is the All-Sufficing, the All-Praised.[249]

> This ordinance is binding upon everyone, and by observing it one will be raised to honour inasmuch as it will serve to purify one's possessions and will impart blessing, and added prosperity.[250]

Pilgrimage

In the Bahá'í scriptures there are provisions made for a full pilgrimage (*ḥajj*). This, however, is not possible at present as it involves going to certain sites in Iran and Iraq that are not now accessible to Bahá'ís. Bahá'ís do, however, visit the shrine of Bahá'u'lláh at Bahjí and the shrine of the Báb on Mount Carmel (see p. 170) and there is a specific prayer revealed for recital at these shrines.

Laws Relating to Marriage and Divorce

Bahá'í law allows only monogamous marriage between a man and a woman. The taking of more than one wife or husband at a time is prohibited. Marriage is conditional upon the free consent of both of the parties getting married as well as upon the consent of both sets of parents, if they are alive. The reason for this is given by Shoghi Effendi:

> Bahá'u'lláh has clearly stated the consent of all living parents is required for a Bahá'í marriage . . . This great law He has laid down to strengthen the social fabric, to knit closer the ties of the home, to place a certain gratitude and respect in the hearts of the children for those who have given them life and sent their souls out on the eternal journey towards their Creator.[251]

The only obligatory part of the Bahá'í marriage ceremony is the mutual exchange of marriage vows. The couple are free to devise the rest of the marriage ceremony as they wish. The amount of the dowry payable is strictly limited by Bahá'u'lláh.

Divorce can be initiated by either the husband or wife. It is only permitted if there are irreconcilable differences and antipathy between the two. If a couple wish to divorce, they must separate for one year. During this time, efforts are made to reconcile the couple. If by the end of this time there is still no reconciliation, then the divorce may proceed.

Death, Burial and Inheritance

The Bahá'í scriptures give instructions for how the body of a deceased person should be prepared for burial. There is a specific obligatory prayer to be said at the funeral service, although other prayers may also be said if the deceased's family wish it.

The Bahá'í scriptures command all Bahá'ís to draw up their own wills and to dispose of their property as they wish. If a person dies without making a will, however, then Bahá'u'lláh has revealed instructions as to how that person's property should be divided.

The Bahá'í Calendar

The Bahá'í Faith has its own calendar which was called by Bahá'u'lláh the Badí' (wondrous, new) calendar. It was inaugurated by the Báb and confirmed by Bahá'u'lláh. Each year consists of 19 months of 19 days each. The year begins with the spring equinox on 21 March. The months are named after the names and attributes of Allah.

Months of the Bahá'í Year

Bahá'í month	*Translation*	*Begins*
Bahá	Splendour	21 March
Jalál	Glory	9 April
Jamál	Beauty	28 April
'Aẓamat	Grandeur	17 May
Núr	Light	5 June
Raḥmat	Mercy	24 June
Kalimát	Words	13 July
Kamál	Perfection	1 August
Asmá'	Names	20 August
'Izzat	Might	8 September
Mas͟híyyat	Will	27 September
'Ilm	Knowledge	16 October
Qudrat	Power	4 November
Qawl	Speech	23 November
Masá'il	Questions	12 December
S͟haraf	Honour	31 December
Sulṭán	Sovereignty	19 January
Mulk	Dominion	7 February
'Alá'	Loftiness	2 March

There are four additional (intercalary) days before the last month of the year ('Alá') which make the number of days up to 365. They are increased to five days in a leap year and are therefore called the Ayyám-i-Há (the Arabic letter Há being equivalent to five). They are specially set aside for hospitality and the giving of presents.

Bahá'ís observe nine holy days, most of which commemorate significant events in Bahá'í history. (For historical information on these events, see chapter 8.)

Bahá'í Holy Days

Naw-Rúz (New Year)	21 March
Riḍván – first day	21 April
Riḍván – ninth day	29 April
Riḍván – twelfth day	2 May
The Báb's declaration of his mission	23 May
Passing of Bahá'u'lláh	29 May
Martyrdom of the Báb	9 July
Birth of the Báb	20 October
Birth of Bahá'u'lláh	12 November

Prohibitions

In the Kitáb-i-Aqdas, the law whereby certain things are regarded as impure is abolished. Therefore there are no prohibitions in the Bahá'í Faith on what one may eat, wear or touch. Instead there are general commandments regarding cleanliness and moderation, which are given as the guide to human action.

There is, however, in the Bahá'í teachings a prohibition on the consumption of any substances that cause human beings to lose control of their mental, rational faculties. 'Abdu'l-Bahá states:

> Intellect and the faculty of comprehension are God's gifts whereby man is distinguished from other animals. Will a wise man want to lose this Light in the darkness of intoxication? No, by God! This will not satisfy him! He will, rather, do that which will develop his powers of intelligence and understanding, and not increase his negligence, heedlessness and decline. This is an explicit text in the perspicuous Book, wherein God hath set forth every goodly virtue, and exposed every reprehensible act.[252]

Substances that causes human beings to lose control of their mind, substances such as alcohol, opium and other narcotic drugs, are therefore prohibited in Bahá'í law. Smoking is not prohibited although it is strongly condemned as an unclean, unhealthy habit.

The Bahá'í scriptures also specifically prohibit backbiting, the saying of bad things about a person when he or she is not present:

> That seeker should also regard backbiting as grievous error, and keep himself aloof from its dominion, inasmuch as backbiting quencheth the light of the heart, and extinguisheth the life of the soul.[253]

Also prohibited by Allah in the Bahá'í revelation are such human actions as cruelty to animals, gambling, adultery, homosexuality, promiscuity, begging, priesthood, monasticism, the confession of sins, the kissing of hands, the waging of holy war, the burning of books and the muttering of sacred verses while walking along the street.

Laws, Teachings and the Maturity of Humanity

The Islamic system is very much based on laws. Everything that one does during the day is governed by the *Sharí'ah*, the Holy Law. According to Bahá'í teachings, this was necessary in an earlier age when humanity was less mature and therefore needed many rules to keep it in check. Bahá'u'lláh states that this is now the age of the maturity of humanity and that the laws that govern the people in their maturity are different from those that applied in a less mature age.

> Consider that which hath been sent down unto Muḥammad, the Apostle of God. The measure of the Revelation of which He was the bearer had been clearly foreordained by Him Who is the Almighty, the All-Powerful. They that heard Him,

> however, could apprehend His purpose only to the extent of their station and spiritual capacity. He, in like manner, uncovered the Face of Wisdom in proportion to their ability to sustain the burden of His Message. No sooner had mankind attained the stage of maturity, than the Word revealed to men's eyes the latent energies with which it had been endowed – energies which manifested themselves in the plenitude of their glory when the Ancient Beauty appeared, in the year sixty, in the person of 'Alí-Muḥammad, the Báb.[254]

Therefore, although there are laws in the Bahá'í Faith governing things such as prayer, fasting, marriage and certain religious taxes, there is a tendency in the matter of personal matters and interpersonal relations for the Bahá'í scriptures to lay down general principles and to leave it to the individual to apply these as he or she believes fit. Thus, for example, in Islam, according to the Traditions (*ḥadíths*), the wearing of silk or yellow clothes is prohibited,[255] the moustache is to be cut while the beard is to be allowed to grow.[256] In relation to these types of laws, the Bahá'í scriptures sweep away all such specific laws and instead lay down the general principle that there should be nothing in one's demeanour of which sound and upright minds would disapprove. They then go on to make the point that rather than being too concerned with our physical clothes, we should pay more attention to the ethical clothes we wear, our character and conduct:

> It hath been . . . permitted you to attire yourselves in silk. The Lord hath relieved you, as a bounty on His part, of the restrictions that formerly applied to clothing and to the trim of the beard. He, verily, is the Ordainer, the Omniscient. Let there be naught in your demeanour of which sound and upright minds would disapprove, and make not yourselves the playthings of the ignorant. Well is it with him who hath adorned himself with the vesture of seemly conduct and a praiseworthy character. He is assuredly reckoned with those

> who aid their Lord through distinctive and outstanding deeds.[257]

This concept that humanity has now collectively reached the stage of maturity is explained further by 'Abdu'l-Bahá in a talk given in North America:

> The world of humanity shall become the manifestation of the lights of Divinity, and the bestowals of God shall surround all. From the standpoints of both material and spiritual civilization extraordinary progress and development will be witnessed. In this present cycle there will be an evolution in civilization unparalleled in the history of the world. The world of humanity has, heretofore, been in the stage of infancy; now it is approaching maturity. Just as the individual human organism, having attained the period of maturity, reaches its fullest degree of physical strength and ripened intellectual faculties so that in one year of this ripened period there is witnessed an unprecedented measure of development, likewise the world of humanity in this cycle of its completeness and consummation will realize an immeasurable upward progress, and that power of accomplishment whereof each individual human reality is the depository of God – that outworking Universal Spirit – like the intellectual faculty, will reveal itself in infinite degrees of perfection.[258]

8

History of the Bahá'í Faith

In the middle of the 19th Christian century, the 13th Islamic century, there were stirrings of expectancy throughout the Muslim world. There were many who thought that there were clear signs that the time of the expected Mahdi was imminent. There were various causes for this feeling of expectancy. During the first few decades of the 19th century there had been a profound shock to the Muslim world. For centuries Muslims had been used to thinking of themselves as the most powerful advanced civilization in the world. Then, during this period, the Muslim world experienced a series of military defeats that made it clear that this was no longer the case: Napoleon's occupation of Egypt in 1798, Ottoman defeat at the hands of Russia in 1806, Iran's two disastrous wars against Russia, 1804–13 and 1826–8, the French occupation of Algiers in 1830 and the gradual British annexation of the Mughal Empire in India. In addition to military defeats there was the increasing evidence of the trading and manufacturing supremacy of the European states, forcing many merchants and craftsmen in the Middle East out of business. From the 1830s onwards cholera epidemics raged throughout the Muslim world. In all, many Muslims began to see in these events the signs of the advent of the Mahdi:

> The Last Hour will not come before the Romans (Christians) will equip themselves against the Muslims . . . There would be a terrible fight and the Muslims would prepare a detachment . . . and they would fight until evening and neither side

> would obtain a victory and the squad would be wiped out . . . and they would fight such a fight the like of which has never been seen, so much that even if a bird were to pass their flanks, it would fall down dead before reaching the end of them. Were a count to be taken of one hundred related men, it would be found that only one has survived . . . They would be in this very state when they would hear of a calamity more horrible than this. And a cry would reach them: 'The Dajjál (Antichrist) has taken your place among your off-spring.'[259]

In addition to these factors, many had calculated from prophecies in the Qur'án and the Traditions (*ḥadíths*) that it was the time for those prophecies related to the Mahdi and the time of the end to occur. First there was the verse of the Qur'án that stated that the *amr* (command, cause) of the Prophet Muḥammad (blessings and peace be upon him) would return to heaven after one thousand years.

> He establishes His decree (*al-amr*) from the heavens unto the earth and it will go up to Him in a Day, the length of which is one thousand years in your reckoning. (32:5; see pp. 119–20)

Thus people had been looking for some great event from about 1602, one thousand Islamic years after the death of Muḥammad, or after 1631, since some Traditions dated this one thousand years as being from the death of the fourth of the rightly-guided caliphs, 'Alí.[260] Some had considered that Islam would go into decline at this time[261] and that the Mahdi would appear somewhat later once the decline was established. It was also possible to speculate that the first phrase of this verse referred to the establishment of the Cause or Decree (*al-amr*) of Muḥammad and that this could not be considered to have occurred until the middle of the 3rd Islamic century, when the legal schools were established (later Muslim scholars decreed that this was the time when the gate of *ijtihad* was closed). According to this line of reasoning, the one thousand year period would end in the middle of the 13th Islamic century (i.e. about 1250 AH or 1834 AD). The Shi'is looked to the Islamic year 1260 (1844), one thousand years after the disappearance of the twelfth Imám.[262] Throughout the Muslim world, then, in the early part of the 19th Christian century, these expectations grew to a climax. Many began to preach that the promised Mahdi would soon appear. Reports of such an expectation can be found from India, Iran, the Caucasus, Iraq and the Sudan.[263]

It was in such circumstances that one of the prominent *'ulamá* of the period, Shaykh Aḥmad of al-Aḥsá in Arabia, began to preach a new doctrine that soon attracted a large number of followers. Among his doctrines was that the Traditions related to the coming of the Mahdi were to be understood as spiritual truths not literal physical truths. After his death in 1826 his successor Sayyid Káẓim Rashtí continued his teachings at the holy city of Karbalá in Iraq. At his classes he would tell his students of the near advent of the fulfilment of these prophecies. Before he died in 1843 he refused to name a successor but told his students to seek out the truth for themselves.

The Báb

One of the students of Sayyid Kaẓim Rashtí was Mullá Ḥusayn Bushrú'í and in early 1844 he set out in obedience to his master's instructions. In Shiraz he came across a young man, Sayyid 'Alí Muḥammad, who was a descendant of the Prophet Muḥammad through the line of Fáṭimah. On the evening of 23 May 1844 Sayyid 'Alí Muḥammad made a declaration to Mullá Ḥusayn that he was the awaited Mahdi. This declaration at first stunned Mullá Ḥusayn but during the course of the evening he gradually became convinced of the truth of the young man's claims. The young man fulfilled the physical requirements of the Mahdi and during the evening he revealed the first chapter of a book, the Qayyúm al-Asmá, which Mullá

Ḥusayn, familiar as he was with the Islamic scriptures, was convinced could only be a result of divine revelation. The young man took the title of the Báb (meaning the Gate).

Words of the Báb
Written on the Night of the Declaration of His Mission

All praise be to God Who hath, through the power of Truth, sent down this Book unto His servant, that it may serve as a shining light for all mankind . . . Verily this is none other than the sovereign Truth; it is the Path which God hath laid out for all that are in heaven and on earth. Let him then who will, take for himself the right path unto his Lord. Verily this is the true Faith of God, and sufficient witness are God and such as are endowed with the knowledge of the Book. This is indeed the eternal Truth which God, the Ancient of Days, hath revealed unto His omnipotent Word – He Who hath been raised up from the midst of the Burning Bush. This is the Mystery which hath been hidden from all that are in heaven and on earth, and in this wondrous Revelation it hath, in very truth, been set forth in the Mother Book by the hand of God, the Exalted . . .

O concourse of kings and of the sons of kings! Lay aside, one and all, your dominion which belongeth unto God . . .

Let not thy sovereignty deceive thee, O Sháh, for 'every soul shall taste of death' [Qur'án 3:185] and this, in very truth, hath been written down as a decree of God.[264]

Sayyid 'Alí Muḥammad, the Báb, had been born in Shiraz on 20 October 1819. His family were well-known in Shiraz as being descendants of the Prophet Muḥammad, through his daughter Fáṭimah. (See p. 121 for Islamic prophecies that the Mahdi would be a descendant of Muḥammad through Fáṭimah.) During the summer of 1844 the Báb collected 18 disciples and set them off in all directions to announce his advent. Among these 18 was a woman, Ṭáhirih, who was the only one who was not present in Shiraz. She was accepted into the group by virtue of a letter that she wrote. These 18 disciples were called by the Báb the Letters of the Living. Together with the Báb himself they formed the first group, which the Báb called the first *wáḥid* (one, unity) of the Báb's dispensation. These 19 are considered by Bahá'ís to be the 19 that the Qur'án states are appointed by Allah as guardians over the entrance to hell. Those that truly believe are saved by the 19, while those 'in whose hearts is a disease' fall to their doom.

> Soon will I cast him into Hell-Fire! And what will explain to thee what Hell-Fire is? Naught doth it permit to endure, and naught doth it leave alone! – Darkening and changing the colour of man!
>
> Over it are Nineteen. And We have set none but angels as guardians of the Fire; and We have fixed their number only as a trial for Unbelievers, – in order that the People of the Book may arrive at certainty, and the Believers may increase in Faith, – and that no doubts may be left for the People of the Book and the Believers, and that those in whose hearts is a disease and the Unbelievers may say, 'What symbol doth Allah intend by this?' Thus doth Allah leave to stray whom He pleaseth, and guide whom He pleaseth: and none can know the forces of thy Lord, except He. And this is no other than a warning to mankind. (Qur'án 74:26–31)

It is of interest to note that the whole of the religion of the Báb can be said to revolve around the number 19. There are 19 days in the month and 19 months in the year. Thus the Bábís were to meet every 19 days at the beginning of each month. There were 19 chapters in each of the sections of his main book, the Bayán. Those who have opposed the Báb have ridiculed these provisions and have asked: 'What symbol doth Allah intend by this?' This is, of course, exactly the same question as is reported in the above verse of the Qur'án to have been asked by those 'in whose hearts is a disease'.

The Báb himself set off to perform the pilgrimage to Mecca. While there he fulfilled another Islamic prophecy by announcing his claim between the Rukn (corner of the Ka'ba) and Maqám (station, buildings in the courtyard of the Great Mosque) in Mecca.[265] Upon his return the Báb was arrested and put under house arrest for a time in Shiraz. During this period, two of the very learned *'ulamá* of Iran, Mullá Muḥammad 'Alí Zanjání, the Ḥujjat al-Islám, and Sayyid Yaḥyá Ka<u>sh</u>fí Dárábí, who was the personal emissary of the Shah sent to investigate the Báb, became his followers, both as a result of reading the writings of the Báb, and in the latter case, meeting him. Indeed, almost all of the leading disciples of the Báb were from the class of the *'ulamá*, men who were learned in Islam and had spent their whole lives studying the Qur'án. They recognized in the books of the Báb the same voice that spoke from the pages of the Qur'án.

In 1846 the Báb moved to Isfahan where he succeeded in enlisting the governor of the city among his followers. Just as the previous Messengers of Allah were opposed, however, the Báb also encountered opposition from both the civil and religious leaders of Iran. The success of the Báb brought about the enmity of the Prime Minister, Ḥájjí Mírzá Áqásí, who feared that the Báb might replace him as the Shah's confidant and adviser. Bahá'ís regard this Prime Minister as the Dajjál of the Báb's revelation. At the same time as the Shah was becoming curious to meet the Báb, who had caused such a stir in his kingdom, the Prime Minister was plotting to prevent any such meeting. He persuaded the Shah to have the Báb removed to the far north-west of his kingdom, to the prison-fortress of Mákú, in 1847.

Just as Muḥammad had delayed about 12 years into his ministry before finalizing his break with Judaism and Christianity by changing the direction of prayer from Jerusalem to the Ka'ba and beginning to enact the laws of his religion, so also the Báb delayed openly announcing his break with Islam and his revelation of new laws until about 1848. It was in about that year, while the Báb was in Mákú, that he revealed the Bayán, his book of laws, in which the laws of the Qur'án were replaced by new ones, such as those of prayer, fasting and pilgrimage. After this the Báb was removed to a fortress-prison at Chihríq, also in the north-west of Iran.

During the summer of 1848 the followers of the Báb, the Bábís, gathered at a village called Badasht in north-east Iran and there proclaimed the start of a new dispensation. A prominent part in this conference was played by Ṭáhirih, the Báb's leading female disciple, who had throughout the whole of this period played a prominent role in the Bábí movement. By this she set the tone for the Bábí and Bahá'í religions, indicating that, in these religions, there would be equality between women and men. At the conference at Badasht she appeared unveiled before those present, thus dramatically demonstrating the fact that the Islamic dispensation had ceased and that new laws were in operation. On this occasion the Quranic Súrah of Wáqi'ah, which refers to the Day of Judgement, was recited:

> When the Event Inevitable cometh to pass,
> Then will no (soul) entertain falsehood concerning its coming.
> (Many) will it bring low; (many) will it exalt;
> When the earth shall be shaken to its depths,
> And the mountains shall be crumbled to atoms,
> Becoming dust scattered abroad . . .
> And those Foremost (in Faith) will be foremost (in the Hereafter).
> These will be those Nearest to Allah
> In Gardens of Bliss. (56:1–6, 10–12)

At the same time the Báb himself was summoned to the provincial capital, Tabriz, where a trial was held in the presence of the heir to the throne. Here he, three times, made the public pronouncement:

> I am, I am, I am, the promised One! I am the One whose name you have for a thousand years invoked, at whose

> mention you have risen, whose advent you have longed to witness, and the hour of whose Revelation you have prayed God to hasten. Verily I say, it is incumbent upon the peoples of both the East and the West to obey My word and to pledge allegiance to My person.[266]

The leading religious dignitary present, the Niẓám al-'Ulamá, sought clarification:

> 'That is to say you are the Mahdí, the Lord of Religion?'
> 'Yes,' answered the Báb.[267]

Later in the course of the proceedings, the Niẓám al-'Ulamá posed this challenge:

> 'The claim which you have advanced is a stupendous one; it must needs be supported by the most incontrovertible evidence.'
>
> 'His own word,' said the Báb, 'is the most convincing evidence of the truth of the Mission of the Prophet of God.' And He quoted from the Qur'án a verse [29:51] in support of His argument: 'Is it not enough for them that We have sent down to Thee the Book?'[268]

The Báb was further questioned by the *'ulamá* and, according to an eyewitness report written by the heir apparent, refused to retract his claim.[269] He was then subjected to the bastinado, a beating on the soles of the feet, and returned to the prison-fortress of C̲h̲ihríq.

Throughout Iran the message of the Báb was spreading rapidly and gaining large numbers of new followers from every class and sector of society. While some of the *'ulamá* joined the new religion, many opposed it, some because they considered that the Báb was wrong but some also fearing that it would result in an end to their livelihood. One particular centre for the spread of the new religion was the city of Mashhad in the province of Khurasan. Here Mullá Ḥusayn

Bushrú'í and others were actively seeking to spread the new religion. In the summer of 1848 Mullá Ḥusayn, on the instructions of the Báb, raised a black standard and set off from Khurasan to assist Quddús, one of the leading Bábís who was imprisoned in Mazandaran. In this way Mullá Ḥusayn fulfilled the prophecy common to both Sunnis and Shi'is that the coming of the Mahdi would be accompanied by the raising of a black standard in Khurasan (see p. 121).

In Mazandaran, at a shrine called Shaykh Ṭabarsí, Mullá Ḥusayn and Quddús were surrounded by royal troops and forced to take up defensive positions. The old king had died and the new Shah, Náṣir ad-Dín Sháh, advised by his new Prime Minister, Mírzá Taqí Khán, had determined to crush the new religious movement. Although greatly outnumbered by the royal troops who were assisted by cannons and local militia and although they were defending a religious shrine with no natural defences, the Bábís resisted the royal forces for seven months. On several occasions they inflicted great defeats upon the royal troops. Eventually the royal prince leading the besieging army was forced to resort to deception and betrayal. He swore upon the Holy Qur'án safe passage for the remaining Bábís and invited their leaders to come for talks. Then he fell upon those to whom he had granted safe passage and massacred them.

Even members of the besieging army saw in the events of those days a resemblance to the events at Karbalá where Ḥusayn, the grandson of the Prophet Muḥammad, had been betrayed and martyred. One of the leaders of the royal forces is reported to have said:

> The truth of the matter is that anyone who had not seen Karbilá would, if he had seen Ṭabarsí, not only have comprehended what there took place, but would have ceased to consider it; and had he seen Mullá Ḥusayn of Bushrúyih he would have been convinced that the Chief of Martyrs [Ḥusayn] had returned to earth; and had he witnessed my

> deeds, he would assuredly have said: 'This is Shimr [the man who slew Ḥusayn] come back with sword and lance' . . . But in truth I know not what had been shown to these people, or what they had seen, that they came forth to battle with such alacrity and joy, and engaged so eagerly and gladly in the strife, without displaying in their countenance any trace of fear or apprehension. One would imagine that in their eyes the keen sword and blood-spilling dagger were but means to the attainment of everlasting life, so eagerly did their necks and bosoms welcome them . . . And the astonishing thing was that all these men were scholars and men of learning, sedentary recluses of the college and the cloister, delicately nurtured and of weakly frame, inured indeed to austerities, but strangers to the roar of cannon, the rattle of musketry, and the field of battle.[270]

The whole of Iran was stirred by the events at Shaykh Ṭabarsí. The number of the Báb's disciples continued to increase and another two episodes occurred at Zanján and Nayríz in 1850. These two episodes were led by the two learned disciples of the Báb mentioned above, Mullá Muḥammad 'Alí Zanjání and Sayyid Yaḥyá Kashfí Dárábí. In both cases the Bábís held out valiantly against much greater numbers and superior weapons. In all, many thousands of Bábís were martyred for the sake of their Cause. Bahá'ís consider that they were each a testimony to the words of the Qur'án: 'Then seek for death if ye are sincere' (2:94, 62:6).

In the middle of 1850, while the upheaval at Zanján was still going on, the Prime Minister decided that the only way to put an end to this religious movement would be to kill its author, the Báb. Accordingly, he gave orders that the Báb be brought from Chihríq to Tabriz and there put to death. The martyrdom of the Báb occurred on 9 July 1850. The execution was itself not without incident since an entire regiment discharged its rifles at him and yet failed to kill him. The Báb was nowhere to be seen. They searched for him and found him finishing off some dictation to his secretary. And so they brought him back to the place of execution and a second regiment was brought which succeeded in accomplishing its task. The British Minister in Tehran at that time, Justin Sheil, confirmed these facts in his reports to the British Foreign Secretary:

> The founder of this sect has been executed at Tabreez. He was killed by a volley of musketry, and his death was on the point of giving his religion a lustre which would have largely increased its proselytes. When the smoke and dust cleared away after the volley, Bâb was not to be seen, and the populace proclaimed that he had ascended to the skies. The balls had broken the ropes by which he was bound, but he was dragged from the recess where after some search, he was discovered, and shot.[271]

The body of the Báb was recovered and hidden by his disciples. Many years later it was transported out of Iran and interred in a shrine that now forms the centre of a group of Bahá'í buildings on the slopes of Mount Carmel.

Prayer of the Báb

I am aware, O Lord, that my trespasses have covered my face with shame in Thy presence, and have burdened my back before Thee, have intervened between me and Thy beauteous countenance, have compassed me from every direction and have hindered me on all sides from gaining access unto the revelations of Thy celestial power.

O Lord! If Thou forgivest me not, who is there then to grant pardon, and if Thou hast no mercy upon me who is capable of showing compassion? Glory be unto Thee, Thou didst create me when I was non-existent and Thou didst nourish me while I was devoid of any understanding. Praise be unto Thee, every evidence of bounty proceedeth from Thee and every token of grace emanateth from the treasuries of Thy decree.[272]

Bahá'u'lláh

Bahá'u'lláh was born in Tehran on 12 November 1817. He was the son of a Minister in the Shah's government and was thus brought up in comfortable circumstances. When the call of the Báb was raised in 1844, Bahá'u'lláh immediately responded, although it soon became clear that by doing so he risked wealth and status. Bahá'u'lláh's home in Tehran became a focal point for the Bábís of that city and he was frequently able to give assistance to his fellow-believers who were being persecuted. He was able to assist Ṭáhirih to flee her hometown of Qazvin and he sent supplies and assistance to the defenders at Shaykh Ṭabarsí.

After the martyrdom of the Báb, Bahá'u'lláh, owing to his close association with the new religion, was forced to leave Iran and spent some months at the shrine cities of Iraq. He returned to Iran just at the time that a small group of Bábís made a futile and ill-fated attempt on the life of Náṣir ad-Dín Sháh in August 1852. The result of this was a fierce renewal of persecutions. Many Bábís were put to death under terrible conditions. A Swiss-Austrian military instructor, Captain von Gumoens, who was in Tehran at the time, recorded his observations which were published in several European journals and newspapers:

> But follow me, my friend, you who lay claim to a heart and European ethics, follow me to the unhappy ones who, with gouged-out eyes, must eat, on the scene of the deed, without any sauce, their own amputated ears; or whose teeth are torn out with inhuman violence by the hand of the executioner; or whose bare skulls are simply crushed by blows from a hammer; or where the bazaar is illuminated with unhappy victims, because on right and left the people dig deep holes in their breasts and shoulders, and insert burning wicks in the wounds. I saw some dragged in chains through the bazaar, preceded by a military band, in whom these wicks had burned so deep that now the fat flickered convulsively in the wound like a newly extinguished lamp.

> Not seldom it happens that the unwearying ingenuity of the Oriental leads to fresh tortures. They will skin the soles of the Babis' feet, soak the wounds in boiling oil, shoe the foot like the hoof of a horse, and compel the victim to run. No cry escaped from the victim's breast; the torment is endured in dark silence by the numbed sensation of the fanatic; now he must run; the body cannot endure what the soul has endured; he falls. Give him the coup de grace! Put him out of his pain! No! The executioner swings the whip, and – I myself have had to witness it – the unhappy victim of hundredfold tortures runs! This is the beginning of the end. As for the end itself, they hang the scorched and perforated bodies by their hands and feet to a tree head downwards, and now every Persian may try his marksmanship to his heart's content from a fixed but not too proximate distance on the noble quarry placed at his disposal. I saw corpses torn by nearly 150 bullets . . .
>
> When I read over again what I have written, I am overcome by the thought that those who are with you in our dearly beloved Austria may doubt the full truth of the picture, and accuse me of exaggeration. Would to God that I had not lived to see it! But by the duties of my profession I was unhappily often, only too often, a witness of these abominations. At present I never leave my house, in order not to meet with fresh scenes of horror . . .[273]

Bahá'u'lláh was among those arrested as a result of the attempt on the life of the Shah. At this time he lost all of the remaining family wealth. He was placed along with the other Bábís in a damp underground chamber that had been a water cistern and was now simply called the Síyáh-Chál (the Black Hole). It was here that he had an experience that Bahá'ís regard as being the equivalent of what Muḥammad experienced on Mount Hira when the angel Gabriel first appeared to him. The following is Bahá'u'lláh's own account of this:

> While engulfed in tribulations I heard a most wondrous, a most sweet voice, calling above My head. Turning My face,

> I beheld a Maiden – the embodiment of the remembrance of the name of My Lord – suspended in the air before Me. So rejoiced was she in her very soul that her countenance shone with the ornament of the good-pleasure of God, and her cheeks glowed with the brightness of the All-Merciful. Betwixt earth and heaven she was raising a call which captivated the hearts and minds of men. She was imparting to both My inward and outer being tidings which rejoiced My soul, and the souls of God's honoured servants. Pointing with her finger unto My head, she addressed all who are in heaven and all who are on earth, saying: 'By God! This is the Best-Beloved of the worlds, and yet ye comprehend not. This is the Beauty of God amongst you, and the power of His sovereignty within you, could ye but understand. This is the Mystery of God and His Treasure, the Cause of God and His glory unto all who are in the kingdoms of Revelation and of creation, if ye be of them that perceive.'[274]

Bahá'ís regard this episode as marking the beginning of Bahá'u'lláh's mission, the start of Allah's revelation to Bahá'u-'lláh. In January 1853 Bahá'u'lláh was freed from the Síyáh-Chál but ordered into exile. Rejecting an offer of asylum in Russia, he travelled with his family over snow in the middle of winter to Baghdad, which at that time was part of the Ottoman Empire.

Baghdad had been the capital of the 'Abbasid caliphate and was then given the title Dár as-Salám, the Abode of Peace. Bahá'ís regard Bahá'u'lláh's arrival in Baghdad as the fulfilment of the Quranic verse: 'But Allah doth call to the Home [Abode] of Peace: He doth guide whom He pleaseth to a way that is straight' (10:25). During his time there Bahá'u'lláh rebuilt the Bábí community, which had been shattered by five years of intense persecutions. He wrote works such as the Kitáb-i-Íqán, in which he set out to prove the truth of the new religion, the Seven Valleys, a mystical work written to a Sufi shaykh, and the Hidden Words, a series of epigrammatic utterances summarizing the spiritual and ethical principles of all religions. Bahá'u'lláh was faced with opposition from some of the Bábís and in particular his own half-brother Azal, who had been given a role as a figurehead by the Báb. In order to prevent division in the ranks of the Bábís, Bahá'u'lláh withdrew for two years, at first to wander as a recluse in the hills around Sulaymániyyah and then to spend some time in a Sufi *takiyyah* (retreat) in Sulaymániyyah.

Just as every Messenger of Allah has experienced opposition primarily from the religious leaders of his time, so Bahá'u'lláh began to encounter opposition from some of the Islamic *'ulamá* in Baghdad and the shrine cities of Iraq. On one occasion, they attempted to assassinate him; on another they tried to entrap him into a test which they thought he would fail:

> . . . the Persian 'ulamá who were at Karbilá and Najaf chose a wise man whom they sent on a mission to him; his name was Mullá Ḥasan-i-'Amú. He came into the Holy Presence, and proposed a number of questions on behalf of the 'ulamá, to which Bahá'u'lláh replied. Then Ḥasan-i-'Amú said: 'The 'ulamá recognize without hesitation and confess the knowledge and virtue of Bahá'u'lláh, and they are unanimously convinced that in all learning he has no peer or equal; and it is also evident that he has never studied or acquired this learning'; but still the 'ulamá said: 'We are not contented with this, we do not acknowledge the reality of his mission by virtue of his wisdom and righteousness. Therefore we ask him to show us a miracle in order to satisfy and tranquillize our hearts.'
>
> Bahá'u'lláh replied: 'Although you have no right to ask this, for God should test His creatures, and they should not test God, still I allow and accept this request. But the Cause of God is not a theatrical display that is presented every hour, of which some new diversion may be asked for every day. If it were thus, the Cause of God would become mere child's play.
>
> 'The 'ulamá must therefore assemble and with one accord choose one miracle, and write that after the performance of this miracle they will no longer entertain doubts about me,

> and that all will acknowledge and confess the truth of my Cause. Let them seal this paper and bring it to me. This must be the accepted criterion: If the miracle is performed, no doubt will remain for them; and if not, we shall be convicted of imposture.' The learned man, Ḥasan-i-'Amú, rose and replied, 'There is no more to be said'; he then kissed the knee of the Blessed One although he was not a believer, and went. He gathered the 'ulamá and gave them the sacred message. They consulted together and said, 'This man is an enchanter: perhaps he will perform an enchantment, and then we shall have nothing more to say.' Acting on this belief, they did not dare to push the matter further.
>
> This man, Ḥasan-i-'Amú, mentioned this fact at many meetings. After leaving Karbilá he went to Kirmánshah and Ṭihrán, and spread a detailed account of it everywhere, laying emphasis on the fear and the withdrawal of the 'ulamá.[275]

Bahá'u'lláh's fame and prestige gradually grew and eventually the Shah asked the Ottoman government either to hand Bahá'u'lláh back to the Iranian government or to remove him from proximity to the borders of Iran. It was at the time of Bahá'u'lláh's departure from Baghdad that a very important event occurred. Bahá'u'lláh had received intimation of his mission in the Síyáh-Chál in 1852–3 but he had not announced this to the Bábís, although a few of them had become aware of it. Between 21 April and 3 May 1863, while residing at a garden outside Baghdad making preparations to leave, Bahá'u'lláh disclosed his mission and station to a few of his companions. The garden is called by Bahá'ís the garden of Riḍván and the occasion is celebrated each year by Bahá'ís as the festival of Riḍván.

Bahá'u'lláh was exiled for a time to Istanbul and then to Edirne in European Turkey, where he remained until 1868. During this time Bahá'u'lláh issued a general proclamation of his claims and his mission to the Bábís in Iran, to the people of the world in general, to the rulers of the world and to the religious leaders of all religions. Just as the Prophet Muḥammad had addressed the great rulers of the world of his time, the Emperors of Byzantium and Persia, so did Bahá'u'lláh address the great kings of his time: Emperor Napoleon III, Queen Victoria, the Tsar of Russia, Sulṭán 'Abd al-Ḥamíd of the Ottoman Empire and Náṣir ad-Dín Sháh of Iran. To the religious leaders generally he addressed these words:

> Say: O leaders of religion! Weigh not the Book of God with such standards and sciences as are current amongst you, for the Book itself is the unerring Balance established amongst men. In this most perfect Balance whatsoever the peoples and kindreds of the earth possess must be weighed, while the measure of its weight should be tested according to its own standard, did ye but know it.[276]

Also during the Edirne period there occurred the final separation between Bahá'u'lláh and his half-brother Azal. The latter was encouraged in his opposition to Bahá'u'lláh by Sayyid Muḥammad Iṣfahání, whom Bahá'ís regard as the Dajjál of the Bahá'í dispensation.[277] Jealous of the increasing number of Bábís who were turning to Bahá'u'lláh and finding himself completely inadequate to oppose Bahá'u'lláh openly, Azal began to plot against Bahá'u'lláh secretly. Assisted by Iṣfahání, he tried on one occasion to poison Bahá'u'lláh and, when this failed, he made false accusations against Bahá'u'lláh to the Ottoman authorities. Bahá'u'lláh has explained that the Dajjál is a universal or archetypal figure who appears in each dispensation. The same idea is implied in the Islamic Traditions. Muḥammad is recorded as having said: 'I warn you of him [the Dajjál], and there was no prophet but warned his followers of him.'[278] The Dajjál is the one who recognizes the truth of the Messenger of Allah and yet opposes him and tries to destroy him. In the dispensation of Jesus, it was Judas Iscariot; in the dispensation of Muḥammad, it was 'Abdu'llah ibn 'Ubayy, the leader of the *munáfiqún*, the hypocrites; in the dispensation of the Báb, it was, as mentioned above, Ḥájjí Mírzá Áqásí.

Just as the *munáfiqún*, the hypocrites, in the time of Muḥammad had sought to undermine and betray the Prophet, so too did Azal and his associates seek to work against Bahá'u-'lláh. There was at this time a great deal of political instability and rebellious activity in the area of the Balkans and, when Azal began to make accusations against Bahá'u'lláh, the Ottoman authorities decided to exile Bahá'u'lláh away from this area. Bahá'u'lláh was sent to 'Akká, which was at that time in the Ottoman province of Syria. Being a walled city, it was used by the Ottomans as a prison for dangerous political prisoners and criminals.

During his ministry Bahá'u'lláh and his followers experienced much persecution from the Muslim *'ulamá*. Addressing one of the most prominent religious leaders in Iran, Bahá'u-'lláh wrote:

> O S͟hayk͟h! We have learned that thou hast turned away from Us, and protested against Us, in such wise that thou hast bidden the people to curse Me, and decreed that the blood of the servants of God be shed . . . Verily I say: Whatever befalleth in the path of God is the beloved of the soul and the desire of the heart. Deadly poison in His path is pure honey, and every tribulation a draught of crystal water. In the Tablet to His Majesty the S͟háh it is written: 'By Him Who is the Truth! I fear no tribulation in His path, nor any affliction in My love for Him. Verily God hath made adversity as a morning dew upon His green pasture, and a wick for His lamp which lighteth earth and heaven.'[279]

During Bahá'u'lláh's time in 'Akká, Sayyid Muḥammad Iṣfahání was sent to live there also and to spy on Bahá'u'lláh for the Ottoman authorities. He lived by the land gate of 'Akká that leads out towards Ludd (Lod) and Jerusalem. In this position he was able to keep a close watch on the exiles and reported any of Bahá'u'lláh's followers who had come from Iran and elsewhere to see him so that they were arrested as they arrived. Although Bahá'u'lláh counselled his followers to be patient, a few of them were unable to tolerate this situation and killed Iṣfahání in his house at the gate of 'Akká.

After living for two years in the citadel-prison of 'Akká and seven years under house arrest in various houses in the town, Bahá'u'lláh moved out of 'Akká and in 1879 established himself in a mansion known as Bahjí just outside the city. During these years in and around 'Akká he wrote numerous books and many of his followers travelled thousands of miles to visit him. It was at Bahjí that he passed away on 29 May 1892 and was buried in a small house nearby that is now his shrine.

Through Bahá'u'lláh's exile to 'Akká the Ottoman authorities unwittingly caused Bahá'u'lláh to fulfil many prophecies that occur in the books of *ḥadí<u>th</u>s*. Bahá'ís consider that Bahá'u-'lláh is the return of Christ (al-Masíḥ) about which there are many prophecies in the Traditions. It is stated that the return of Christ will occur after the emergence of the Mahdi.[280] The Tradition that speaks of the last of the supporters of the Mahdi reaching 'Akká has already been cited (see p. 127–8), as have numerous other Traditions relating to Syria and 'Akká (see pp. 132–5). Islamic Traditions had stated that when Christ returned he would descend at a white minaret to the east of Damascus. Baghdad is to the east of Damascus and the Qamariyyah Mosque in Baghdad has a large white minaret. This is where Bahá'u'lláh's mission began. The same Tradition, as reported by Ibn Májah, then goes on to say that Christ will seek out the Dajjál until he finds him at the Ludd gate and will kill him there, a reflection of what happened to Iṣfahání (see above). The same Tradition then says that after this:

> . . . a people whom Allah has protected from him [the Dajjál] will come to Jesus and he will wipe their faces and will relate to them their station in paradise. Meanwhile, Allah will reveal to Jesus: 'O Jesus, I have brought forth servants of mine whom none can overcome in battle. Gather my servants to the mountain.'[281]

This prophecy of gathering Allah's servants to the mountain can be considered to have been fulfilled when, towards the end of his life, Bahá'u'lláh visited Haifa and instructed his son 'Abdu'l-Bahá to begin the process that has led to the establishment of the World Centre of the Bahá'í Faith on the side of Mount Carmel (see p. 170).

Another Tradition which appears to refer to the successive stages of the exile and migration of Bahá'u'lláh states:

> There will be emigration after emigration, but the best people on earth will be those who cleave most closely to the places to which Abraham emigrated. (Abú Dáwud)[282]

Abraham migrated from Mesopotamia until eventually he reached Syria and Palestine. Bahá'u'lláh and his companions also were, at the beginning of his ministry, in Baghdad, which is in Mesopotamia, and after several exiles they ended up in 'Akká on the boundary of Syria and Palestine.

The Ottomans had caused Bahá'u'lláh to be imprisoned in the part of the province of Syria that had historically been known as the land of Palestine. Islamic Traditions state that when Christ returns he will appear in Palestine. A frequently repeated *ḥadíth* says that one of the signs of the Hour will be that 'the sun will arise from its setting-place'.[283] Bahá'ís, as previously discussed (see pp. 87–90), believe that 'sun' here refers to the spiritual sun which is the Messenger of Allah. One Bahá'í interpretation of this Tradition is that the sun of Christ which set in Palestine two thousand years ago has arisen in the same place in the person of Bahá'u'lláh.

There are many Islamic Traditions that state that the Mahdi and Christ on their return will institute a period of peace and justice. The following is part of a long *ḥadíth*. After relating points about the Dajjál and other matters similar to a Tradition given previously (concerning the actions of Christ in breaking crosses, etc.; see p. 126), it goes on to say that at the time of the return of Christ:

> Mutual hatred and rancour will disappear. The ability to injure will be removed from every injurious thing. Thus a boy will touch a snake and it will not injure him, and a girl will run from a lion and it will not harm her; and the wolf will be with the sheep, as though it is their sheep-dog. And the earth will be filled with peace, just as water fills a jug. And the word will be one, and only Allah will be worshipped, and war will lay down its burdens. (Ibn Májah)[284]

Bahá'u'lláh states that his mission is to bring peace to the world and unity to the religions (see pp. 151–60). Many of his teachings revolve around the concept of justice. Thus the above prophecy summarizes well the aims of Bahá'u'lláh's mission.

Some of the eminent Islamic scholars who met Bahá'u'lláh have written testimonies to his greatness. Thus for example, S͟hayk͟h Mahdí al-Azharí recorded the following words of Fáḍil Mawlaví about Bahá'u'lláh:

> I only met him once at which time I was able to examine all aspects of him. Seeing him was the equivalent for me of seeing half of the inhabitants of the world . . . Knowledge itself burst forth from him and wisdom and authority emanated from his environs. I learned from just one session in his presence more than I learned from years with others.[285]

Another who merely saw Bahá'u'lláh was the eminent Lebanese writer Amír Amín Arslan. He wrote:

> His appearance struck my imagination in such a way that I cannot better represent it than by evoking the image of God the Father, commanding, in his majesty, the elements of nature, in the middle of clouds.[286]

'Abdu'l-Bahá

Bahá'u'lláh established a covenant with his followers that after his passing they would turn to 'Abdu'l-Bahá as the authorized interpreter of Bahá'í scripture and the Perfect Exemplar of the Bahá'í teachings. 'Abdu'l-Bahá was born on 23 May 1844. He had accompanied his father through every stage of his exiles and had been in charge of all of Bahá'u'lláh's affairs during Bahá'u'lláh's last years in 'Akká.

'Abdu'l-Bahá exhibited great ability and had excited the admiration of many who had come into contact with him. At an age of less than 20, for example, he had composed for an Ottoman official, 'Alí Shevket Pasha, a treatise on the Holy Islamic Tradition (*ḥadíth qudsí*): 'I was a Hidden Treasure and desired to be known, therefore I created the creation in order that I might be known.' At the age of 31 he produced another work, *The Secret of Divine Civilization*, which is still much studied today and in which he gave the outline of what is needed for the progress and prosperity of societies as they emerge into the modern age. He was in contact with many of the great reformers of the Muslim world, including such leaders of the Young Ottomans movement as Namik Kemal and Bereketzade Ismail Hakki Effendi, and other reformers such as Midhat Pasha and Sayyid Jamál ad-Din 'al-Afghání'.[287] The great Islamic revivalist and scholar Muḥammad 'Abduh (1849–1905) met 'Abdu'l-Bahá in Beirut in the 1880s. The following is the text of a conversation in 1897 between 'Abduh and his student Muḥammad Rashíd Riḍá (1865–1935), another great Islamic scholar, about 'Abdu'l-Bahá, whom they call 'Abbás Effendi, the name by which 'Abdu'l-Bahá was generally known:

Riḍá: (Then I asked him about 'Abbás Effendi ['Abdu'l-Bahá]): 'I hear that he excels in religious science and in diplomacy (*as-siyásah*), and that he is wise enough to satisfy all who seek his company.' *'Abduh*: Yes, 'Abbás Effendi transcends all that. He is, in fact, a great man; he is the man to whom it is right to apply that epithet.[288]

An eminent Lebanese writer, Amír Amín Arslan, attested in 1896 to 'Abdu'l-Bahá's intelligence and his mastery of the Arabic language:

> He ['Abdu'l-Bahá] is a man of rare intelligence, and although Persian, he has a deep knowledge of our Arabic language, and I possess some Arabic letters from him which are masterpieces in style and thought . . .[289]

During the first years of his ministry 'Abdu'l-Bahá was opposed by his half-brother, who contested the leadership of the Bahá'í Faith. But owing to the fact that 'Abdu'l-Bahá's appointment was in a written document and after seeing for themselves 'Abdu'l-Bahá's superior abilities and character, the overwhelming majority of Bahá'ís followed 'Abdu'l-Bahá and rejected his half-brother's claims.

'Abdu'l-Bahá supervised the spread of the Bahá'í Faith to North America and Europe, the construction of a shrine for the Báb in Haifa on the slopes of Mount Carmel and the growth of Bahá'í literature and institutions. He travelled to Egypt where he met many of the eminent Islamic scholars and thinkers of the day. Shaykh Muḥammad Bakhít, the Muftí of Egypt, called on him and Shaykh 'Alí Yúsuf, the owner and editor of *al-Mu'ayyad* newspaper, who had been hostile towards the new religion, wrote the following in his newspaper, after meeting 'Abdu'l-Bahá:

> He is a venerable person, dignified, possessed of profound knowledge, deeply versed in theology, master of the history of Islám, and of its denominations and developments . . .

> whosoever has consorted with him has seen in him a man exceedingly well-informed, whose speech is captivating, who attracts minds and souls, who is dedicated to belief in the oneness of mankind . . . His teaching and guidance revolve round the axis of relinquishing prejudices: religious, racial, patriotic.[290]

The prominent Arabic newspaper *Al-Ahrám* on 19 January 1911 published this description of 'Abdu'l-Bahá from the pen of Shukrí Effendi:

> In regard to his morality and character, he is the pattern of dignity and perfection. He is gracious, generous, noble-minded, philanthropic, charitable and full of benevolence . . . To him all are the same, he looks upon them as part of the same family of humanity . . . This is just a short sketch of his generous qualities and I must confess my inability to do it justice. His physical appearance is medium size, white hair, penetrating eyes, smiling face and wonderful countenance, courteous, and his manner, simplicity itself, disliking any ostentation and show. He is a wise man, a philosopher and his knowledge of Turkish, Persian and Arabic is unsurpassed.
>
> He knows the history of nations and understands the causes of their rise and fall.[291]

From Egypt, 'Abdu'l-Bahá went on to travel in North America and Europe in 1911–13, before returning to Egypt and then to Haifa. He spent the years of the First World War in Palestine and died in 1921 in Haifa. At his funeral, Muslim, Christian and Jewish religious leaders paid tribute to his life, which had been devoted to bringing about peace and reconciliation. The following are the words of Muḥammad Murád, the Mufti of Haifa:

> I do not wish to exaggerate in my eulogy of this great one, for his ready and helping hand in the service of mankind

and the beautiful and wondrous story of his life, spent in doing that which is right and good, none can deny, save him whose heart is blinded . . .

O thou revered voyager! Thou hast lived greatly and hast died greatly! This great funeral procession is but a glorious proof of thy greatness in thy life and in thy death. But O, thou whom we have lost! Thou leader of men generous and benevolent! To whom shall the poor now look? Who shall care for the hungry? and the desolate, the widow and the orphan?

May the Lord inspire all thy household and thy kindred with patience in this grievous calamity, and immerse thee in the ocean of his grace and mercy! He verily, is the prayer-hearing, prayer-answering God.[292]

Shoghi Effendi and the Universal House of Justice

'Abdu'l-Bahá gave instructions in his Will and Testament that he should be succeeded as leader of the Bahá'í community and authorized interpreter of the Bahá'í scriptures by his grandson, Shoghi Effendi, to whom he gave the title Guardian of the Bahá'í Faith. This appointment is regarded by Bahá'ís as the continuation of the covenant made by Bahá'u'lláh giving authority to 'Abdu'l-Bahá.

Shoghi Effendi was born in 1897 in 'Akká and was educated in Haifa and at the American University in Beirut before going on to the University of Oxford. He was thus only 24 years of age when he became the Guardian of the Bahá'í Faith. He guided the Bahá'í community in the establishment of the Bahá'í administration (see pp. 167–9) and later in its spread to all parts of the world in the Ten Year Crusade that he instituted in 1953. He wrote many works and translated much of the scriptures of the Bahá'í Faith into English.

During Shoghi Effendi's ministry an important court case was heard in Egypt in 1925. This case was brought before the Appellate Religious Court of Beba in the province of Beni Suef in Upper Egypt, being appealed from two previous cases in

1923 and 1924. On 10 May 1925 the judge Maḥmúd 'Abdu'lláh Sa'ad, in the presence of the secretary of the Court, Shaykh Muḥammad Sayyid Aḥmad, delivered a lengthy judgement. Part of this judgement affirmed the independent nature of the Bahá'í Faith:

> All these prove definitely that the Bahá'í religion is a new religion, with an independent platform of laws and institutions peculiar to it, and show a different and contradictory belief to the beliefs and laws and commandments of Islám. Nor can we state a Bahá'í to be a Muslim, or the reverse; as we cannot say of a Buddhist or a Brahman or a Christian that he is a Muslim or the reverse.[293]

Shoghi Effendi passed away in 1957 and when the Ten Year Crusade that he had initiated finished in 1963, the Universal House of Justice was elected. The authority for this body is to be found in the writings of Bahá'u'lláh. It is now the head of the Bahá'í Faith and has continued to guide the Bahá'í community in its expansion and development.

The Bahá'í World Today

The Bahá'í world today is a community that is extremely diverse in its ethnicity, its social class composition and in the cultural and religious background of its adherents. Despite its diversity, it manages to enable the Bahá'ís to work together to pursue goals of international cooperation and development. Bahá'ís now reside in almost every country of the world and there are organized Bahá'í communities in most of these countries, except where persecution and opposition has made this impossible.

The expansion of the Bahá'í Faith takes place mainly through person-to-person contact. If anyone shows interest in learning more about the religion, he or she is often invited to an introductory meeting. There is no ritual or ceremony of conversion. If someone accepts the claims that Bahá'u'lláh has made about his station and mission, agrees to follow the Bahá'í laws, accepts the station of Bahá'u'lláh's successors, 'Abdu'l-Bahá and Shoghi Effendi, as well as the authority of the Universal House of Justice, which was ordained by Bahá'u'lláh, then that person is a Bahá'í. In order to become part of the worldwide Bahá'í community, however, it is usually necessary to register with one's local Bahá'í community. The spread of the Bahá'í Faith takes place through the movement of individual Bahá'ís to new locations. Such persons are usually self-supporting, taking up their normal occupation in their new place of residence and spreading the Bahá'í Faith among their new acquaintances.

Some idea of the growth of the Bahá'í Faith in the last half century can be gained from the fact that in 1954 there were about 200,000 Bahá'ís in the world, with 12 National Spiritual Assemblies, 708 Local Spiritual Assemblies, and some 3,117 localities where Bahá'ís resided. There are at present (2000), over five million Bahá'ís, 182 National Spiritual Assemblies, over 12,000 Local Spiritual Assemblies and over 125,000 localities where Bahá'ís reside. Bahá'í literature has been translated into some 800 languages.[294] The largest Bahá'í community is currently in India but there are also large Bahá'í communities in Southeast Asia, sub-Saharan Africa, South America and the Pacific.

In some Muslim countries, such as Iran, Iraq, Egypt and Morocco, the Bahá'í Faith has been persecuted in recent years. In other Muslim countries, such as Pakistan, Bangladesh, Malaysia and the Gambia, its existence as a separate world religion is officially recognized.

The Bahá'í community has had a close relationship with the United Nations ever since its formation. Bahá'ís do not consider the present structure and constitution of the United Nations to be ideal. Nevertheless, they consider its objectives to be close to those of the Bahá'í Faith and therefore worthy of support. Over the last few decades the Bahá'í International

Community has been one of the most active of the non-governmental organizations at the United Nations. It has had consultative status with some of its subsidiary organizations such as ECOSOC and UNICEF and has also had a significant presence at all of the major United Nations conferences.

Although several attempts were made as early as the closing decades of the 19th century in the Iranian Bahá'í community to begin projects for social development, these did not flourish owing to the atmosphere of repression against the Bahá'í community. The numerous schools started by the Iranian Bahá'ís, for example, were all closed in 1934 on the orders of the government. In recent decades, which have seen the emergence of large Bahá'í communities in the poorer parts of the world, there has been a renewed impetus towards social and economic development plans. These plans are usually developed by the local communities with some assistance from the national level. They cover such areas as education and literacy, health, agriculture, community development and capacity-building.

9

Some Further Considerations

In this final chapter some of the objections that a few Muslim scholars have raised against the Bahá'í Faith will be considered. In the second part of the chapter some historical points will be discussed and some Bahá'í interpretations of a few further verses of the Qur'án will be given.

The Sovereignty and Victories of the Mahdi

The Islamic Traditions (*ḥadí<u>th</u>s*) seem to indicate that the Mahdi and also Christ on his return would lead armies of Muslims to a great victory over their enemies.[295] It would appear that no such event happened in the time of the Báb and Bahá'u'lláh; indeed, the Báb was even executed. And so, it is asked, how can these prophecies be said to be have been fulfilled in the Bahá'í Faith? This matter is discussed at length in the Bahá'í scriptures[296] and only a brief account of it will be given here.

Firstly, the Bahá'í scriptures state that 'the terms sovereignty, wealth, life, death, judgement and resurrection, spoken of by the scriptures of old, are not what this generation hath conceived and vainly imagined'.[297] We have seen in other chapters of this book (see pp. 87–111) that the Bahá'í scriptures have interpreted many of the words and phrases that refer to the Day of Judgement and Resurrection as referring to spiritual realities rather than physical ones: thus the 'sun being darkened' represents the loss of power and spiritual strength of religion and 'the stars falling' or 'failing to give their light' refers to the loss of true spiritual leadership among the religious leaders, while the 'earth shaking' refers to the hearts of the believers being in turmoil (see pp. 87–90); by 'resurrection' is meant the spiritual raising up of the spiritually dead to life (pp. 103–8). It is true that physical battles also occurred and the Muslim world was badly affected by the aggression against it by imperialist forces (see pp. 125, 187) but these are not the main meaning of these prophecies. What affected the Muslim world to a much greater extent and in a more widespread manner was the spiritual turmoil and distress that occurred.

This spiritual interpretation of prophecies also refers to those passages in the Qur'án and the Traditions that refer to the battles that are to be fought by the Mahdi and the returned Christ, the victories that they will win and the sovereignty that will be theirs. These are spiritual battles, spiritual victories and a spiritual sovereignty. Regarding this spiritual sovereignty, the Bahá'í scriptures explain that:

> . . . by sovereignty is meant that sovereignty which in every dispensation resideth within, and is exercised by, the person of the Manifestation, the Day-star of Truth. That sovereignty is the spiritual ascendancy which He exerciseth to the fullest degree over all that is in heaven and on earth, and which in due time revealeth itself to the world in direct proportion to its capacity and spiritual receptiveness, even as the sovereignty of Muḥammad, the Messenger of God, is today apparent and manifest amongst the people.[298]

The Bahá'í scriptures also remind us that this sovereignty has been ascribed to the Messenger of God in every dispensation and is nothing to do with whether or not he has achieved an earthly sovereignty.

> This sovereignty, however, is not the sovereignty which the minds of men have falsely imagined. Moreover, the Prophets of old, each and every one, whenever announcing to the people of their day the advent of the coming Revelation, have invariably and specifically referred to that sovereignty with which the promised Manifestation must needs be invested. This is attested by the records of the scriptures of the past . . . the attribute of sovereignty and all other names and attributes of God have been and will ever be vouchsafed unto all the Manifestations of God . . . inasmuch as these Manifestations, as it hath already been explained, are the Embodiments of the attributes of God, the Invisible, and the Revealers of the divine mysteries.[299]

The Qur'án is also quite clear that earthly sovereignty is not a proof of having been sent by Allah. Indeed, it expressly states that some of those sent by Allah have been killed while others persecuted (2:87, 91). The Bahá'í scriptures give the example of the Prophet Muḥammad (blessings and peace be upon him). They remind us how in the early part of Muḥammad's ministry he had been persecuted and humiliated.

> You are well aware of what befell His [Muḥammad's] Faith in the early days of His dispensation. What woeful sufferings did the hand of the infidel and erring, the divines of that age and their associates, inflict upon that spiritual Essence, that most pure and holy Being! How abundant the thorns and briars which they have strewn over His path! It is evident that wretched generation, in their wicked and satanic fancy, regarded every injury to that immortal Being as a means to the attainment of an abiding felicity; inasmuch as the recognized divines of that age, such as 'Abdu'lláh-i-Ubayy, Abú-'Ámir, the hermit, Ka'b-Ibn-i-As͟hraf, and Naḍr-Ibn-i-Ḥárit͟h, all treated Him as an impostor, and pronounced Him a lunatic and a calumniator . . .
>
> Consider, how great is the change today! Behold, how many are the Sovereigns who bow the knee before His name! How numerous the nations and kingdoms who have sought

the shelter of His shadow, who bear allegiance to His Faith, and pride themselves therein! From the pulpit-top there ascendeth today the words of praise which, in utter lowliness, glorify His blessed name; and from the heights of minarets there resoundeth the call that summoneth the concourse of His people to adore Him . . . Such is His earthly sovereignty, the evidences of which thou dost on every side behold. This sovereignty must needs be revealed and established either in the lifetime of every Manifestation of God or after His ascension unto His true habitation in the realms above.[300]

Another example of the power and sovereignty of Muḥammad is the power of the Word of Allah that he uttered:

The following is an evidence of the sovereignty exercised by Muḥammad, the Day-star of Truth. Hast thou not heard how with one single verse He hath sundered light from darkness, the righteous from the ungodly, and the believing from the infidel? . . . These revealed words were a blessing to the righteous who on hearing them exclaimed: 'O God our Lord, we have heard, and obeyed.' They were a curse to the people of iniquity who, on hearing them affirmed: 'We have heard and rebelled.' Those words, sharp as the sword of God, have separated the faithful from the infidel, and severed father from son . . .

Our purpose in setting forth these truths hath been to demonstrate the sovereignty of Him Who is the King of kings. Be fair: Is this sovereignty which, through the utterance of one Word, hath manifested such pervading influence, ascendancy, and awful majesty, is this sovereignty superior, or is the worldly dominion of these kings of the earth who, despite their solicitude for their subjects and their help of the poor, are assured only of an outward and fleeting allegiance, while in the hearts of men they inspire neither affection nor respect? Hath not that sovereignty, through the potency of one word, subdued, quickened, and revitalized the whole world? What! Can the lowly dust compare with Him Who is the Lord of Lords?[301]

This sovereignty of the Messengers of Allah is not something which they have at one time and not at another. It is an essential part of their nature that is with them always. At times, however, it may be hidden from certain human beings who lack the discernment to see it.

> That spiritual ascendancy, however, which is primarily intended, resideth within, and revolveth around Them from eternity even unto eternity. It can never for a moment be divorced from Them. Its dominion hath encompassed all that is in heaven and on earth.[302]

Another example is that of Jesus Christ. The Jews were expecting their Messiah to be a military leader who would lead them to victory against the Romans. Jesus came as a lowly carpenter's son and made no attempt to gain power or military victory. And so the majority of Jews rejected him for the same reason that some Muslims now object to the Báb and Bahá'u-'lláh; where, they asked, was the sovereignty and the victory that is so clearly described in their prophecies?

Thus the sovereignty and the mighty battles and victories that are described in the prophecies related to the Mahdi and the Return of Christ in the Islamic Traditions relate not to physical events but to spiritual realities. They refer to a spiritual sovereignty that exceeds all worldly might and power and to spiritual battles and victories won over the powers of darkness. In the same way that Christ and Muḥammad stood firm against the persecutions and humiliations heaped upon them and eventually their Cause won through and they were rendered victorious, so the Báb and Bahá'u'lláh persevered in the face of persecution and exile and eventually prevailed against their enemies.

One further point worth making is that it is not correct to say that the Islamic Traditions only show the Mahdi and the returned Christ as being victorious over their opponents. They also relate the opposition that the Muslim *'ulamá* will put up against the Mahdi and the returned Christ[303] and the martyrdom of many of their followers.[304] And this of course is what happened with the coming of the Báb and Bahá'u'lláh (see chapter 8).

Consensus (*Ijmá'*) as Evidence

Many Muslim writers have declared that Bahá'u'lláh's claim to be a Messenger of Allah after Muḥammad is against the consensus (*ijmá'*) of the Islamic community. Since there are some Traditions that state that the Muslim community will not agree about something that is erroneous,[305] this is considered to be a proof against Bahá'u'lláh and the Bahá'í Faith. It is necessary to study carefully what the uses of consensus (*ijmá'*) are and what its limitations are. While it may be regarded as a proof in relation to the rituals and practices of Islam (the *Sharí'ah*), there is much evidence in the Qur'án and in the Traditions that consensus (*ijmá'*) cannot be regarded as a proof or evidence when it comes to the matter of deciding upon the claims of Bahá'u'lláh.

In the first place, if consensus (*ijmá'*) was a proof, then Muḥammad himself must be considered in error as, during Muḥammad's lifetime, there was a clear *ijmá'* among Jews and Christians that Muḥammad was a false prophet. Both Jews and Christians have a consensus among themselves that theirs is the last religion from Allah before the Day of Judgement and no other revelation is needed.

Secondly, the Qur'án clearly states that in the matter of deciding what is true religion and what is not, one must not rely on the consensus of either one's family or the elders of one's community:

> When it is said to them: 'Follow what Allah hath revealed': they say: 'Nay! we shall follow the ways of our fathers.' What! even though their fathers were void of wisdom and guidance? (2:170)

> And they would say: 'Our Lord! We obeyed our chiefs and our great ones and they misled us as to the (right) path. Our Lord! give them double Penalty and curse them with a very great Curse!' (33:67–8)

Only what one has come to know as a result of one's own enquiry will be acceptable before Allah:

> And pursue not that of which thou hast no knowledge; for every act of hearing or of seeing or of (feeling in) the heart will be enquired into (on the Day of Reckoning). (17:36)

These verses apply as much to Muslims today as they did to those whom Muḥammad addressed over a thousand years ago. The Qur'án explicitly condemns the idea of consensus (*ijmá'*) when applied to such matters. Indeed it proclaims that the majority of the people are usually wrong:

> Wert thou to follow the common run of those on earth, they will lead thee away from the Way of Allah. They follow nothing but conjecture: they do nothing but lie. (6:116)

Further evidence that consensus (*ijmá'*) is not a reliable guide to the truth comes from the fact that, as pointed out in previous chapters, according to reliable Traditions, only one group of Muslims is on the path of truth and all the rest are in error:

> A party of my people will be aided upon the right path, and those who oppose them shall not harm them, until the Cause of Allah shall come. (Ibn Májah)[306]

In summary, then, consensus is not a valid basis on which to decide the truth of Bahá'u'lláh's claim to be a new Messenger of Allah. In this matter the Qur'án requires every individual to investigate the truth for himself or herself. No excuse for avoiding this responsibility is acceptable.

Miracles

There are many stories circulating in the Muslim community about the miracles performed by the Prophet Muḥammad. It has been suggested by some Muslims that since Bahá'ís claim that the Báb and Bahá'u'lláh are also Messengers of Allah, then it should also be possible to produce evidence of miracles they performed.

The Bahá'ís answer this by making several points. First, it should be noted that there is no basis in Allah's Word, the Qur'án, for raising this as an issue. Nowhere in the Qur'án does Allah ask people to believe in Muḥammad because of a miracle that he produced. Indeed, the Qur'án does not really ascribe any miracles to Muḥammad. Most of the miracles that are related about him among Muslims are not to be found in the Qur'án nor indeed in the more reliable and authentic histories of his life.

The Qur'án states that miracles have never been a proof that has convinced peoples of the past of the mission of a Messenger of Allah. In the following translations from the Qur'án, it should be remembered that the word *áyah* (plural *áyát*) in Arabic can be translated as 'miracle', 'sign' or 'verse' (see Yusuf Ali's comment on this point on pp. 152–3). Therefore wherever the word 'sign' appears in the following translations, it could equally well be translated as 'miracle'. One example of the uselessness of miracles that is given in the Qur'án is provided by Moses. Despite the numerous miracles shown to Pharaoh, he still did not believe in Moses' mission:

> 'Now put thy hand into thy bosom, and it will come forth white without stain (or harm): (these are) among the nine Signs (thou wilt take) to Pharaoh and his people: for they are a people rebellious in transgression.' But when Our Signs came to them that should have opened their eyes they said: 'This is sorcery manifest!' And they rejected those Signs in iniquity and arrogance . . . (27:12–14)

Even the people of Israel were not convinced by the miracles of Moses and went on to worship the golden calf. Allah reminds Muḥammad of this fact when the Jews asked him for a miracle, to make a book descend from heaven:

> The People of the Book ask thee to cause a book to descend to them from heaven: indeed they asked Moses for an even greater (miracle), for they said: 'Show us Allah in public,' but they were dazed for their presumption, with thunder and lightning. Yet they worshipped the calf even after Clear Signs had come to them; even so We forgave them; and gave Moses manifest proofs of authority. (4:153)

Not only does the Qur'án refrain from using miracles as proof of Muḥammad's mission, it even states that when Muḥammad was asked by the people for a miracle, he was instructed to refuse this request and to point out that this was a useless request since previous Messengers of Allah had come with miracles and had been rejected by the people.

> They (also) said: 'Allah took our promise not to believe in a Messenger unless He showed us a sacrifice consumed by fire (from heaven).' Say: 'There came to you Messengers before me, with Clear Signs and even with what ye ask for: why then did ye slay them, if ye speak the truth?' (3:183)

> But (now), when the Truth has come to them from Ourselves, they say, 'Why are not (Signs) sent to him like those which were sent to Moses?' Do they not then reject (the Signs) which were formerly sent to Moses? They say: 'Two kinds of sorcery, each assisting the other!' And they say: 'For us, we reject all (such things)!' (28:48)

Muḥammad is told in the Qur'án that even if he had been sent with miracles, the people would have treated him in the same way as previous Messengers of Allah and would have called him a magician or trickster as they had called Moses (see above):

> Verily We have coined for mankind in the Qur'án all kinds of similitudes; and indeed if thou camest unto them with a miracle, those who disbelieve would verily exclaim: 'Ye are but tricksters!' (30:58)[307]

> They swear their strongest oaths by Allah, that if a (special) Sign [miracle] came to them, by it they would believe. Say: 'Certainly (all) signs are in the power of Allah: but what will make you (Muslims) realize that even if (special) signs came, they will not believe?' (6:109)

It is stated in the Qur'án that because earlier peoples had rejected the Messengers of the past despite the miracles that had been performed, Allah had sent Muḥammad without any accompanying miracles:

> And We refrain from sending the Signs [miracles], only because the men of former generations treated them as false: We sent the She-camel to the Thamúd to open their eyes, but they treated her wrongfully. (17:59)

That Allah only gave Muḥammad the revelation of the Qur'án as proof of his prophethood and not miracles is also confirmed in the Traditions. The following is from the *Saḥíḥ* of al-Bukhárí:

> Narrated Abú Hurayra: The Prophet said, 'Every Prophet was given miracles because of which people believed, but what I have been given is Divine Inspiration which Allah has revealed to me. So I hope that my followers will outnumber the followers of the other Prophets on the Day of Resurrection.'[308]

In view of these verses of the Qur'án and the above Tradition, it is surprising that some Muslims cling to miracles as necessary proofs of a Messenger of Allah. According to the Qur'án, when people came to Muḥammad asking for miracles, he was told to direct them to the Qur'án itself, wherein was the true miracle of Allah's guidance:

> Yet they say: 'Why are not Signs [miracles] sent down to him from his Lord?' Say: 'The Signs are indeed with Allah: and I am indeed a clear Warner.' And is it not enough for them that We have sent down to thee the Book which is rehearsed to them? Verily in it is Mercy and a Reminder to those who believe. (29:50–1)

As noted above, in the Arabic of the Qur'án the same word *áyah* is used for 'miracle', 'sign' and 'verse' and thus no distinction is made between the concept of a 'miracle' and the concept of a 'verse' of the Qur'án. For the Qur'án, therefore, proofs are not to be found in miracles but rather in the scriptures themselves. It is ridiculous for people to pray for divine guidance and then, when that is sent to them in the form of scriptures, to ask for a miracle:

> And they say: If only he would bring us a miracle from his Lord! Hath there not come unto them the proof of what is in the former Scriptures? And if We had destroyed them with some punishment before it, they would assuredly have said: Our Lord! If only Thou hadst sent unto us a Messenger, so that we might have followed Thy revelations before we were (thus) humbled and disgraced! Say: Each is awaiting; so await ye! Ye will come to know who are the owners of the path of equity, and who is right.' (20:133–5)[309]

The Bahá'í scriptures take the same attitude to miracles as the Qur'án does. They argue that the proof of miracles is not relevant to the claim made by the Messenger of Allah and that to wish for them is really only a measure of the perversity of the people.

> The people derisively observed saying: 'Work thou another miracle, and give us another sign!' One would say: 'Make

> now a part of the heaven to fall down upon us' [Qur'án 26:187]; and another: 'If this be the very truth from before Thee, rain down stones upon us from heaven.' [Qur'án 8:32] Even as the people of Israel, in the time of Moses, bartered away the bread of heaven for the sordid things of the earth, these people, likewise, sought to exchange the divinely-revealed verses for their foul, their vile, and idle desires. In like manner, thou beholdest in this day that although spiritual sustenance hath descended from the heaven of divine mercy . . . yet these people, ravenous as the dogs, have gathered around carrion, and contented themselves with the stagnant waters of a briny lake. Gracious God! how strange the way of this people! They clamour for guidance, although the standards of Him Who guideth all things are already hoisted. They cleave to the obscure intricacies of knowledge, when He, Who is the Object of all knowledge, shineth as the sun. They see the sun with their own eyes, and yet question that brilliant Orb as to the proof of its light. They behold the vernal showers descending upon them, and yet seek an evidence of that bounty. The proof of the sun is the light thereof, which shineth and envelopeth all things. The evidence of the shower is the bounty thereof, which reneweth and investeth the world with the mantle of life. Yea, the blind can perceive naught from the sun except its heat, and the arid soil hath no share of the showers of mercy. 'Marvel not if in the Qur'án the unbeliever perceiveth naught but the trace of letters, for in the sun, the blind findeth naught but heat.'[310]

It should be noted, however, that although the Bahá'í scriptures discount miracles as being proof of the station of the Messenger of Allah, there are numerous accounts of various miracles that occurred during the lifetimes of the Báb and Bahá'u'lláh. Perhaps the most well-known of these is the events that happened at the martyrdom of the Báb in 1850 (see pp. 196–7). Bahá'u'lláh, moreover, on at least two occasions publicly announced that he would perform any miracle requested of him by the Islamic *'ulamá* provided they first agreed among themselves what it should be and also agreed that if Bahá'u'lláh performed this, they would no longer oppose him. The first occasion was in Baghdad (see pp. 201–2). The second occasion was in Bahá'u'lláh's letter to Náṣir ad-Dín Sháh of Iran, which was delivered to the Shah by a young Bahá'í, named Badí'. 'Abdu'l-Bahá, the son of Bahá'u'lláh describes Bahá'u'lláh's challenge thus:

> If we carefully examine the text of the Torah, we see that the Divine Manifestation never said to those who denied Him, 'Whatever miracle you desire, I am ready to perform, and I will submit to whatever test you propose.' But in the Epistle to the Sháh, Bahá'u'lláh said clearly, 'Gather the *'ulamá*, and summon Me, that the evidences and proofs may be established.'[311]

On both occasions the *'ulamá*, realizing that they would be compelled to acknowledge Bahá'u'lláh if he succeeded, refused to agree upon a miracle. This shows how useless miracles are as proof. Even were a Messenger of Allah to perform a miracle, the crowds would come back to demand a more difficult one or would ascribe it to satanic sorcery. Miracles are, moreover, only evidence to those who witness them. They are of no value to those who are absent or who are born to later generations and thus have no way of verifying what occurred. A miracle is no evidence at all to anyone not present. Even for those present it is of questionable value (as the above verses from the Qur'án demonstrate); after all, great wonders are also related of the great magicians of the past.[312]

The Correctness and Form of Bahá'u'lláh's Writings

Since the Qur'án states that the greatest miracle produced by the Prophet Muḥammad was the Qur'án itself, some Muslims have argued that the main miracle of the Qur'án is the fact that its Arabic is of such eloquence and stylistic excellence (*balághah*) and of such marvellous literary and grammatical correctness (*faṣáḥah*) that it is not humanly possible to produce anything like it. They have based this concept of the inimitability of the Qur'án (*i'jáz al-Qur'án*) on verses such as the following:

> Say: If the whole of mankind and Jinns were to gather together to produce the like of this Qur'án, they could not produce the like thereof, even if they backed up each other with help and support. (17:88)

Following on from this, one of the objections that some Muslims raise to the truth of the Bahá'í Faith revolves around the correctness of the Arabic in the Bahá'í scriptures. They have examined the scriptures revealed by Bahá'u'lláh and the Báb and have declared that since they have detected grammatical errors in these texts, they could not be divine revelation. They argue that the Allah who produced the Qur'án would not produce works that have errors in them.

The Bahá'ís respond to this objection in several ways. First Bahá'ís point out that there is much evidence that the meaning ascribed to the above verse may not be correct; in other words, that the inimitability implied in the above verse may not refer to the Qur'án's eloquence and rhetorical style. Indeed, there are several indications in the text of the Qur'án itself that this was not the meaning that was intended by this verse. Nowhere in the Qur'án itself does it state that its inimitability is due to its eloquence and rhetorical style. The Qur'án, in fact, implies and the histories confirm that Muḥammad's opponents, among whom were several, such as Ka'b ibn Zuhayr and Ka'b ibn Ashraf, who were orators and poets, did not find the Qur'án to be of such marvellous eloquence that they could not produce anything like it. Thus, for example, we find Muḥammad's opponents raising the following objection to the text of the Qur'án:

> When Our Signs are rehearsed to them, they say: 'We have heard this (before): if we wished, we could say (words) like these: these are nothing but tales of the ancients.' (8:31)

As the above verse indicates and the Muslim histories record, opponents of Muḥammad, on several occasions, described the Qur'án as being merely mediocre poetry and produced verses that they claimed surpassed it.[313] Indeed, since the time of Muḥammad, there have been many prominent figures in Arab literature who have been Christians and denied that the Qur'án is of miraculous eloquence. Additionally, Christian Arab writers have produced lists of grammatical errors in the Qur'án.[314] Thus Christian Arabs have made exactly the same sort of accusations about the Arabic of the Qur'án that some Muslim scholars have made about the Arabic of the Bahá'í scriptures.

In any case, Bahá'ís consider that this line of argument and counter-argument is erroneous and ill-conceived in that it misses the point of the inimitability of the Qur'án. What, they ask, would be the point of the eloquence and rhetorical excellence of the Arabic of the Qur'án being a proof for the people when only a small proportion of the people of the world understand Arabic sufficiently to be able to judge such a proof? Not even all Arabs would be able to judge such a matter but only such as were educated in literature. If this were to be a proof of the truth of the Qur'án, then the majority of people would have no choice but to follow the opinion of others rather than to judge for themselves and following the opinions of others is not permissible in matters of faith, according to the Qur'án.[315] Even then it would not be a decisive proof, since eloquence and style are matters of taste and people will differ on such matters. Thus we find well-qualified Christian writers differing with Muslims over the eloquence of the Qur'án and well-qualified Bahá'í scholars differing with Muslims over the eloquence of the Bahá'í scriptures. Furthermore, if the eloquence of the Qur'án were the indisputable proof of the Qur'án, then why is it that we find, as noted above, that in the time of Muḥammad those who were masters of eloquence and rhetoric rejected the Qur'án, while those who were illiterate or foreigners with no appreciation of Arabic, such as Bilál, Salmán and Abú Dharr, accepted it.

Bahá'ís consider that if we look carefully at the text of the Qur'án, we can discover the true meaning of the inimitability of this holy book. On one occasion, when Muḥammad was being instructed in the Qur'án to throw down a challenge to his opponents to produce a work comparable to the Qur'án, the following was stated:

> Say (unto them, O Muḥammad): Then bring a Scripture from the presence of Allah that giveth clearer guidance (*ahdá*) than these two (that) I may follow it, if ye are truthful. (28:49)[316]

It can be seen that the criterion here for the challenge of bringing of a book that is better than the Qur'án is that is should be better or clearer in the guidance that it gives (*ahdá*) than the Qur'án; it does not say that it should be more eloquent in language (*afsáḥ*). There are numerous similar passages that could be cited in this connection in the Qur'án.[317] This then is the criterion on which the Qur'án's inimitability should be judged: its ability to guide humanity to the truth, to Allah and to salvation, its ability to inspire people with devotion and to constrain people to act in ways that are moral and righteous. This, Bahá'ís believe, is the true meaning of the inimitability of the Qur'án (*i'jáz al-Qur'án*). This is a proof that all can judge for themselves. Even those who are opposed to Islam cannot deny that the Qur'án has inspired great devotion in its followers.

Bahá'u'lláh contends that such criteria as eloquence and grammatical correctness have never been the proofs or standards of the divine scriptures. The holy books and the divine teachings have always been accessible to all classes of people, even the uneducated and poor. Indeed, if we examine religious history, we can see that the earliest followers of Jesus were not the educated Jewish religious leaders but rather illiterate fishermen; similarly in the time of Muḥammad, most of his earliest followers were not to be found among the religious leaders and educated men of Mecca and Medina but among the uneducated and the slaves. Bahá'u'lláh makes this point:

> Heed not the idle contention of those who maintain that the Book and verses thereof can never be a testimony unto the common people, inasmuch as they neither grasp their meaning nor appreciate their value. And yet, the unfailing testimony of God to both the East and the West is none other than the Qur'án. Were it beyond the comprehension of men, how could it have been declared as a universal testimony unto all people? . . .
>
> Such contention is utterly fallacious and inadmissible. It is actuated solely by arrogance and pride. Its motive is to lead the people astray from the Riḍván [Paradise] of divine good-pleasure and to tighten the reins of their authority over the people. And yet, in the sight of God, these common people are infinitely superior and exalted above their religious leaders who have turned away from the one true God. The understanding of His words and the comprehension of the utterances of the Birds of Heaven are in no wise dependent upon human learning. They depend solely upon purity of heart, chastity of soul, and freedom of spirit.[318]

Thus when Muslim scholars have objected to the Arabic of both the Báb and Bahá'u'lláh, claiming that these have grammatical errors in them, they are repeating the mistake of those learned Arabs, such as Ka'b ibn Zuhayr and Ka'b ibn A<u>sh</u>raf, who objected to the Arabic of the Qur'án. They are also contradicting the testimonies of many Arab scholars, poets and writers who met Bahá'u'lláh or read his writings and praised him greatly. (For some examples, see pp. 207–8.)[319] Bahá'ís claim that the Bahá'í scriptures pass both the test of content and of form. Those who read these scriptures impartially find that they contain guidance that is beyond anything that human beings can give (see chapters 2, 5, 6 and 7), while the words are also of great eloquence (see pp. 243–5).

Some Muslim scholars have also claimed that the Bahá'í scriptures cannot be of the same status as the Qur'án since the Qur'án is the Word of Allah while the scriptures revealed by Bahá'u'lláh appear to be Bahá'u'lláh's own words. A more thorough study of both the Qur'án and the Bahá'í scriptures demonstrates, however, that the Messenger of Allah, whether in the Qur'án or in the Bahá'í scriptures, sometimes reveals words that appear to be Allah Himself speaking to humanity and sometimes reveals words that appear to be his own.

The following are some words from the Qur'án and from the Bahá'í scriptures where the direct words of Allah Himself are revealed:

> So We opened the gates of heaven with water pouring forth. And We caused the earth to gush forth with springs. So the waters met (and rose) to the extent decreed. But We bore him [Noah] on an (Ark) made of broad planks and caulked with palm-fibre . . . But how (terrible) was My Penalty and My Warning? And We have indeed made the Qur'án easy to understand and remember: then is there any that will receive admonition? (Qur'án 54:11–13, 16–17)

> O Son of Man! Veiled in My immemorial being and in the ancient eternity of My essence, I knew My love for thee; therefore I created thee, have engraved on thee Mine image and revealed to thee My beauty. (Bahá'u'lláh)

> O Son of Man! I loved thy creation, hence I created thee. Wherefore, do thou love Me, that I may name thy name and fill thy soul with the spirit of life. (Bahá'u'lláh)[320]

There are also passages in both the Qur'án and the Bahá'í scriptures which are the words of the Messenger of Allah, Muḥammad or Bahá'u'lláh.

> For me, I have been commanded to serve the Lord of this City, Him Who has sanctified it and to Whom (belong) all things: and I am commanded to be of those who bow in Islam to Allah's Will . . . (Qur'án 27:91)

> I was but a man like others, asleep upon My couch, when lo, the breezes of the All-Glorious were wafted over Me, and taught Me the knowledge of all that hath been. This thing is not from Me, but from One Who is Almighty and All-Knowing. (Bahá'u'lláh)[321]

And sometimes the words revealed by these Messengers is intended by them to be recited by us as prayers or words to address Allah.

> In the name of Allah, Most Gracious, Most Merciful. Praise be to Allah, the Cherisher and Sustainer of the Worlds; Most Gracious, Most Merciful; Master of the Day of Judgement. Thee do we worship, and Thine aid we seek. Show us the straight way, the way of those on whom Thou hast bestowed Thy Grace, Those whose (portion) is not wrath and who go not astray. (Qur'án 1:1–7)

> O my God! O my God! Unite the hearts of Thy servants, and reveal to them Thy great purpose. May they follow Thy commandments and abide in Thy law. Help them, O God, in their endeavour, and grant them strength to serve Thee. O God! Leave them not to themselves, but guide their steps by the light of Thy knowledge, and cheer their hearts by Thy love. Verily, Thou art their Helper and their Lord. (Bahá'u'lláh)[322]

Forgery and History

Within the Islamic world, a number of false statements have been made about the origins and history of the Bahá'í Faith. As stated in the Introduction to this book, because Bahá'ís have not had a chance to publicly demonstrate the falsity of these accounts, they have been accepted by Muslims as true and are even incorporated into official statements as though they were the undoubted truth. Although these points are not strictly concerned with the subject-matter of this book, nevertheless, because these historical errors have become part of the standard account believed by Muslims about the Bahá'í Faith, it is not inappropriate to deal with them here.

The nature of some of these accusations and forgeries is no better demonstrated than the assertion in many works (for example in English: *Bahaism: its origins and its role,* published by the Revolutionary Government of Iran in the early 1980s) that the Bábí and Bahá'í Faiths were started by both the British and Russian governments. The authors of such works are apparently unaware that the British and Russian governments were deadly enemies in Iran throughout the whole of the 19th century. They were vying with each other to prevent the spread of the other's influence into areas that they each considered vital to their national interests. The British wanted to prevent Russia from spreading its influence southward and thus threatening British India, while the Russians were wary of any extension of British influence northwards into the areas of Caucasia and Central Asia which they were conquering and subjugating. Throughout the Middle East, Britain and Russia kept up this enmity during the whole of the 19th century, coming to a head in the Crimean War of 1853–6. The idea that two such bitter rivals and enemies would join together to create the Bábí and Bahá'í Faiths could only have been the creation of people who knew nothing of history.

A short work such as this cannot deal at any length with all of the numerous historical allegations that have been made in various publications. A single example of the sort of forgery and falsification that has gone on must suffice. Among the documents that is most frequently cited as supporting evidence for the allegations that are made is what is known as the *Political Confessions of Prince Dolgoruki* (*I'tirafát Siyásí-yi Kinyáz*

Dolgoruki). It is certainly true that Dolgoruki was the Russian Minister in Iran in the 1840s but the location of the original manuscript on which this book is based has never been stated nor has it ever been published in Russian. The first that anyone knew of such a work was its publication in Persian at Mashhad in 1943. Shortly after its first publication, it was republished in Tehran with some of the more glaring historical errors corrected. Despite this attempt to cover up its origins, the book still contains errors of fact on almost every page. A few of these are cited here as examples.

Regarding the Báb, it is stated in the Khurasan edition of the book that when he advanced his claims, the Báb's father threw him out of the house. Realizing that this was an error, since the Báb's father is well-known to have died when the Báb was only a child, the Tehran edition corrects this to saying that the Báb's family threw him out. Even this correction is, however, erroneous for none of the Báb's family opposed him (even though most of them did not at that time become believers in him) and the uncle who brought him up even gave his life as a martyr in the Cause of the Báb.

With regard to Bahá'u'lláh, Dolgoruki is given to say that for a few years after his arrival in Tehran, he used to attend evening gatherings at the home of Ḥakím Aḥmad Gílání and among his companions at those gatherings were Bahá'u'lláh and his half-brother Azal, who were servants of Áqá Khán Núrí. This account is self-evidently erroneous on several counts. First, the book itself states elsewhere that Ḥakím Aḥmad Gílání died in 1251/1835, three years before Dolgoruki's arrival in Tehran, according to the Khurasan edition. Second, Bahá'u'lláh and Azal as sons of a minister and members of the nobility would never have been servants of Áqá Khán Núrí. Third, at the suggested date (i.e. before the death of Gílání in 1835), Bahá'u'lláh would have been 17 years of age but Azal would only have been a child of five – hardly the sort of ages that would make them suitable evening companions for senior statesmen such as Gílání and

Dolgoruki. Indeed the book is very confused about the age and status of Bahá'u'lláh, the Khurasan edition describing him as a Bedouin and the Tehran edition describing him at this time as 'an old man'. The statement in the Khurasan edition that Dolgoruki provided money for Bahá'u'lláh to build a house in 'Akká is changed to a house in Edirne in the Tehran edition, no doubt when someone realized that Dolgoruki was in fact dead by the time that Bahá'u'lláh was in 'Akká.

Far more seriously awry are the historical details about Dolgoruki himself. The book gives the inherently improbable story that Dolgoruki first came to Iran in 1838 (Khurasan edition) or 1834 (Tehran edition), converted to Islam and set out for Karbalá to study the Islamic sciences at a religious college. For some reason that is not explained in the book, Dolgoruki now turns against Islam and meets the Báb, whom he instigates to put forward his claim as a way of ruining both Iran and Islam. It is stated that Dolgoruki not only assisted the Báb in his ministry but that later he was responsible for assisting Bahá'u'lláh. It is even claimed that the writings of Bahá'u'lláh were composed by the Foreign Ministry in Russia and then sent to Bahá'u'lláh in Baghdad, Edirne and 'Akká.

Unfortunately for those who concocted this forgery, they made a rather bad choice in the person whom they chose as the purported author of their work. For Prince Dolgoruki was a career diplomat from one of the most prominent families in Russia. There is an entry for him in the authoritative Russian biographical dictionary, *Russkii Biograficheski Slovar* (vol. 6, St Petersburg, 1905), and for those who do not read Russian, his diplomatic career can be followed by consulting the successive editions of almanacs and yearbooks such as the *Almanach de Gotha*. These show that during the years that the forged *Political Confessions* would have him in Iran and Karbalá, converting to Islam and first contacting the Báb, the real Dolgoruki was at several diplomatic posts in Europe (the Hague 1832–7, Naples 1837–42 and Istanbul 1842–5). Dolgoruki was the Russian Minister in Iran from 1845 to 1854 but, unfortunately for the authors of this forged work, a Russian scholar, Mikhail S. Ivanov, researched the Russian diplomatic reports of Dolgoruki and published these as an addendum to a book on the Bábís that he wrote (*Babidskie vostaniya v Irani, 1848–52*, Moscow, 1939). Ivanov, who was a communist scholar and therefore himself not friendly to the Bábí and Bahá'í Faiths, shows in the dispatches that he published that Dolgoruki was not even aware of the Bábí movement until about 1847, three years after it started. Even then, the information that he sends to the Russian Foreign ministry is incomplete and inaccurate.[323] If anything, these dispatches show Dolgoruki to have been antagonistic to the Báb. Fearing that a spread of the Bábí movement into Caucasia would disrupt the newly-established hold that Russia had over those regions, he insisted that the Báb be moved away from Mákú on the Russian border.[324] Since Dolgoruki retired from the Russian diplomatic service in 1854 and died in 1867, it was clearly impossible for him to have later been helping Bahá'u'lláh in the ways that are described above.

Several distinguished Iranian historians and academics who are not Bahá'ís have recorded their belief that these memoirs are a forgery. 'Abbás Iqbál, Professor of History at the University of Tehran, in the well-known journal of history and literature *Yádgár*, stated:

> Concerning the matter of Prince Dolgoruki, the truth of the matter is that this is a complete fabrication and the work of some forgers. Apart from the fact that no one knew of the existence of such a document until now, it contains so many ridiculous historical errors that these are in themselves sufficient to refute this work.[325]

A similar statement was made by Mujtabá Mínuví, Professor in the College of Divinity and Islamic Sciences of the University of Tehran, writing in the journal *Ráhnimá-yi Kitáb*: 'I am certain that these memoirs attributed to Dolgoruki are forged.'[326] Even the famous Aḥmad Kasraví of Tabriz, although he was an enemy of the Bahá'í Faith and wrote a book, *Bahá'í-garí*, attacking it, stated that these *Political Confessions* were a forgery and he even states that he knew the identity of the forger.[327]

One would have thought that with all of this evidence against this book, it would have quietly slipped into oblivion. But the fact that the Bahá'ís are unable to put these points publicly and the number of non-Bahá'ís daring to state the truth about this work is very small, the work has lived on and continues to be used as supporting evidence for various attacks on the Bahá'í Faith up to the present day.

In recent years, many assertions have been made that some of the former Shah's key supporters were Bahá'ís, including high-ranking officials in SAVAK. Almost all of these assertions are false. Bahá'í principles clearly prohibit Bahá'ís from engaging in political activity. This rule was strictly enforced in Iran. In a few cases, Bahá'ís who disobeyed this rule and took up high government positions under the Shah were expelled from the Bahá'í community. Thus most of those who were accused of having been Bahá'ís and working for the Shah are people who had either been expelled from the Bahá'í community or who merely had Bahá'í ancestors but had never been Bahá'ís themselves. It is no more appropriate to condemn the Bahá'í community for the actions of these people than it is to condemn Islam because the overwhelming majority of the members of the former Shah's government were avowed Muslims.

The Bahá'í World Centre and the State of Israel

Some Muslims have criticized and even attacked the Bahá'í Faith because the Bahá'í World Centre is located in the state of Israel. They have accused the Bahá'ís of receiving money from and of being agents of the Israeli government or of Zionism. As was described above, the Bahá'í World Centre was established in the Haifa–'Akká area by virtue of the facts that Bahá'u'lláh was exiled there by the Ottoman authorities, that he died there and that his shrine there is the holiest spot in the world for Bahá'ís. All this occurred long before the state of Israel came into being. Therefore the Bahá'ís have no choice but to have their World Centre in Israel.

As far as the relationship between the Bahá'í World Centre and the government of Israel is concerned, the Bahá'ís have been anxious to assert their rights as an independent religion. Thus for example, since Jewish, Christian and Muslim religious shrines are exempt from taxes, the Bahá'ís have also claimed this right and have been granted it but the Bahá'ís do not receive from the Israeli government any rights or privileges that are not also given to the Christian and Muslim religious communities in Israel. The Bahá'í teachings include the obligation to be obedient to the government and obey the laws under which one lives. This principle was established by both Bahá'u'lláh and 'Abdu'l-Bahá and thus predates the establishment of the state of Israel by many years. It applies, of course, to Bahá'ís living in any country whether Israel, Iran, an Arab country or anywhere else.

Accusations have also been made that Bahá'ís send money to support the state of Israel. This is false. Money sent to Israel by Bahá'ís is sent directly to the Bahá'í World Centre and it is used by the Bahá'í authorities to support the Bahá'í holy places and for other religious purposes of the Bahá'í Faith.

Some Bahá'í Interpretations of the Qur'án

In this section, a few Bahá'í interpretations of certain passages in the Qur'án are mentioned. As distinct from those passages discussed above and in chapters 3 and 4, these interpretations are matters of opinion in that no decisive proof can be produced to support these interpretations and Muslim scholars have objected to some of them. They are included here for completeness, however.

1. The Bayán. Bahá'ís believe that, after the dispensation of Muḥammad, the next Messenger of Allah to come to the world was the Báb. Thus after the Qur'án, the next major holy scripture to be revealed was the holy book of the Báb's dispensation, the Bayán, which means in Arabic 'the Explanation'. The Báb taught that the true explanation of each holy book was not known to human beings until the coming of the next Messenger of Allah. Thus the true meaning of the obscure passages of the Christian Gospel only became known with the coming of Muḥammad and the revelation of the Qur'án. Similarly, the true meaning of the Qur'án only became known with the coming of the Báb and the revelation of his book the Bayán. This Bahá'ís believe explains the following two sets of verses of the Qur'án, each set showing the coming of the Bayán after the Qur'án:

> (Allah) Most Gracious!
> It is He Who has taught the Qur'án.
> He has created man:
> He has taught him the Bayán. (55:1–4)

> And when We read it, follow thou the reading [Qur'án];
> Then lo! upon Us (resteth) the explanation [Bayán] thereof.
> (75:18–19)[328]

2. The Name of the Báb. The name of the Báb appears in several places in the Qur'án. Bahá'ís find the following occurrence the most interesting, as it directly foretells the function of the Messenger of Allah which the Báb describes in more detail in his writings. The Báb says that the coming of each Messenger of Allah causes the separation between those who truly believe and those who either do not believe or the hypocrites who are false in their belief. Similarly, the following verse foretells that in the future a wall will be put up between the believers on the one side and those who do not believe and the hypocrites on the other. The Messenger of Allah himself is the gate (*báb*) in that wall through which the unbelievers can come to belief:

> So a wall will be put up betwixt them, with a gate (*báb*) therein. Within it will be Mercy throughout, and without it all alongside, will be (wrath and) Punishment! (57:13)

3. The Name of Bahá'u'lláh. In Islamic Traditions, there is mention of the Greatest Name of Allah, which is concealed. It is stated that if anyone were to ask Allah anything by that name, Allah would grant it.

> The Greatest Name of Allah is the one which if He [Allah] is called [prayed to] by it, he will answer. (Ibn Májah)[329]

Bahá'ís believe that *Bahá'* is the Greatest Name of Allah, a name which was kept concealed throughout the Islamic dispensation and which has now been revealed. Since the Greatest Name of Allah was concealed in the Islamic dispensation, the word *Bahá'* does not appear in the Qur'án but an indication of its importance and status as the Greatest Name of Allah is to be found in a verse in the Súrah of *al-Ḥaqqah*, the same súrah that Bahá'ís believe contains many other allusions to the coming of Bahá'u'lláh (see pp. 95–6). In this súrah, after describing what the Inevitable or the Sure Reality is and stating that on that Day the Great Event (*al-Wáqi'ah*), the Day of Judgement, will come to pass, it states that:

> . . . and eight will, that Day, bear the Throne of thy Lord above them. (69:17)

Bahá'ís point out that the number that is borne on eight is, of course, nine. According to the Arabic (Abjad) system where each letter has a numerical equivalent, *Bahá'* is equivalent to nine (B+h+á+' = 2+5+1+1).

In another passage describing the Day of Judgement, the Qur'án states that, on that Day, 'the Earth will shine with the glory of its Lord' (39:69). Although the Qur'án here uses the word *núr*, which can mean 'light', or as Yusuf Ali has translated it here, 'glory', this has almost the same range of meanings as the word *bahá'*. Thus Bahá'ís read this phrase as saying that on that day the earth will be illumined by the glory of Allah, Bahá'u'lláh.

Furthermore, according to Traditions cited by such eminent scholars as aṭ-Ṭabarí and Ibn Kathír, the letter 'B' at the beginning of the words *Bismalláh* (In the name of Allah) which open almost every súrah of the Qur'án stands for 'Bahá'u'lláh'. In his commentary on the *Bismalláh*, at the beginning of his authoritative *tafsír*, aṭ-Ṭabarí writes:

> The Messenger of Allah (the peace and blessings of Allah be upon him) said that Jesus was handed by his mother Mary over to a school in order that he might be taught. [The teacher] said to him: 'Write "Bism (In the name of)".' And Jesus said to him: 'What is "Bism"?' The teacher said: 'I do not know.' Jesus said: 'The "Bá" is Bahá'u'lláh (the glory of Allah), the "Sín" is His Saná' (radiance), and the "Mim" is His Mamlakah (sovereignty).'[330]

Thus it can be seen that, since every súrah (except Súrah 9 – at-Tawbah) begins with *Bismalláh*, Bahá'ís maintain that the name of Bahá'u'lláh is mentioned at the beginning of every súrah of the Qur'án.

The Writings of Bahá'u'lláh

In order to give those readers who know Arabic a chance to read some of the revelation given to Bahá'u'lláh and to judge his Arabic for themselves, a sample of this is given along with the English translation. The first passage is from his Tablet to the Shah of Iran in which he puts forward his claim that his words and actions are not his own but are God's. Following this are some of Bahá'u'lláh's Hidden Words. This book contains a summary of the eternal spiritual and ethical teachings brought by all of the Messengers of God.

O King! I was but a man like others, asleep upon My couch, when lo, the breezes of the All-Glorious were wafted over Me, and taught Me the knowledge of all that hath been. This thing is not from Me, but from One Who is Almighty and All-Knowing. And He bade Me lift up My voice between earth and heaven, and for this there befell Me what hath caused the tears of every man of understanding to flow. The learning current amongst men I studied not; their schools I entered not. Ask of the city wherein I dwelt, that thou mayest be well assured that I am not of them who speak falsely. This is but a leaf which the winds of the will of thy Lord, the Almighty, the All-Praised, have stirred. Can it be still when the tempestuous winds are blowing? Nay, by Him Who is the Lord of all Names and Attributes! They move it as they list.[331]

O Son of Spirit!

My first counsel is this: Possess a pure, kindly and radiant heart, that thine may be a sovereignty ancient, imperishable and everlasting.[332]

O Son of Spirit!

The best beloved of all things in My sight is Justice; turn not away therefrom if thou desirest Me, and neglect it not that I may confide in thee. By its aid thou shalt see with thine own eyes and not through the eyes of others, and shalt know of thine own knowledge and not through the knowledge of thy neighbour. Ponder this in thy heart; how it behoveth thee to be. Verily justice is My gift to thee and the sign of My loving-kindness. Set it then before thine eyes.[333]

O Son of Man!

Veiled in My immemorial being and in the ancient eternity of My essence, I knew My love for thee; therefore I created thee, have engraved on thee Mine image and revealed to thee My beauty.[334]

يا سلطان انى كنت كاحد من العباد و راقداً على المهاد مرّت علىّ نسائم السّبحان و علّمنى علم ما كان ليس هذا من عندى بل من لدن عزيز عليم و امرنى بالنّدآء بين الارض و السّمآء و بذلک ورد علىّ ما تذرّفت به عيون العارفين. ما قرئت ما عند النّاس من العلوم و ما دخلت المدارس فاسئل المدينة الّتى كنت فيها لتوقن بانّى لست من الكاذبين. هذا ورقة حرّكتها ارياح مشيّة ربّک العزيز الحميد. هل لها استقرار عند هبوب ارياح عاصفات لا و مالک الاسمآء و الصّفات بل تحرّكها كيف تريد.

﴿ يا ابنَ الرُّوح ﴾

فى أوّل القول إملكْ قلباً جيّداً حسناً منيراً لِتَمْلِكَ ملكاً دائماً باقياً أزلاً قديماً *

﴿ يا ابنَ الرُّوح ﴾

أحَبُّ الأشياءِ عِندي الإنصاف لا تَرْغَبْ عنه إن تكنْ إلىّ راغباً ولا تَغفُلْ منه لتكون لى أميناً وانت تُوفَّقُ بذلك أنْ تُشاهِدَ الأشياءَ بعينك لا بعين العباد وتَعْرِفَها بمعرفتك لا بمعرفة أحدٍ فى البلاد فكّر فى ذلك كيف ينبغى أن يكون ذلك من عطيّتى عليك وعنايتى لك فاجعله أمام عينيك *

﴿ يا ابنَ الإنسانِ ﴾

كنتُ فى قِدم ذاتى وأزلية كينونتى عرَفْتُ حُبّى فيك خلقتك وألقيتُ عليك مِثالي وأظهرتُ لك جمالى

Bibliography

This bibliography contains only the most important works used. Bibliographical details for other works can be found where they occur in the notes. Where English translations of texts are available, I have used these but I have tried to give sufficient information in the notes so that whoever wishes to find the original text can do so.

'Abdu'l-Bahá. *Paris Talks*. London: Bahá'í Publishing Trust, 1967.

— *The Promulgation of Universal Peace*. Wilmette, IL: Bahá'í Publishing Trust, 1982.

— *The Secret of Divine Civilization*. Wilmette, IL: Bahá'í Publishing Trust, 1990.

— *Selections from the Writings of 'Abdu'l-Bahá*. Haifa: Bahá'í World Centre, 1978.

— *Some Answered Questions*. Wilmette, IL: Bahá'í Publishing Trust, 1981.

'Abdu'l-Bahá in London. London: Bahá'í Publishing Trust, 1987.

Abú Dáwud al-Sijistání al-Azdí. *Sunan*. Cairo: Maṭba'ah Muṣṭafá al-Bábí al-Ḥalabí, 1371/1952.

Áfáqí, Ṣábir. *Proofs from the Holy Qur'án (Regarding the Advent of Bahá'u'lláh)*. New Delhi: Mir'át Publications, 1993.

Ál-Muḥammad, Aḥmad Ḥamdí. *Ad-Dalíl wa'l-Irshád*. Beirut: Maṭábi' al-Bayán, 3rd printing, 1966.

— *Ar-Rá'id wa 'd-Dalíl*. Beirut: Dár ar-Rayḥání, 1969.

— *At-Tibyán wa 'l-Burhán*. 2 vols. Beirut: Maṭba'ah al-Bayán, 3rd printing, 1966.

Bahá'í Prayers: A Selection of Prayers revealed by Bahá'u'lláh, the Báb and 'Abdu'l-Bahá. Wilmette, IL: Bahá'í Publishing Trust, 1991.

Bahá'í World Faith. Wilmette, IL: Bahá'í Publishing Trust, 2nd edn. 1976.

Bahá'u'lláh. *Epistle to the Son of the Wolf* (trans. Shoghi Effendi). Wilmette, IL: Bahá'í Publishing Trust, 1988.

— *Gleanings from the Writings of Bahá'u'lláh* (trans. Shoghi Effendi). Wilmette, IL: Bahá'í Publishing Trust, 1983.

— *The Hidden Words* (trans. Shoghi Effendi et al.). Wilmette, IL: Bahá'í Publishing Trust, rev. edn. 1990.

— *The Kitáb-i-Aqdas*. Haifa: Bahá'í World Centre, 1992.

— *The Kitáb-i-Íqán, the Book of Certitude* (trans. Shoghi Effendi). Wilmette, IL: Bahá'í Publishing Trust, 2nd edn. 1989.

— *Prayers and Meditations* (trans. Shoghi Effendi). Wilmette, IL: Bahá'í Publishing Trust, 1987.

— *The Proclamation of Bahá'u'lláh*. Haifa: Bahá'í World Centre, 1967.

— *The Seven Valleys and the Four Valleys* (trans. Marzieh Gail in consultation with Ali-Kuli Khan). Wilmette, IL: Bahá'í Publishing Trust, 1991.

— *Tablets of Bahá'u'lláh*. Wilmette, IL: Bahá'í Publishing Trust, 1988.

Balyuzi, H. M. *'Abdu'l-Bahá: The Centre of the Covenant of Bahá'u'lláh*. Oxford: George Ronald, 2nd edn. with minor corr. 1987.

— *The Báb: The Herald of the Day of Days*. Oxford: George Ronald, 1973.

— *Bahá'u'lláh, The King of Glory*. Oxford: George Ronald, 1980.

al-Bayḍáwí, 'Abdu'lláh. *Anwár at-Tanzíl*. 5 vols. Cairo: Dár al-Kutub al-'Arabí al-Kubrá, 1330/1912.

Bible. Revised Standard Version.

al-Bukhárí, Muḥammad. *Saḥíḥ* (trans. Muhammad Muhsin Khan). 9 vols. Chicago: Kazi Publications, 3rd edn., 1979.

Compilation of Compilations, The. Prepared by the Universal House of Justice 1963–1990. 2 vols. [Sydney]: Bahá'í Publications Australia, 1991.

ad-Dárimí, 'Abdu'lláh. *Sunan*. 2 vols. Cairo: Dár al-Maḥásin, 1386/1966.

Directives from the Guardian. Compiled by Gertrude Garrida. New Delhi: Bahá'í Publishing Trust, 1973.

Fananapazir, Enayat. *Islam: a Pathway to the Bahá'í Faith*. Mimeographed publication.

Faris, Nabih Amin. *The Foundations of the Articles of Faith*. Lahore: Sh. Muhammad Ashraf, 1963.

Fazel, Seena, and Khazeh Fananapazir. 'A Bahá'í Approach to the Claim of Finality in Islam'. *Journal of Bahá'í Studies*, vol. 5, no. 3, 1993, pp. 17–40.

Friedmann, Yohanan. *Prophecy Continuous*. Berkeley: University of California, 1989.

al-Ghazálí, Muḥammad. *Iḥyá' 'Ulúm ad-Dín*. Cairo: Dár Iḥyá Turáth al-'Arabí, n.d.

Gulpáygání, Abu'l-Faḍl. *Al-Fará'id*. Cairo, 1315 AH.

— *Faṣl al-Khiṭáb*. Dundas, Ont.: Institute for Bahá'í Studies in Persian, 1995.

— *Miracles and Metaphors* (trans. J.R. Cole). Los Angeles: Kalimát Press, 1981.

Hadith Encyclopedia (al-Ḥadíth ash-Sharíf). CD. Cairo: Harf, 1988.

al-Ḥákim an-Naysabúrí. *Al-Mustadrak 'alá 'l-Saḥíḥayn fí 'l-Ḥadíth*. Riyáḍ: Maktabah an-Naṣr, 1968.

Ibn al-'Arabí, Muḥyi ad-Dín. *Al-Futúḥát al-Makkiyyah*. Beirut: Dar Ṣádir [1968?] (Reprint of Cairo: Dár al-Kutub, 1329/1911)

Ibn Ḥanbal, Aḥmad. *Musnad*. 6 vols. Cairo: Maṭba'ah al-Maymániyyah, 1313/1896.

Ibn Kat͟hír. *Tafsír al-Qur'án al-'Aẓím*. 4 vols. Cairo: Dár at-Turát͟h al-Arabí, 1385/1965.

Ibn Májah, Muḥammad. *Sunan* (ed. Muḥammad Fu'ád 'Abd al-Báqí). 2 vols. Cairo: Dár Iḥyá al-Kutub al-'Arabiyyah, 1372–3/1952–3.

al-Irbilí, 'Alí. *Kas͟hf al-G͟hummah*. 3 vols. Tabriz: Maktabah Baní Hás͟him, 1381/1961.

al-Jaṣáṣ ar-Rází, Abu Bakr Aḥmad. *Kitáb Aḥkám al-Qur'án*. 2 vols. Maṭba'ah al-Awqáf al-Islámiyyah, 1335.

Kazemi, Zekrullah. *The Great Call*, Abidjan: Editions Nur, 1995.

Lane, Edward. *Arabic-English Lexicon*. 8 vols. Beirut: Librairie du Liban, 1968.

Lights of Guidance: A Bahá'í Reference File. Compiled by Helen Hornby. New Delhi: Bahá'í Publishing Trust, 2nd edn. 1988.

Majlisí, Muḥammad Báqir. *Biḥár al-Anwár*. Lithograph edn., 25 vols. Tehran, 1301–15/1884–97; otherwise 110 vols. Tehran: Maṭba'ah al-Islámiyyah, 1376–92/1956–72.

Momen, Moojan. *The Bábí and Bahá'í Religions, 1844–1944. Some Contemporary Western Accounts*. Oxford: George Ronald, 1981.

Monjazeb, Arashmidos. *A Closer Look: Reading the Quran for Central Meanings*. Private publishing, n.p., 1997.

Mubárakfúrí, Muḥammad 'Abd al-Raḥmán. *Tuḥfat al-aḥwád͟hí bi-sharḥ Jámi' al-Tirmid͟hí* ('Abd al-Raḥman Muḥammad 'Ut͟hmán, ed.). 10 vols. Beirut: Dár al-Kutub al-'Ilmiyyah, 2nd edn. [1963–7].

al-Mufíd, Muḥammad. *Kitáb al-Irs͟hád* (trans. I.K.A. Howard). Horsham: Balagha Books, 1981.

Muslim ibn al-Ḥajjáj. *Ṣaḥíḥ* (trans. 'Abdul Hamid Siddiqi). Lahore: Sh. Muhammad Ashraf, 1975.

Mustafa, Muhammad. *Bahá'u'lláh: The Great Announcement of the Qur'án.* Dhaka, Bangladesh: Bahá'í Publishing Trust, n.d.

al-Muttaqí al-Hindí, 'Alá ad-Dín 'Alí. *Kanz al-'Ummál.* 16 vols. Aleppo: Maktabah at-Turáth al-Islámí, 1389–97/1969–77.

Nabíl-i-A'ẓam. *The Dawn-Breakers: Nabíl's Narrative of the Early Days of the Bahá'í Revelation* (trans. Shoghi Effendi). Wilmette, IL: Bahá'í Publishing Trust, 1970.

Holy Qur'án. Except where indicated otherwise, I have used A. Yusuf Ali's translation (Islamic Propaganda Centre International, n.d.). In a few places, where I have felt that the translations of Marmaduke Pickthall (New York: Dorset Press, n.d.) or N. J. Dawood (*The Koran*, Harmondsworth: Penguin, 1974) are clearer, I have used these.

Rashíd Riḍá, Muḥammad. *Táríkh al-ustádh al-imám ash-Shaykh Muḥammad 'Abduh.* 2 vols. Cairo: Maṭba'ah al-Manár, 1350/1931.

Rawshaní, Rúḥí. *Khátamiyyat.* Dundas, Ont.: Institute for Bahá'í Studies in Persian, 2nd edn. 1993.

ar-Rází, Fakhr ad-Dín. *At-Tafsír al-Kabír.* 32 vols. Cairo: al-Maṭba'ah al-Bahiyyah al-Misriyyah, [1938].

ash-Sha'rání, 'Abd al-Wahháb. *Al-Yawáqít wa'l-Jawáhir.* 2 vols. Cairo: Maṭba'ah Muṣṭafá al-Bábí al-Ḥalabí, 1378/1959.

Shoghi Effendi. *The Advent of Divine Justice.* Wilmette, IL: Bahá'í Publishing Trust, 1990.

— *Bahá'í Administration.* Wilmette, IL: Bahá'í Publishing Trust, 1968.

— *God Passes By.* Wilmette, IL: Bahá'í Publishing Trust, rev. edn. 1974.

— *The Promised Day is Come.* Wilmette, IL: Bahá'í Publishing Trust, rev. edn. 1980.

— *The World Order of Bahá'u'lláh.* Wilmette, IL: Bahá'í Publishing Trust, 1991.

as-Suyúṭí, Jalál ad-Dín. *Ad-Durr al-Manthúr fi't-Tafsír bi'l-Ma'thúr*. 6 vols. Beirut: Muḥammad Amín Damaj, n.d. (facsimile of Cairo, 1314/1896 edn.).

aṭ-Ṭabarí, Abu Ja'far Muḥammad. *Jámi' al-Bayán fi Tafsír al-Qur'án*. 30 vols. Cairo: Maṭba'ah al-Maymániyyah, 1321/1903.

at-Tibrízí, al-Khaṭíb. *Mishkat al-Maṣábiḥ* (trans. James Robson). 4 vols. Lahore: Sh. Muhammad Ashraf, 1963.

at-Tirmidhí, Muḥammad. *Ṣaḥíḥ* (together with the *Sharḥ* of Imám Abú Bakr ibn al-'Arabí al-Málikí). 13 vols. Cairo: Maṭba'ah as-Ṣáwí, 1353/1934.

Wright, W. *A Grammar of the Arabic Language*. 2 vols. Cambridge: Cambridge University Press, 1964.

az-Zamakhsharí, Abu'l-Qásim Maḥmúd. *Al-Kashsháf 'an Ḥaqá'iq at-Tanzíl*. 3 vols. Cairo: al-Maṭba'ah al-Kubrá al-Amíriyyah, 2nd printing, 1318–19.

References and Notes

*Chapter 1: **The Prophet Muḥammad and Islam***

1. Bahá'u'lláh, *Tablets*, pp. 162–3.
2. Bahá'u'lláh, *Kitáb-i-Iqán*, p. 199.
3. ibid. p. 149.
4. ibid. p. 162.
5. ibid. p. 65.
6. ibid. pp. 49–50.
7. ibid. pp. 111–13.
8. ibid. pp. 109–10.
9. Bahá'u'lláh, *Gleanings*, no. 23, p. 57.
10. 'Abdu'l-Bahá, *Promulgation*, pp. 346–7.
11. Published in the *Christian Commonwealth*, 29 September 1911; see 'Abdu'l-Bahá, *'Abdu'l-Bahá in London*, pp. 42–3.
12. Bahá'u'lláh, *Kitáb-i-Aqdas*, Questions and Answers, p. 139.
13. Bahá'u'lláh, *Kitáb-i-Íqán*, p. 210.
14. ibid. pp. 200–1.
15. 'Abdu'l-Bahá, *Some Answered Questions*, pp. 23–4.
16. See ibid. pp. 18–24.
17. 'Abdu'l-Bahá, *Promulgation*, p. 201.
18. 'Abdu'l-Bahá, *Some Answered Questions*, p. 21.
19. 'Abdu'l-Bahá, *Secret of Divine Civilization*, pp. 89–91.
20. Shoghi Effendi, *Promised Day is Come*, pp. 108–9.
21. From a letter written on behalf of Shoghi Effendi to an individual, 27 April 1936, in *Lights of Guidance*, p. 496, no. 1664; see also pp. 497–9.
22. ibid.
23. From a letter written on behalf of Shoghi Effendi to an individual, 14 August 1939, in ibid. p. 562, no. 1903.
24. From a letter written on behalf of Shoghi Effendi to an individual, 27 April 1936, in ibid. p. 496, no. 1664.

25. From a letter written on behalf of Shoghi Effendi to an individual, 30 July 1941, in ibid. p. 497, no. 1665.

Chapter 2: ***Spiritual and Ethical Teachings***

26. Bahá'u'lláh, *Gleanings*, no. 94, p. 192.
27. ibid. no. 27, pp. 64–5.
28. Pickthall's translation (10:66).
29. Bahá'u'lláh, *Epistle to the Son of the Wolf*, pp. 102–3.
30. Bahá'u'lláh, *Gleanings*, no. 129, p. 284.
31. Bahá'u'lláh, *Tablets*, p. 110.
32. Bahá'u'lláh, *Gleanings*, no. 20, p. 49.
33. Bahá'u'lláh, *Kitáb-i-Íqán*, p. 99.
34. This verse can be compared to the assertion in the Bible by Jesus to the Jews that 'had ye believed Moses, ye would have believed me: for he wrote of me'. (John 5:46)
35. Bahá'u'lláh, *Kitáb-i-Íqán*, p. 4.
36. Pickthall's translation (5:73).
37. 'Abdu'l-Bahá, *Some Answered Questions*, pp. 7–10.
38. Pickthall's translation; cf. 2:285, 3:84, 4:152.
39. Al-Bukhárí, *Ṣaḥíḥ*, Book 55 (Prophets), no. 652, vol. 4, p. 434; cf. Ibn Ḥanbal, *Musnad*, vol. 2, p. 406.
40. Bahá'u'lláh, *Gleanings*, no. 24, p. 59.
41. Bahá'u'lláh, in *Bahá'í Prayers*, p. 212.
42. Pickthall's translation.
43. For verse 29, I have here used the translation of N. J. Dawood, 1974, as this is closest to the original. A literal translation of the Arabic is: 'each day He is upon an affair (*sha'n*).'
44. Bahá'u'lláh, *Gleanings*, no. 34, p. 80.
45. ibid. no. 109, p. 215.
46. ibid. no. 34, p. 81.
47. Bahá'u'lláh, *Hidden Words*, Arabic no. 67.
48. Pickthall's translation.
49. Pickthall's translation.
50. Bahá'u'lláh, *Kitáb-i-Íqán*, pp. 152–4.
51. ibid. p. 176.
52. ibid. p. 177.
53. Bahá'u'lláh, *Hidden Words*, Persian no. 29.

54. 'Abdu'l-Bahá, *Paris Talks*, p. 60.
55. Pickthall's translation.
56. Bahá'u'lláh, *Prayers and Meditations*, p. 311.
57. Bahá'u'lláh, *Epistle to the Son of the Wolf*, p. 132.
58. In many editions of the Qur'án this is verse 119.
59. Bahá'u'lláh, *Kitáb-i-Aqdas*, para. 76.
60. Bahá'u'lláh, *Hidden Words*, Arabic no. 2.
61. Bahá'u'lláh, quoted in *Lights of Guidance*, p. 231, no. 768.
62. Bahá'u'lláh, *Kitáb-i-Aqdas*, para. 120.
63. Bahá'u'lláh, *Gleanings*, no. 109, p. 215.
64. Bahá'u'lláh, *Tablets*, pp. 72–3.
65. Bahá'u'lláh, *Hidden Words*, Arabic nos. 55–6.
66. Bahá'u'lláh, *Hidden Words*, Persian no. 49.
67. Bahá'u'lláh, *Gleanings*, no. 110, p. 215.
68. ibid. no. 130, p. 285.

Chapter 3: ***The Claim of Bahá'u'lláh***

69. Bahá'u'lláh, *Tablets*, p. 244.
70. Bahá'u'lláh, *Epistle to the Son of the Wolf*, p. 161.
71. Bahá'u'lláh, *Gleanings*, no. 34, p. 80.
72. Among the large numbers of books and articles containing Bahá'í proofs for Muslims which the author has consulted in drawing up this chapter and chapters 4, 8, and 9 are, in English: Ṣábir Áfáqí, *Proofs from the Holy Qur'án*; Muhammad Mustafa, *Bahá'u'lláh: The Great Announcement of the Qur'án*; Zekrullah Kazemi, *The Great Call*; E. Fananapazir, *Islam: a Pathway to the Bahá'í Faith*; Fazel and Fananapazir, 'A Bahá'í Approach to the Claim of Finality in Islam'. In Arabic: Aḥmad Ál-Muḥammad, *Ad-Dalíl wa'l-Irshád* and *At-Tibyán wa'l-Burhán*. In Persian: Gulpáygání, *Al-Fará'id* and *Faṣl-al-Khiṭáb*; Rawḥání, *Khátimiyyat*. The author is also grateful to the Internet, Usenet and WWW postings of Abir Majid and Kamran Hakim and for the comments of the latter on this manuscript.
73. Bahá'u'lláh, *Proclamation*, p. 111.
74. ibid. pp. 111–12.
75. *Ad-Durr al-Manthúr*, vol. 5, p. 204.
76. ibid.

77. Commentary on *Sunan* of Tirmidhí by Mubárakfúrí, *Tuḥfat al-Aḥwádhí bi-Sharḥ at-Tirmidhí*, vol. 9, p. 70, in explanation of the *ḥadíth* which at-Tirmidhí gives in his section on 'Tafsír al-Qur'án' in commentary on Qur'án 33:40.
78. *Jámi' al-Bayán*, vol. 6, p. 183.
79. See, for example, ash-Sháfi'í, *al-Fiqh al-Akbar* (Cairo, n.d.), p. 28.
80. See Wright, *Grammar of the Arabic Language*, vol. 2, pp. 333–4.
81. Az-Zamakhsharí, *al-Kashsháf*, vol. 2, p. 433. Since al-Bayḍáwí is based on az-Zamakhsharí, it is not surprising that al-Bayḍáwí gives a very similar explanation of this verse, *Anwár at-Tanzíl*, vol. 4, p. 164.
82. Ibn Májah, *Sunan*, Kitáb al-Janá'iz, ch. 27, nos. 1510–11, vol. 1, p. 484; Ibn Ḥanbal, *Musnad*, vol. 4, p. 353.
83. An-Nawawí, *Tahdhíb al-Asmá wa'l-Lughát*, quoted in I. Goldziher, *Muslim Studies* (London: George Allen and Unwin, 1971), vol. 2, p. 104 and Friedmann, *Prophecy Continuous*, p. 62.
84. Ibn Májah, *Sunan*, Kitáb al-Janá'iz, ch. 27, nos. 1510–11, vol. 1, p. 484; Ibn Ḥanbal, *Musnad*, vol. 4, p. 353.
85. Ar-Rází, *At-Tafsír al-Kabír*, vol. 25, p. 214.
86. Al-Bukhárí, *Ṣaḥíḥ*, Book 24 (al-Anbiyá), no. 661, vol. 4, pp. 439–40; Muslim, *Ṣaḥíḥ*, Kitáb al-Imárah, ch. 763, vol. 3, p. 1025, no. 4543; Ibn Májah, *Sunan*, al-Jihád, ch. 42, vol. 1, op. 958–9, no. 2871; Ibn Ḥanbal, *Musnad*, vol. 2, p. 297.
87. Muslim, *Ṣaḥíḥ*, Kitáb Faḍá'il as-Ṣaḥábah, ch. 996, vol. 4, p. 1284, no. 5913; see also nos. 5914–16, pp. 1284–5; Ibn Májah, *Sunan*, al-Muqadimah, ch. 11, vol. 1, pp. 42–3, no. 115; p. 45, no. 121; Ibn Ḥanbal, *Musnad*, vol. 1, pp. 170, 174–5, 179, 182–3, 184, 331; vol. 3, pp. 32, 338; vol. 6, pp. 369, 438.
88. Az-Zamakhsharí, *al-Kashsháf*, vol. 2, p. 433. Al-Bayḍáwí, *Anwár at-Tanzíl*, vol. 4, p. 164.
89. See, for example, Marshall Hodgson, *Venture of Islam* (Chicago: University of Chicago Press, 1974), vol. 1, pp. 197–8. Apart from those well-known claimants to prophethood who were contemporaries of Muḥammad such as Musaylima and al-Aswad al-'Ansí, among those who later rebelled against the caliphate claiming to be prophets were al-Ḥárith ibn al-Sa'íd

(executed during the caliphate of 'Abd al-Malik), Muḥammad ibn Sa'íd al-Maṣlúb (executed during the reign of al-Manṣur), Maḥmúd ibn al-Faraj (executed c. 235/849–50). Among Shi'is who claimed prophethood were: Bayán ibn Sam'án at-Tamímí, founder of the Bayániyyah; Hashim ibn al-Ḥakím, known as al-Muqanna', founder of the Muqanniyyah; 'Abdu'lláh ibn Mu'áwiya, founder of the Janáḥiyyah; Mughíra ibn Sa'íd al-'Ijlí, founder of the Mughíriyyah; Abu'l-Khaṭṭáb al-Asadí, founder of the Khaṭṭábiyyah; Mu'ammar ibn Kaytham, founder of the Mu'ammariyyah; and Muḥammad ibn Nuṣayr an-Namírí, founder of the Nuṣayriyyah. All of the above were either executed or killed.

90. Thus, for example, *kháatam* or closely related words such as *khatama* and *khuttám* can be found thus: Ibn Khallikán calls a poet '*khatama ash-shu'ara*' (the seal of the poets); Ibn al-'Arabí is described as '*khuttám al-'ulamá*' (the sealer of the scholars) by Ibn Bashkuwál; I. Goldziher, *Gesammelte Scriften* (Hildesheim: Georg Olms), vol. 1, p. 288n. Goldziher here also refers to the usage *khátam al-muḥaqqiqín*. Clearly in none of these usages is it implied that the person thus described is the last in this category.
91. These two literary examples are cited in Friedmann, *Prophecy Continuous*, p. 57. This poem of Umayya ibn Abí aṣ-Ṣalt has been published in *Umajja ibn Abi s Salt* (trans. Friedrich Schulthess, Leipzig: J.C. Hinrichs, 1911), p. 24.
92. See A. J. Wensinck, *The Muslim Creed* (Cambridge: University Press, 1932), p. 192, article 9. See also Montgomery Watt, *Islamic Creeds* (Edinburgh University Press, 1994), pp. 41–7.
93. The *Fiqh Akbar I* (dated to early 9th century AD and attributed to a pupil of Abú Ḥanífa), which is not as comprehensive as the *Fiqh Akbar II*, also does not contain any reference to the doctrine of the finality of prophethood. See Wensinck, *The Muslim Creed*, pp. 124–31 and Watt, *Islamic Creeds*, pp. 57–61. For Ibn Ḥanbal see Watt, *Islamic Creeds*, pp. 30–2.
94. In the second section of *Iḥyá' 'Ulúm ad-Dín*, al-Ghazálí discusses prophethood and the station of Muḥammad in the first and third chapters (chapters 16 and 19 of the whole book). See vol. 1, pp. 91–2, 113. This section of the *Iḥyá' 'Ulúm ad-Dín* has been translated in English by Nabih Amin

Faris under the title *The Foundations of the Articles of Faith*. The passages dealing with prophethood and the station of Muḥammad are on pp. 6–9 and 90–1. It should be noted, however, that Faris has translated the phrase 'Seal of the Prophets (*khátam an-nabiyyin*)' as 'last of the prophets' (p. 90). Thus what is published as 'God sent Muḥammad as the last of the prophets' should read 'God sent Muḥammad as the seal of the prophets'. A translation of part of this creed can also be found in Watt, *Islamic Creeds*, pp. 73–9.

95. Al-G͟hazálí, *Iḥyá' 'Ulúm ad-Dín*, vol. 1, p. 113. Faris, *Foundations of the Articles of Faith*, p. 90 but see comment upon this translation in the previous note.
96. Pickthall's translation (10:48).
97. Pickthall's translation.
98. See Edward Lane's *Arabic-English Lexicon*, vol. 1, p. 90. Lane draws his meanings from all of the major classical dictionaries of Arabic, especially the *Táj al-'Arús* of al-Zabídí and the *Lisán al'Arab* of Ibn Mukarram. In relation to these particular meanings of *ummah*, Lane cites these sources and others including Firúzábádí, *al-Qámús*; al-Azharí, *Tahd͟híb al-Lughah*, Ibn Sída, *al-Muḥkam* and al-Jawharí, *al-Ṣiḥáḥ*.
99. I have here translated *áyah* as 'verse' instead of 'sign' (see p. 222) and *ajal* as 'fixed term' rather than 'period' as that is how I have rendered it in the preceding paragraphs.
100. Pickthall's translation.
101. Bahá'u'lláh, *Kitáb-i-Íqán*, pp. 153–4.
102. ibid. pp. 20–1.
103. ibid. pp. 21–2.
104. ibid. pp. 161–2.
105. Ibn Kat͟hír, *Tafsír al-Qur'án*, vol. 3, p. 494. Similar statements can be found in two Traditions that may be found in Ibn Hanbal, *Musnad*, vol. 4, pp. 126, 127.
106. Muslim, *Ṣaḥíḥ*, Kitáb al-Ḥajj, no. 3211, vol. 3, pp. 697–8. An equivalent Shi'i Tradition records that 'Alí stated: 'Muḥammad is the Seal of the Prophets and I am the Seal of the Successors (to the Prophet).' For Twelver Shi'is, of course, there were eleven further Imáms after 'Alí and so 'Alí was not the last of the successors to the Prophet; Majlisí, *Biḥár al-Anwár*, vol. 26, pp. 4–5; vol. 39, p. 36, no. 5.

107. Al-Jaṣáṣ ar-Rází, *Aḥkám al-Qur'án*, vol. 2, p. 16.
108. Ibn Kat͟hír, *Tafsír*, vol. 3, p. 393.
109. 'No Messenger has been sent except with Islam.' *ad-Durr al-Manthúr*, vol. 2, p. 12.
110. In translating the last phrase using 'Muslims', I have indicated the word that appears in the Arabic (*muslimún*), rather than the translation given by Yusuf Ali, which is 'and to Allah do we bow our will (in Islam)'.
111. See also other similar passages in the Hebrew Bible affirming certain specific laws or the law in general as being 'for ever': Exodus 12:14, 17, 24; 27:21; 28:43; 29:28; 30:21; Leviticus 6:18, 22; 7:34, 36; 10:9, 15; 16:29, 31; 17:7; 23:14, 21, 31, 41; 24:3; Numbers 10:8; 15:14–15; 18:8, 11, 19, 23; 19:10; Psalms 111:7–8; 119:44.
112. Al-Buk͟hárí, *Ṣaḥíḥ*, Book 1 – Revelation, no. 6, vol. 1, pp. 7–10.
113. Bahá'u'lláh, *Kitáb-i-Íqán*, pp. 136–8.
114. ibid. pp. 5–6.
115. Muslim, *Ṣaḥíḥ*, Kitab al-'Ilm, chap. 3, no. 6448; al-Buk͟hárí, *Ṣaḥíḥ*, Book 24 (Anbiyá), no. 662, vol. 4, p. 440. A similar *ḥadít͟h* states that the followers of Muḥammad asked him to make for them a special tree (with magical properties) as the polytheists had. Muḥammad protested that this is exactly what the Israelites asked of Moses, that he set up a god for them that they could worship. Then he said: 'By the One in whose hand is my soul! Truly you will travel along the very same path as those before you.' At-Tirmid͟hí, *Ṣaḥiḥ*, vol. 9, pp. 26–8.
116. Ibn Májah, *Sunan*, 36 (Kitáb al-Fitan), ch. 26, no. 4048, vol. 2, p. 1344. For a Shi'i Tradition on this theme see note 122.
117. ibid. pp. 254–5.
118. Pickthall's translation.
119. Yusuf Ali translates *ta'wíl* here as 'fulfilment' but this is not a usual translation of this word. Indeed both Yusuf Ali and Pickthall translate *ta'wíl* elsewhere as 'interpretation' or 'elucidation' (10:39, 12:6, 21, 44, 45, 101; 18:78, 82).
120. Bahá'u'lláh, *Kitáb-i-Íqán*, pp. 238–42.
121. Pickthall's translation.

122. Narrated 'Abdu'lláh ibn 'Amr ibn al-'As; al-Bukhárí, *Ṣaḥíḥ*, Book 3 (Knowledge), no. 100, vol. 1, p. 80. There are similar Shi'i Traditions that state that: The Messenger of Allah said: 'There will come a time for my people when there will remain nothing of the Qur'án except its outward form and nothing of Islam except its name and they will call themselves by this name even though they are the people furthest from it. Their mosques will be full of people but they will be empty of right guidance. The religious leaders [*fuqahá*] of that day will be the most evil religious leaders under the heavens; sedition and dissension will go out from them and to them will it return.' Ibn Bábúya, *Thawáb al-A'mál*, quoted in Majlisí, *Biḥár al-Anwár* (lithograph ed.), vol. 13, p. 152. A very similar passage can be found in the *Nahj al-Balaghah*, the collection of the speeches and writings of 'Alí ibn Abú Ṭálib, which is accepted by both Sunnis and Shi'is, Khuṭbah no. 150 (in some editions, this is given as Khuṭbah no. 146).

123. While the Qur'án states that it is not possible for a false claimant to divine revelation to survive, the converse of this is not true. In other words, the fact that the Báb was killed in early life is not a proof of the falsity of the Báb, for the Qur'án states that it is possible for a true prophet or Messenger to be killed. (2:91)

124. Yusuf Ali begins this verse: 'And if the Messenger were to invent . . .' but the Arabic text does not contain the word *rasúl* (Messenger); therefore I have corrected this.

125. See note 89.

126. Qur'án 3:105. There are also many Traditions on this theme; in the most well-known Muḥammad states that 'my community will be split into seventy-three (or seventy-two) sects'. Ibn Májah, *Sunan*, 36 (Kitáb al-Fitan), ch. 17, nos. 3991–3, vol. 2, pp. 1321–2; Ibn Ḥanbal, *Musnad*, vol. 2, p. 332; vol. 3, p. 145; cf. al-Ḥákim, *al-Mustadrak*, vol. 4, p. 430.

Chapter 4: ***Islamic Prophecies***

127. Dawood's translation.

128. This interpretation is also supported by the following Tradition, narrated by Ibn 'Umar: The Prophet said, 'Oppression

will be a darkness on the Day of Resurrection.' Al-Bukhárí, *Ṣaḥíḥ*, Book 43 (al-Maẓálim), no. 627, vol. 3, p. 376.

129. This matter is explained in detail in Bahá'u'lláh's *Kitáb-i Íqán*, pp. 24–49; although Bahá'u'lláh bases his explanations upon a verse of the Christian Bible that prophesies events on the Day of Judgement, the terms that Bahá'u'lláh explains in this passage are the same terms that are found in the Qur'án. Indeed, Bahá'u'lláh quotes parallel Quranic verses in his explanation; see for example p. 44, where he quotes Qur'án 82:1.
130. Al-Bukhárí, *Ṣaḥíḥ*, Book 88 (Fitan), no. 184, vol. 9, p. 150. Shi'i Traditions also speak of much death and destruction in Syria and Iraq: al-Mufíd, *al-Irshád*, pp. 542, 544, 548.
131. Al-Bukhárí, *Ṣaḥíḥ*, Book 88, no. 231, vol. 9, pp. 177–8; cf. Muslim, *Ṣaḥíḥ*, Kitáb al-Fitan, ch. 1205, no. 6948, p. 1506.
132. Pickthall's translation.
133. Pickthall's translation.
134. Muslim, *Ṣaḥíḥ*, vol. 4, ch. 1214 on 'Approach of the Last Hour', no. 7049, p. 1527. Six other similar traditions are cited in this chapter. See also Ibn Májah, *Sunan*, 36 (Kitáb al-Fitan), ch. 25, no. 4040, vol. 2, p. 1341; at-Tirmidhí, *Ṣaḥíḥ*, Abwáb al-Fitan, vol. 9, p. 60.
135. Pickthall's translation.
136. Qur'án 44:10; Ibn Májah, *Sunan*, 36 (Kitáb al-Fitan), ch. 25, no. 4041, vol. 2, p. 1341.
137. Qur'án 2:210.
138. Bahá'u'lláh, *Kitáb-i-Íqán*, pp. 71–4.
139. ibid. pp. 76–7.
140. Bahá'u'lláh, *Epistle to the Son of the Wolf*, pp. 131–4.
141. Pickthall's translation.
142. See also Qur'án 3:169, where those slain in the path of Allah are said to be alive (i.e. spiritually alive even though physically dead); while in Qur'án 16:20–1, it is stated that those who are living should be accounted as among the dead if they participate in idolatry. The Qur'án also states that a resurrection occurred with the coming of Moses (2:55–6).
143. Qur'án 40:32.
144. Az-Zamakhsharí, *al-Kashsháf*, vol. 3, p. 134.

145. Ibn Májah, *Sunan*, 5 (Iqámat aṣ-Ṣalát), ch. 196, no. 1405, vol. 1, p. 451.
146. See also Qur'án 46:31–2 where the reference to *ad-dá'í* is also clearly to a Messenger of Allah.
147. See p. 18: 'we make no difference between any of them' (2:136; Pickthall's translation).
148. Pickthall's translation.
149. Bahá'u'lláh, *Gleanings*, no. 10, pp. 12–13.
150. Bahá'u'lláh, *Tablets*, p. 182.
151. See for example what was said to Abraham: 'I will make thee an Imám to the Nations.'(Qur'án 2:124)
152. Yusuf Ali has translated Imám here in the plural but the text clearly has 'Imám' in the singular.
153. The word *liqá* (meeting) occurs in the Qur'án 24 times. On 17 occasions it explicitly refers to the 'meeting with Allah'; on six occasions it implicitly refers to this and there is only one occasion on which it may not do so.
154. Al-Bukhárí, *Ṣaḥíḥ*, 93 (Tawḥíd), no. 531, vol. 9, p. 390. See also nos. 529–30, 532–3, pp. 389–95; Muslim, *Ṣaḥíḥ*, 1 (Kitáb al-Ímán), ch. 81, nos. 349–52, vol. 1, pp. 115–9; and Ibn Ḥanbal, *Musnad*, vol. 2, p. 275.
155. In the *Ṣaḥíḥ* of al-Bukhárí the following is to be found: 'Á'ishah said, 'If anyone tells you that Muḥammad has seen his Lord, he is a liar, for Allah says: "No vision can grasp Him" (Qur'án 6:103). And if anyone tells you that Muḥammad has seen the Unseen, he is a liar, for Allah says: "None has the knowledge of the Unseen but Allah."' al-Bukhárí, *Ṣaḥíḥ*, Book 93 (at-Tawḥíd), no. 477, vol. 9, p. 354; cf. Ibn Ḥanbal, *Musnad*, vol. 6, p. 49. Even in the accounts of the Mi'ráj, the night-ascent into heaven, the Prophet Muḥammad is stopped at the Sadrat al-Muntahá (the furthest lote-tree), beyond which there is no passing, and does not see Allah. See, for example, the accounts of the Mi'ráj in the chapter on al-Isrá' (the Night Journey) in Muslim, *Ṣaḥíḥ*, 1 (Kitáb al-Ímán), ch. 75, nos. 309–22, vol. 1, pp. 100–8.
156. Pickthall's translation.
157. Bahá'u'lláh, *Gleanings*, no. 21, p. 50.
158. 'He who has seen me has indeed seen the Truth (*al-Ḥaqq*).' al-Bukhárí, *Ṣaḥíḥ*, Book 87 (Dreams), no. 125, vol. 9, p. 105;

Muslim, *Ṣaḥíḥ*, *Kitáb al-Ru'ya*, ch. 2, no. 5637. *Al-Ḥaqq* is one of the Names of Allah. In another Tradition, for example, Muḥammad specifically addresses Allah as *al-Ḥaqq*: 'O Allah! Our Lord! . . . Unto Thee be praise, Thou art the light of the heavens and the earth and all who are in them. Thou art the Truth (*al-Ḥaqq*)'; al-Bukhárí, *Ṣaḥíḥ*, Book 93 (at-Tawḥíd), no. 534, vol. 9, pp. 402–3. Although the above Tradition ('He who has seen me has indeed seen the Truth') is placed in a section that is related to dreams and there are several other similar Traditions that relate to dreams of the Prophet Muḥammad, there is nothing in this specific Tradition that states that it relates to dreams.

159. Al-Bukhárí, *Ṣaḥíḥ*, Book 88 (Fitan), no. 241, vol. 9, p. 183; at-Tirmidhí, *Ṣaḥíḥ*, Abwáb al-Fitan, vol. 9, pp. 83–6; see also pp. 98–9.
160. Al-Bukhárí, *Ṣaḥíḥ*, Book 93 (Tawḥíd), no. 532, vol. 9, p. 391.
161. Bahá'u'lláh, *Kitáb-i-Íqán*, pp. 168–70.
162. Whole chapters on prophecies of the appearance of the Mahdi and of the return of Jesus appear in such authoritative collections of Traditions as al-Bukhárí, Muslim, Ibn Májah, Abú Dáwud and at-Tirmidhí. A few Islamic scholars, the most notable of whom is Ibn Khaldún, have tried to maintain that the Mahdi is merely Islamic folklore and not truly part of original Islam. But such doubts regarding the authenticity of the Mahdi have not been endorsed by most scholars. The Traditions about the Mahdi appear in the most reliable collections of *ḥadíths* (as above) and the individual Traditions have been examined by Islamic scholars and pronounced to be reliable. For example, al-Ḥákim an-Naysábúrí has examined the Tradition that states that the coming of the Mahdi is one of the conditions of the Hour (Day of Judgement), that he is of the family of the Prophet and that he will fill the earth with justice. He states that this Tradition is 'sound (*ṣaḥíḥ*) according to the criteria of the two Shaykhs (Muslim and al-Bukhárí)'; *al-Mustadrak*, vol. 4, p. 557.
163. Abú Dáwud, *Sunan*, Kitáb al-Mahdí, vol. 2, p. 422; see also Ibn Májah, *Sunan*, 36 (Kitáb al-Fitan), ch. 34 (Khurúj al-Mahdí), no. 4086, vol. 2, p. 1368. For Shi'is, of course, the Mahdi is the Twelfth Imam, Muḥammad ibn Ḥasan al-

'Askarí, and therefore also a descendant of the Prophet through Fáṭimah.

164. Abú Dáwud, *Sunan*, 36 (Kitáb al-Mahdí,) vol. 2, pp. 421–2, cf. also vol. 2, p. 422. See also al-Ḥákim, *al-Mustadrak*, vol. 4, p. 557. Similar Shi'i Traditions can be found in al-Mufíd, *Irshád*, no. 548, p. 341.

165. Abú Dáwud, *Sunan*, 36 (Kitáb al-Mahdí), vol. 2, p. 422. Some Traditions say seven or nine years (Ibn Hanbal, *Musnad*, vol. 3, p. 27). This may refer to the fact that although the Báb's ministry lasted seven years until he was executed in 1850, his dispensation lasted nine years until the beginning of Bahá'u'lláh's ministry in 1852 (see pp. 198-200). Similar Shi'i Traditions can be found in al-Irbilí, *Kashf al-Ghummah*, vol. 3, pp. 257, 269 and al-Nu'mání, *al-Ghaybah* quoted in Majlisí, *Biḥár al-Anwár* (lithograph ed.), vol. 13, p. 178.

166. Ibn Ḥanbal, *Musnad*, vol. 5, p. 277. English translation in at-Tibrizí, *Mishkat al-Maṣábiḥ*, vol. 3, p. 1142, quoting Ibn Ḥanbal and Bayhaqí, *Dalá'il an-Nubuwwa*. Ibn Májah gives a similar *ḥadíth* which says 'black flags from the East' and adds that 'if you see him then go to pledge obeisance to him even if you have to crawl over the snow'. *Sunan*, 36 (Kitáb al-Fitan), ch. 34 (Khurúj al-Mahdí), no. 4084, vol. 2, pp. 1367 (cf. no. 4082, vol. 2, pp. 1366). At-Tirmidhí gives a version of this Tradition that states that the Black Standard will eventually reach Jerusalem, *Ṣaḥíḥ*, Abwáb al-Fitan, vol. 9, p. 122. See also al-Muttaqí al-Hindí, *Kanz al-'Ummál*, vol. 14, p. 268, no. 38679. Shi'i Traditions include al-Irbilí, *Kashf al-Ghummah*, vol. 3, pp. 262–3 and Shaykh at-Tá'ifa, *al-Ghaybah* quoted in Majlisí, *Biḥár al-Anwár*, vol. 13 (lithograph ed.), p. 159.

167. Al-Ḥákim, *al-Mustadrak*, Kitáb al-Fitan wa al-Maláḥim, vol. 4, p. 550; cf. Muslim, *Ṣaḥíḥ*, Kitáb al-Imára, ch. 1306, nos. 4715–16 and 4719, vol. 3, pp. 1061–2; Ibn Ḥanbal, *Musnad*, vol. 5, p. 278, 279; Abú Dáwud, *Sunan*, al-Fitan wa al-Maláḥim, ch. 1, col. 2, p. 414; Ibn Májah, *Sunan*, 36 (Fitan), ch. 9, vol. 2, p. 1304, no. 3952; ad-Dárimí, *Sunan*, Jihád, ch. 39, vol. 2, p. 132, no. 2437; al-Bukhárí, *Ṣaḥíḥ*, 3 ('Ilm), ch. 14, vol. 1, p. 61, no. 71, 53 (Khums), ch. 7, vol. 4, pp. 223–4, no. 346, 93 – Kitáb at-Tawḥíd, ch. 29, no. 551–2,

vol. 9, pp. 414–15. The last of these Traditions from al-Bukhárí (no. 552) links the future coming of the Cause of Allah (*amr Alláh*) to the people of Syria; see similar Traditions in Ibn Ḥanbal, *Musnad*, vol. 4, p. 101, and al-Muttaqí al-Hindí, *Kanz al-'Ummál*, vol. 14, no. 38224, p. 158. For other Traditions regarding Syria, see p. 132.

168. Az-Zamakhsharí, *Al-Kashsháf*, vol. 2, p. 418; Al-Bayḍáwí, *Anwár at-Tanzíl*, vol. 4, p. 155.
169. Ibn Májah, *Sunan*, 1 (al-Muqaddamah), no. 10, pp. 5–6.
170. Ibn Májah, *Sunan*, 1 (al-Muqaddamah), no. 6, pp. 4–5.
171. Muslim, *Ṣaḥíḥ* (Kitáb al-Imára), ch. 1306, no. 4715–22, vol. 3, p. 1061. Nos. 4715–16 and 4719 have 'until the Cause of Allah shall come' (*ḥattá yá'tí amr Alláh*, given in the translation as 'until Allah's Command is executed'); no. 4718 and 4720 have 'until the Day of Judgement'; and no. 4717 and 4721–2 have 'until the Last Hour is established'.
172. Ibn Ḥanbal, *Musnad*, vol. 5, p. 269.
173. See, for example, in the Qur'án, the occurrence of this phrase *ḥattá ta'tiya-hum* in Qur'án 22:55, where the phrase refers to the future coming of the Hour of Judgement: 'Those who reject Faith will not cease to be in doubt concerning (Revelation) until the Hour (of Judgement) comes suddenly upon them (*ḥattá ya'tiya-hum*) or there comes to them the Penalty of a Day of Disaster.' In the Traditions, see for example al-Bukhárí, *Ṣaḥíḥ*, 93 (Kitáb at-Tawḥíd), ch. 29, no. 551, vol. 9, p. 414, in which Muḥammad states that a group from among his people 'will continue to be victorious until there shall come to them (*ḥattá ya'tiya-hum*) the Cause of Allah'. See also the discussion about the very similar phrase *immá ya'tiyanna-kum* on p. 49.
174. Ash-Sha'rání, *al-Yawáqít wa'l-Jawáhir*, vol. 2, ch. 65, p. 143. Ash-Sha'rání states that he is quoting Ibn 'Arabí, *al-Futúḥát al-Makkiyyah*, apparently from chapter 366 on 'Knowing the station of the supporters of the Mahdi who will appear at the end of time', vol. 3, p. 106 but the wording is slightly different in the text of Ibn 'Arabí in the edition that I have used (see Bibliography). In Shi'i Traditions there are similar statements about the Mahdi: a new book and a new religion: 'He will come with a new Cause – just as Muḥammad, at the

beginning of Islam, summoned the people to a new Cause – and with a new book'; opposition of the *'ulamá* to the Mahdi: 'The Qá'im [Mahdi] will come to a people who will interpret the Book of Allah against him and will bring proofs from it against him'; both Traditions are in al-Nu'mání, *al-Ghayba* quoted in Majlisí, *Biḥár al-Anwár* (lithograph ed.), vol. 13, pp. 192–3.

175. Al-Bukhárí, *Ṣaḥíḥ*, Book 43 (Oppressions), no. 656, vol. 3, p. 395; at-Tirmidhí, *Ṣaḥíḥ*, Abwáb al-Fitan, vol. 9, pp. 75–7.
176. Abú Dáwud, *Sunan*, 37 (Kitáb Al-Maláḥim), vol. 2, p. 432; Ibn Ḥanbal, *Musnad*, vol. 4, p. 406.
177. At-Tirmidhí, *Ṣaḥíḥ*, Abwab at-Tafsír, chapter on the *Tafsír* of Súrah of Muḥammad, vol. 12, p. 146. At-Tirmidhí gives several chains of transmission for this *ḥadíth* and another similar one. English translation may be found in at-Tibrízí, *Mishkat al-al-Maṣábiḥ*, vol. 4, p. 1375. The Shi'i commentary on the Qur'án, al-Fayḍ al-Káshání, *Kitáb as-Ṣáfí* (Tehran: Kitábfurúshí Islámiyyah, 2536 IY), quotes a similar Tradition, vol. 2, pp. 572–3.
178. Ibn al-'Arabí, *al-Futúḥát al-Makkiyyah*, chapter 366 on 'Knowing the station of the supporters of the Mahdi who will appear at the end of time', vol. 3, pp. 106–8. See also ash-Sha'rání, *al-Yawáqít wa'l-Jawáhir*, vol. 2, ch. 65, pp. 143–4.
179. Bahá'u'lláh, *Kitáb-i-Íqán*, pp. 148–9.
180. ibid. pp. 150–1.
181. ibid. pp. 151–2.
182. ibid. pp. 152.
183. Ibn Ḥanbal, *Musnad*, vol. 4, p. 110; Abú Dáwud, *Sunan*, Kitáb al-Jihád, ch. 3 (On the Inhabitants of Syria), vol. 2, p. 4; al-Muttaqí al-Hindí, *Kanz al-'Ummál*, vol. 14, p. 162, no. 38239. See also the translation in at-Tibrízi, *Mishkat al-al-Maṣábiḥ*, vol. 4, p. 1381.
184. Al-Muttaqí al-Hindí, *Kanz al-'Ummál*, vol. 14, p. 161, no. 38234.
185. At-Tirmidhí, *Sunan*, Abwáb al-Fitan, vol. 9, p. 62; cf. al-Muttaqí al-Hindí, *Kanz al-'Ummál*, vol. 14, p. 161, no. 38235. See also the translation in at-Tibrízi, *Mishkat al-Maṣábiḥ*, vol. 4, p. 1380.

186. Yáqút, *Mu'jam al-Buldán* (Maṭba'a as-Sa'áda, Cairo, 1324/1906), vol. 6, p. 206.
187. These Traditions on 'Akká are to be found in Abu'l-Ḥasan ar-Ruba'í, *Faḍá'il as͟h-S͟hám wa Dimas͟hq*, in the chapter 'Faḍá'il 'Akká wa 'Asqalán'. The section on 'Akká and Askalon have been omitted from two recent editions of this work. I possess a photocopy of an old lithographed edition of this work that does not show a date of publication and has no page numbers. This does have these Traditions. I have also used the citation of this work in Ál-Muḥammad, *ad-Dalíl wa'l-Irs͟hád*, pp. 166–9.

Chapter 5: ***Bahá'í Spirituality***

188. Bahá'u'lláh, *Gleanings*, no. 106, p. 213.
189. Bahá'u'lláh, *Hidden Words*, Arabic no. 13.
190. ibid. Arabic no. 56.
191. ibid. Arabic no. 62.
192. ibid. Persian no. 45.
193. ibid. Persian no. 20.
194. ibid. Persian no. 13.
195. ibid. Persian no. 40.
196. ibid. Persian no. 14.
197. ibid. Arabic no. 15.
198. Shoghi Effendi's translation.
199. Bahá'u'lláh, *Hidden Words*, Persian no. 7.
200. ibid. Arabic no. 5.
201. Bahá'u'lláh, *Gleanings*, no. 114, pp. no. 114, 237–8.
202. Bahá'u'lláh, *Hidden Words*, Persian no. 26.
203. Bahá'u'lláh, *Kitáb-i-Íqán*, pp. 192–3.
204. ibid. pp. 193–4.
205. Bahá'u'lláh, *Seven Valleys*, pp. 8, 11.
206. 'Abdu'l-Bahá, *Paris Talks*, p. 178.
207. Bahá'u'lláh, *Hidden Words*, Arabic no. 51.
208. 'Abdu'l-Bahá, *Bahá'í Prayers*, p. 136.
209. Bahá'u'lláh, *Kitáb-i-Íqán*, pp. 15–16.
210. Bahá'u'lláh, *Tablets*, p. 24.
211. Bahá'u'lláh, *Hidden Words*, Persian no. 29.

Chapter 6: ***Social Teachings***

212. Yusuf Ali, *Holy Qur'an*, p. 46, note 107.
213. Bahá'u'lláh, *Gleanings*, no. 34, p. 80.
214. Bahá'u'lláh, *Kitáb-i-Aqdas*, para. 75.
215. Bahá'u'lláh, *Tablets*, p. 22.
216. Bahá'u'lláh, *Gleanings*, no. 112, p. 218.
217. Ibn Májah, *Sunan*, 36 (Kitáb al-Fitan), ch. 33, no. 4077, vol. 2, p. 1362.
218. Bahá'u'lláh, *Epistle to the Son of the Wolf*, p. 30.
219. ibid. pp. 30–1.
220. Shoghi Effendi, *World Order*, pp. 162–3.
221. ibid. p. 203; emphasis added.
222. ibid. pp. 203–4.
223. ibid. p. 204.
224. 'Abdu'l-Bahá, *Promulgation*, p. 232.
225. 'Abdu'l-Bahá, *Paris Talks*, pp. 136–7.
226. Bahá'u'lláh, in *Compilation*, vol. 2, p. 357, no. 2093.
227. 'Abdu'l-Bahá, *Promulgation*, pp. 135–7.
228. ibid. p. 167.
229. 'Abdu'l-Bahá, *Paris Talks*, p. 143.
230. Bahá'u'lláh, *Gleanings*, no. 122, pp. 259–60.
231. 'Abdu'l-Bahá, *Selections*, p. 139.
232. 'Abdu'l-Bahá, *Selections*, pp. 136–7.
233. 'Abdu'l-Bahá, in *Compilation*, vol. 1, p. 391, no. 839.
234. 'Abdu'l-Bahá, *Promulgation*, p. 168.
235. Shoghi Effendi, *Advent of Divine Justice*, p. 54.
236. 'Abdu'l-Bahá, *Selections*, pp. 291–2.
237. From a letter written on behalf of Shoghi Effendi to the National Spiritual Assembly of the United States and Canada, 30 May 1930, in *Lights of Guidance*, p. 2, no. 5.
238. From a letter written on behalf of Shoghi Effendi to two Bahá'ís, 14 October 1941 in *Compilation*, vol. 2, p. 59, no. 1405.
239. Bahá'u'lláh, in *Compilation*, vol. 1, p. 93, no. 170.
240. 'Abdu'l-Bahá cited in Shoghi Effendi, *Bahá'í Administration*, pp. 21–2.
241. 'Abdu'l-Bahá, *Selections*, p. 209.
242. Bahá'u'lláh, *Kitáb-i-Aqdas*, para. 37.

243. From a letter written on behalf of Shoghi Effendi to the National Spiritual Assembly of the United States and Canada, 2 October 1935, in *Lights of Guidance*, p. 440, no. 1436.

Chapter 7: ***Bahá'í Law***

244. Bahá'u'lláh, *Prayers and Meditations*, pp. 314–16.
245. 'Abdu'l-Bahá, *Bahá'í World Faith*, p. 368.
246. Bahá'u'lláh, *Prayers and Meditations*, p. 248.
247. ibid. pp. 262–3.
248. Shoghi Effendi, in *Directives of the Guardian*, no. 71, pp. 28–9.
249. Bahá'u'lláh, in *Compilation*, vol. 1, p. 490, no. 1102.
250. Bahá'u'lláh in ibid. p. 503, no. 1140.
251. From a letter written of behalf of Shoghi Effendi, in Bahá'u-'lláh, *Kitáb-i-Aqdas*, note 92, p. 207.
252. 'Abdu'l-Bahá, in *Compilation*, vol. 2, p. 247, no. 1790.
253. Bahá'u'lláh, *Kitáb-i-Íqán*, p. 193.
254. Bahá'u'lláh, *Gleanings*, no. 33, p. 77.
255. See for example Muslim, *Ṣaḥíḥ*, Kitáb al-Libás wa'l-Zínah, ch. 1364, nos. 5129, 5134, 5140–67, pp. 1140–5 regarding silk; ch. 1356, no. 5173–8, p.1146 regarding yellow clothes.
256. At-Tibrízí, *Mishkat al-Maṣábiḥ*, Book 21 (Clothing), ch. 4, vol. 3, p. 929.
257. Bahá'u'lláh, *Kitáb-i-Aqdas*, para. 159. A similar point is made in the Qur'án where, after the story is told of Adam and Eve eating of the tree which brought about their fall, Allah says: 'O ye Children of Adam! We have bestowed raiment upon you to cover your shame, as well as to be an adornment to you. But the raiment of righteousness, – that is the best. Such are among the Signs of Allah, that they may receive admonition!' (Qur'án 7:26)
258. 'Abdu'l-Bahá, *Promulgation*, pp. 37–8.

Chapter 8: ***History of the Bahá'í Faith***

259. Tradition narrated by Yusayr ibn Jábir, Muslim, *Ṣaḥíḥ*, Kitáb al-Fitan, ch. 1200, tradition 6927, p. 1502. See also translation of the same tradition in at-Tibrízí, *Mishkat al-Maṣábiḥ*,

vol. 3, p. 1132. Shi'i Traditions also paint a picture of much conflict and death, see note 130.

260. See ash-Sha'rání, *al-Yawáqít wa'l-Jawáhir*, vol. 2, pp. 142–3.
261. See ibid. vol. 2, p. 143.
262. Accounts of such Shi'i expectations can be found in the references given in the next note.
263. For such expectation in India, see Cole, *Roots of North Indian Shi'ism in Iran and Iraq* (Berkeley: University of California Press, 1988), pp. 100–1; for India, Iran, Iraq and the Caucasus, see Abbas Amanat, *Resurrection and Renewal: the Making of the Bábí Movement in Iran, 1844–1850* (Ithaca: Cornell University Press), pp. 70–105; for the Sudan, see accounts of Muḥammad Aḥmad, the Sudanese Mahdí of 1881–5 in P. M. Holt, *The Mahdist State in the Sudan* (Oxford: Clarendon, 1958).
264. The Báb, *Selections*, p. 41.
265. There are several prophecies that state that the claim of the Mahdi will be announced between the Rukn and the Maqám and that obeisance will be pledged to him there. See for example Abú Dáwud, *Sunan*, 36 (Kitáb al-Mahdí) vol. 2, pp. 422–3. A similar Shi'i Tradition can be found in Majlisí, *Biḥár al-Anwár* (lithograph ed.), vol. 13, pp. 163, 186.
266. Nabíl, *Dawn-Breakers*, pp. 315–16.
267. Balyuzi, *The Báb*, p. 142.
268. ibid. pp. 143–4.
269. ibid. p. 145n.
270. Nabíl, *Dawn-Breakers*, pp. 413–15, footnote citing the *Taríkh-i-Jadíd*, pp. 106–9.
271. Momen, *Bábí and Bahá'í Religion*, p. 78. See also Balyuzi, *The Báb*, p. 202.
272. The Báb, *Selections*, p. 182.
273. Captain Alfred von Gumoens' account was first published in an Austrian journal, *Oesterreichischer Soldatenfreund*, on 12 October 1852. It was later published in English in *The Times* on 23 October 1852. Browne published a translation in *Materials for the Study of the Bábí Religion* (Cambridge: Cambridge University Press, 1918), pp. 268–71. See also Shoghi Effendi, *God Passes By*, pp. 65–6 and Momen, *Bábí and Bahá'í Religions*, pp. 132–4.

274. Shoghi Effendi, *God Passes By*, pp. 101–2.
275. Balyuzi, *King of Glory*, pp. 144–5.
276. Bahá'u'lláh, *Kitáb-i-Aqdas*, para. 99.
277. Interestingly, some of the Islamic Traditions link the Dajjál with Isfahan. One Tradition, for example, says that he will be followed by Jews of Isfahan, at-Tibrízí, *Mishkat al-Maṣábiḥ*, Kitáb al-Fitan, ch. 4, vol. 3, p. 1148.
278. Al-Bukhárí, *Ṣaḥíḥ*, Book 88 (Afflictions), no. 241, vol. 9, p. 183; cf. Abú Dáwud, *Sunan*, vol. 2, pp. 430–1.
279. Bahá'u'lláh, *Epistle to the Son of the Wolf*, p. 17.
280. 'O Uncle of the Prophet [i.e. Abú Ṭálib]! Verily Allah Almighty has begun Islam through me and he will seal Islam through a youth (*ghulám*) from among your descendants [i.e. a descendant of 'Alí and Fáṭimah, who is the Mahdi], and he will precede Jesus son of Mary.' Al-Muttaqí al-Hindí, *Kanz al-'Ummál*, vol. 14, p. 271, no. 38693. The Aḥmadiyyah frequently quote a Tradition from Ibn Májah that says 'There is no Mahdi except Jesus son of Mary' (Kitáb al-Fitan, ch. 24, vol. 2, pp. 1339–40, no. 4036) to support their contention that the Mahdi and the returned Christ are the same person. However, the whole of this Tradition gives a list of things, none of which, it states, will occur except when accompanied by the other – until, at the end of this list, it says: '. . . the [Last] Hour will not arise except with the people becoming evil, nor is there the Mahdi except Jesus the son of Mary.' It is clear that the Tradition is giving a list of things that will accompany one another in the age when the Mahdi is expected. Given this and the fact that there are numerous Traditions that describe the Mahdi and the returned Christ as two different people, then it is clear that the meaning of this Tradition is: '. . . nor is there the [coming of] the Mahdi except [with the coming of] Jesus.' The other Tradition that the Aḥmadiyyah frequently quote is the following: 'For our Mahdi, there are two signs. Since the birth of Universe, these events have never taken place. Those two signs are that there will be a lunar eclipse on the first night of Ramadan and a solar eclipse in the middle of Ramadan.' This Tradition is not found in any of the major books of Traditions; it has not

been attributed to Muḥammad and has been rejected as false by Muslim scholars.

281. This forms part of a long *ḥadíth*; see Ibn Májah *Sunan*, Kitáb al-Fitan, ch. 33, pp. 1357–8. See also at-Tirmidhí, *Ṣaḥíḥ*, Abwáb al-Fitan, vol. 9, pp. 94, 98; al-Ḥákim, *al-Mustadrak*, Kitáb al-Fitan w'al-Maláḥim, vol. 4, p. 493; translation in at-Tibrízí, *Mishkat al-Maṣábiḥ*, book 26 (Kitáb al-Fitan), vol. 3, p. 1146.

282. Abú Dáwud, *Sunan*, Kitáb al-Jihád, ch. 3 (On the Inhabitants of Syria), vol. 2, p. 4. See also the translation in at-Tibrízí, *Mishkat al-Maṣabiḥ*, vol. 4, p. 1380.

283. See, for example, Ibn Májah, *Sunan*, 36 (Kitáb al-Fitan), ch. 32 (The Rising of the Sun from its Setting-Place), vol. 2, pp. 1352–3; this chapter contains three *ḥadíths* on this theme. See also al-Bukhárí, *Ṣaḥíḥ*, Book 88 (Kitáb al-Fitan), no. 237, vol. 9, pp. 180–1. Similar Shi'i Traditions include al-Mufíd, *al-Irshád*, p. 541.

284. Ibn Májah, *Sunan*, 36 (Kitáb al-Fitan), ch. 33, no. 4077, vol. 2, p. 1362. Similar Shi'i Traditions include Shaykh al-Mufíd, *Kitáb al-Irshád*, pp. 343–4; translated in Momen, *Introduction to Shi'i Islam* (Oxford: George Ronald, 1985), p. 169.

285. Article in the journal *Al-Hidáya*, no. 9, Dhu'l-Qa'da 1314, quoted in Gulpáygání, *Fará'id*, p. 512. Gulpáygání quotes the views and poetry of several eminent Arab scholars and poets concerning Bahá'u'lláh, pp. 511–24.

286. Emin Arslan, 'Une Visite au Chef du Babisme,' *Revue Bleu: Revue Politique et Literature*, 4th series, vol. 4, Paris, 1896, p. 316. Translated from the French in Momen, *Bábí and Bahá'í Religions 1844–1944*, p. 225.

287. On contacts with the Ottoman reformers, see Juan Cole, *Modernity and Millennium* (New York: Columbia University Press, 1998), pp. 68–77; on 'al-Afghání', see pp. 74–5.

288. Muḥammad Rashíd Riḍá, *Táríkh al-ustádh al-imám ash-Shaykh Muḥammad 'Abduh* (3 vols., Cairo: al-Manár, 1931), vol. 1, pp. 930–9, translated by J. R. Cole in 'A Dialogue on the Bahá'í Faith', *World Order*, vol. 15, nos. 3/4, Spring/Summer 1981, p. 13.

289. Emin Arslan, 'Une Visite au Chef du Babisme,' *Revue Bleu: Revue Politique et Literature*, 4th series, vol. 4, Paris, 1896, p. 316. Translated from the French in Momen, *The Bábí and Bahá'í Religions 1844–1944*, p. 225.
290. Shaykh 'Alí Yúsuf, *al-Mu'ayyad*, 16 October 1911. Adapted from Balyuzi, *'Abdu'l-Bahá*, pp. 136–7.
291. *Al-Ahrám* translated in *Star of the West*, vol. 1, no. 19 (March 1911), pp. 4–5.
292. Translated in Balyuzi, *'Abdu'l-Bahá*, pp. 468–9.
293. *The Bahá'í World (1928–1930)*, vol. 3, (New York, 1930), pp. 49–50.
294. *Bahá'í World 1998–99* (Haifa: Bahá'í World Centre, 2000), p. 317.

Chapter 9: ***Some Further Considerations***

295. See, for example, Abú Dáwud, *Sunan*, 36 (Kitáb al-Mahdí), vol. 2, pp. 422–3; Ibn Májah, *Sunan*, 36 (Kitáb al-Fitan), ch. 34, no. 4082, vol. 2, p. 1366.
296. Bahá'u'lláh reverts to this theme recurrently throughout pages 106 to 135 of the *Kitáb-i-Íqán*.
297. Bahá'u'lláh, *Kitáb-i-Íqán*, p. 107.
298. ibid. pp. 107–8.
299. ibid. pp. 106–7.
300. ibid. pp. 108–11.
301. ibid. pp. 111–12, 123–4.
302. ibid. p. 111.
303. See prophecy on p. 125.
304. One *ḥadíth* states that a third of the followers of the Mahdi would be killed before the appearance of the returned Christ. Muslim, *Ṣaḥíḥ*, ch. 1198, no. 6924, vol. 4, p. 1501.
305. See for example Abú Dáwud, *Sunan*, Book 35 (al-Fitan wa'l-Maláḥim), no. 4240: 'The Prophet said: Allah has protected you from three things . . . that you should not all agree in an error.'
306. Ibn Májah, *Sunan*, 1 (al-Muqaddamah), no. 10, pp. 5–6.
307. Pickthall's translation.

308. Al-Bukhárí, *Ṣaḥíḥ*, Book 61 (Virtues of the Qur'án), no. 504, vol. 6, p. 474; cf. also Book 92 (Holding Fast to the Qur'án), no. 379, vol. 9, p. 282.
309. Pickthall's translation
310. Bahá'u'lláh, *Kitáb-i-Íqán*, pp. 207–9.
311. 'Abdu'l-Bahá, *Some Answered Questions*, pp. 34–5.
312. For a more extensive discussion of this theme, see Abu'l-Faḍl Gulpáygání, *Miracles and Metaphors*, pp. 99–163.
313. See also Qur'án 37:36, which records the assertion by opponents of Muḥammad that he was merely a 'mad poet'.
314. Gulpáygání (*Fará'id*, pp. 468–7) gives many examples from a treatise by the Protestant missionary George Sale that is in turn based on a work by a Christian Arab, Háshim Shámí. It is difficult in a work written in English to describe the errors that have been pointed out. The following are a few examples. In verse 2:172, the word '*aṣ-ṣábirín*' should be '*aṣ-ṣábirún*'; indeed it is in a parallel construction to the earlier word '*al-mawfún*', which is given correctly. Similarly in 4:162, there is a series of parallel constructions in which the first phrase is given incorrectly: '*al-muqímín aṣ-ṣalát*' but the other phrases are given correctly: '*al-mu'tún az-zakát*' and '*al-mu'minún billáhi*'. In 22:19, the verb is given as '*ikhtaṣamú*' but it should be in the dual form to agree with its subject. The same error occurs in 49:9 where the verb '*iqtatalú*' should be in the dual form. In 9:69, there occurs the phrase '*khuḍtum ka-llathí khádú*'. Here '*allathí*' should be in plural form. The point here is not to establish that there are grammatical errors in the Qur'án but merely to demonstrate that exactly the same claim of error has been made by some Christians about the Qur'án as is now made by some Muslims about the writings of the Báb and Bahá'u'lláh.
315. See for example Qur'án 17:36, 2:170. See also pp. 78–83.
316. Pickthall's translation.
317. For example: 'This is the Book; in it is guidance sure, without doubt, to those who fear Allah' (2:2). Thus this passage, which is, in effect the first verse of the Qur'án after the Fátiḥaḥ, states that the main point of the content of the Qur'án is the guidance found within, not its eloquence. Indeed, the eloquence (*faṣáḥah*) of the Qur'án is not a subject that even occurs in the Qur'án.

318. Bahá'u'lláh, *Kitáb-i-Íqán*, p. 210–11.
319. Gulpáygání records the views and poetry of several eminent Arab scholars and poets concerning Bahá'u'lláh. Gulpáygání, *Fará'id*, pp. 511–27.
320. Bahá'u'lláh, *Hidden Words*, Arabic nos. 3, 4.
321. Bahá'u'lláh, *Epistle to the Son of the Wolf*, p. 11.
322. Bahá'u'lláh, in *Bahá'í Prayers*, p. 204.
323. For translations of some of the despatches of Dolgoruki, see Momen, *Bábí and Bahá'í Religions*, pp. 9–10, 71, 72–3, 75, 77–8, 92–5, 100–1, 103–4, 114–24. The reports on pp. 9–10 in particular show how little Dolgoruki knew of the Bábí movement even as late as 1852.
324. Momen, *Bábí and Bahá'í Religions*, pp. 72–3.
325. *Yádgár*, 5th year, Farvardín/Urdíbihisht 1328, no. 8/9, p. 148.
326. *Ráhnimá-yi Kitáb*, 6th year, Farvardín/Urdíbihisht, 1342, no. 1/2, pp. 25–6.
327. *Bahá'í-garí*, Tehran, 1323, pp. 88–9.
328. Pickthall's translation.
329. Ibn Májah, *Sunan*, 34 (Kitáb ad-Du'á), ch. 9, no. 3856, vol. 2, p. 1267. See also Ad-Dárimí, *Sunan*, 23 (Faḍa'il al-Qur'án), ch. 15, no. 3296, vol. 2, pp. 324–5. Similar statements in the Shi'i Traditions include: Majlisí, *Biḥár al-Anwár*, vol. 26, p. 7.
330. Aṭ-Ṭabarí, *Jámi' al-Bayán*, vol. 1, p. 40. Some of the abbreviated editions of this work (such as the Mu'assasah ar-Risálah, Beirut, 1994, edition) omit this passage as does the translation by J. Cooper (Oxford University Press, 1987). Ibn Kathír records this Tradition, *Tafsír*, vol. 1, p. 17. As-Suyúṭí in *ad-Durr al-Manthúr*, vol. 1, p. 8, also records this Tradition and gives a list of other scholars who have cited it including Abú Na'ím al-Iṣfahání in *Ḥilyat al-Awliya'* and Ibn 'Asákir in *Tarikh Dimashq*.

The Writings of Bahá'u'lláh

331. Bahá'u'lláh, *Proclamation*, p. 57.
332. Bahá'u'lláh *Hidden Words*, Arabic no. 1.
333. ibid. Arabic no. 2.
334. ibid. Arabic no. 3.

Index

This index is alphabetized letter by letter thus 'spirituality' comes before 'spiritual quest'. Hyphens are treated as spaces; the definite articles 'ad-', 'al-', 'as-' and 'at-' as well as 'and', 'for', 'in', 'of' and 'the' in entries are ignored.